Praise for D

"Full of invention and ridic... satire at the expense of the l...
  Irish Independent

"A wildly frenetic read, this, with black humour triumphant. Could it start a cult?"
  The Irish Times

"Certainly a page-turner."
  Woman's Way

"Carson's characters are credibly imperfect."
  Gay Community News

"A delightful . . . fast-paced, easy read. At times rising to pure farce, it is a remarkably amusing book."
  The Tribune Magazine

Praise for *The Knight of the Flaming Heart*

"Via an hilarious version of the Roger Casement story, he sinks his satirical fangs into every breed of sacred cow."
  Books Ireland

"Touching, witty and gripping. In the best entertainment tradition, Michael Carson left me wanting more."
  Catholic Times

"An exquisite modern ghost story."
  Image

A Note on the Author

Michael Carson was born in Merseyside. Educated at Catholic schools, he spent a short period as a novice in a religious order before studying for a degree in education. He has taught English in the Middle East, Nigeria, Brunei, the Bahamas and the US. He is the author of *Serving Suggestions* (a collection of his best radio short stories) and eight previous novels including *Sucking Sherbet Lemons*, *The Knight of the Flaming Heart* and *Dying in Style*. He now lives near Westport, County Mayo.

HUBBIES

MICHAEL CARSON

POOLBEG

Published 1999 by
Poolbeg Press Ltd
123 Baldoyle Industrial Estate
Dublin 13, Ireland

© Michael Carson 1999

The moral right of the author has been asserted.

The Arts Council
An Chomhairle Ealaíon
A catalogue record for this book is available from the British Library.

ISBN 1 85371 678 2

All rights reserved. No part of this publication may be reproduced or transmitted in any form or by any means, electronic or mechanical, including photography, recording, or any information storage or retrieval system, without permission in writing from the publisher. The book is sold subject to the condition that it shall not, by way of trade or otherwise, be lent, resold or otherwise circulated without the publisher's prior consent in any form of binding or cover other than that in which it is published and without a similar condition, including this condition, being imposed on the subsequent purchaser.

Cover illustration by Leonard O'Grady
Cover design by Artmark
Set by Poolbeg Group Services Ltd in Goudy 11/14
Printed by The Guernsey Press Ltd,
Vale, Guernsey, Channel Islands.

**FOR PETER AND
MICHAEL HILLER**

1

The Faulty Swing-Bin Liners

On that significant day, a day commencing like so many others in this hubby's life, it went like this: after I'd taken Jason to school; come home; washed up; made the beds; dusted; double-ducked under the rim; had another go at shifting the unfortunate Jason-spots on the carpet – no go in case you want to know – I joined some of the other Hubbies-Who-Go-Out at the Leisure Centre.

Les was there, lifting bar-bells. To tell you the truth, his singlet and briefs were not really up to snuff. They were – and I'm sorry to have to say this about Les, who was destined to become my best mate – dingy. Still, that's another story. Anyway, Les finished his set and reached for a purple towel which I've a shrewd suspicion he got free for spending over 25 estuarios at Immaculate Linens in that sale they had.

"Oy!" Les said. Like he does. He was once a miner. "How're those spots you were telling me about last week?"

"The unpleasant spots on the Axminster?" I asked, applying talcum to my hands to get a better grip on the dumb-bells, though talcum is awfully drying, have you noticed? Even triple-milled, medicated *Snowy Peak Hi-Performance* talcum with *Lubrehub*.

"Yeah. Did you apply *Lady Macbeth for Stains Organic*, like I told you?"

"Yes, I did, Les, I did just as you advised. But the spots haven't gone completely. They're not what they were, mind. I have hopes that they will go, but they haven't, as you might say, vanished as yet. I'd be telling a lie if I said they had."

Les came over. In spite of his physical exertions, he smelt like *Maine in Fall* which, I'd a shrewd suspicion, was what he was wearing. It suits his skin-chemistry, just like I told him it would. I really was pleased that he had taken my advice and consigned his *Know What I Mean?* roll-on – I mean, it'd had its time, we'd all known for yonks that it meant nothing in particular – to the swing-bin.

But we mustn't get into swing-bins.

"You smell good!" I said, all positive, full-square and upfront, just like I know Les likes me.

"Well," Les said, "you've got to, don't you? I mean, you owe it to the Mrs. She comes home after a hard day kicking arse at the Estuary Nat West. She doesn't want to find me all sweaty and 'orrible, now does she?"

"No, certainly not," I agreed.

Les looked hard into my eyes. I looked back hard. Like you do. "Harry," he said, "Harry, I want you to level with me. You know, hubby to hubby, like."

"Of course, Les," I said. I coughed deep in my throat, drew myself up to be all I could be.

"Did you leave the *Lady Macbeth for Stains Organic* on the unpleasant spots for thirty-six hours, as indicated in the directions?"

I dropped my eyes and confessed that I had not. "You see, Les," I said, "when the spot-remover dries it leaves a white residue which Avril, having come home tired and unemotional from Moseley and Lumumbashi, would be bound to notice. I just didn't want the spots drawing attention to themselves. You can understand that, can't you?"

Les nodded. I knew he understood. Well, you can tell, can't you? He sucked air in through his teeth. "My Mrs is a stickler too."

"So's mine."

"Still, what would we do without them?"

"Search me," I said.

"Touching that stain problem, though," Les said, all serious again. Like he gets. He ushered me to the rest-bench. We sat down, bonding nicely, I thought. "You'd better come clean. You'll see, Avril'll respect you for it."

"Do you think so?" I asked. "Do you really think so?"

"Definitely. My Barbara is always saying as how your Avril likes a hubby who can admit to his weaknesses. She says Avril says it shows her her hubby's human. Remember the swing-bin liners?"

"Les," I said, covered in embarrassment, "don't remind me. It makes me go all giddy just thinking about it."

"Hang about," said Les. "It's no bad thing to remember mistakes." He winked and went off to take over the cross-country skiing machine just vacated by Dave, whose Mrs, Mavis, had identical quads after a shocking few years of trying at the O'Brady Ethical Fertility Centre. Waste of time and money if you want this hubby's opinion when she could have got what she wanted under the counter at Plain Wayne's Hubby Supplies. Still, ethics lets people in for shocking expense, have you noticed? Dave's Mavis is Chief Carer at the Distressed Hubby Drop-In in the Nirvana Precinct and won't use disposable nappies on the nippers on account of the environment. Lucky for Dave, I was able to give him a nudge towards *Napapura*. It contains conditioners which not only prevent redness but delay the onset of unsightly liver-spots by as much as three years and one month, according to extensive research by the Los Angeles Estuary Enclave Pharmacological Association.

I thought about the swing-bin liners while I was lifting the three kilogram dumb-bells. For years, you see, I'd been loyal to *Butch Bags Size 3*. They were a touch more expensive than their nearest competitor. But they were strong – no embarrassing spillages – *and* they had an integral "tie" engineered into the top. It was a very clever idea, this "tie". And like all the best ideas, as simple as a soufflé. It worked on the drawstring principle, and it never failed. It beat those bendy bits of wire – have you noticed they're never long enough, you could break a nail? – even a nail soaked religiously in *Hard As Nails* which contains bull-gelatine. Which just goes to show.

Anyway, I'd better tell you what happened: I was in the Nirvana Precinct and there was this woman selling swing-bin liners outside Hubbies Ah Us plc. Well, I don't know what came over me. Despite priding myself on my brand loyalty, I looked to left and right to make sure there were no hubbies around who might see and report back. I went over and felt one, gave it a good old shake and rip to see if it would stand up. And it did! Then I saw that it had an integral draw-tie – patent pending – and a dozen were *a quarter* of the price I usually paid for *Butch Bags Size 3*. I got that rush of adrenalin you get when you're on the scent of a really fantastic bargain. I pounced on the salesMrs. "How much for the lot?" I asked her.

"For you, 30 estuarios," she said, giving my bum a quick feel.

"Do you mind?" I said, though to tell you the truth I was quite pleased; it had been ages since I'd been touched with intent. I remember I was wearing *BreakOUT For Busy Hubbies*, a roll-on with convenient aerosol back-up. I'd only bought a trial size but it seemed to be passing with flying colours and I remember thinking that perhaps *BreakOUT for Busy Hubbies* was a pleasure I owed myself. After all, I'm worth it. I think.

"I'll give you 25," I said.

"Give us a break, darlin'!" she replied. "I've got a hubby and five kids to support. To tell you not a word of a lie, we're only hanging on at Millennium Mansions by the skin of our orthodontic implants. It'll be the Industrial Nostalgia New Town for us unless I can shift more merchandise. 28."

I shuddered for her at the mention of the Industrial Nostalgia New Town. "I don't know . . . " I said, feeling all sorry for her but still after that bargain . . . Well, you've got to, don't you?

She copped another crafty feel, which ended with a pinch. "Seeing it's you . . . 27.50. A steal for a lifetime's supply of swing-bin liners."

"All right," I said. "They are strong, though, aren't they?"

She gave me one of those straight looks – like the Leader of the rump opposition in the telly ad for *Extra Nude Labour*. "If one breaks, seeps, tears, or in any way lets you down – just one, mind – you know where I am," she said. "I stand full-square behind my product."

Her cast-iron guarantee made me go all tingly. It was just like coming out of a bath liberally spiked with *Ten Thousand Feathers*, which not only rejuvenates the skin as it gently cleanses, but leaves the surface of the bath pristine. In fact, there's a new version of *Ten Thousand Feathers* that tans you while you soak. I don't use it, though. Avril likes me cream-coloured. If she likes me, that is. I'm never quite sure, to tell you the truth.

When I got home – and it wasn't easy I can tell you, it was the devil's own job cramming everything into the basket on the bicycle rickshaw – I announced the bargain to Avril in her office, which also doubles as her rumpus room.

"You and your bargains!" said Avril indulgently. "Any chance of a cup of tea?"

"Darjeeling, Earl Grey, Smoky Robinson, Mississippi Mountain, Ceylon, or the usual?" I asked, like I always do.

"You choose; you know about these things," said Avril, as she always does. She knows exactly how to make me purr. I dusted my hand along the bannister as I waltzed all the way downstairs just for the thrill I get from being really useful.

While I was waiting for the kettle to boil – it's a Swan and Edgar – we've had it seventeen years – ever since I was Head of Parts at Widdecombe Three-Wheeler – and we live in the hardest of hard-water areas. I put down its longevity to the little wire thing I keep inside. It takes the scale to itself and is now like a plug of cement. It was only 30 deci-estuarios but has saved us a fortune on descaler. It may even have stopped the kettle from wearing out and kettles are not inexpensive items. However, as Avril often says in that way she has that makes you think you ought to be writing it down: "It's not the kettle that's the expensive part, but the electrical current that passes through it. Think on it, Harry!" Well, I just nod: "Yes, dear, I'm sure you're right," I always reply. Like you do.

Anyway, while I was waiting I decided to try out a swing-bin liner. I always get a thrill from trying out a new purchase. It's a real little treat, have you noticed? I wafted it about to let the air in and blow me I saw daylight the other end.

The awful heart-stopping feeling that I'd been done came over me. I wafted another one. Daylight. Another and another and there was the daylight of doom, like they say in the adverts for sun mousse. Avril was shouting for her tea; the de-rehumidifier was telling me that it needed a new *DioxinGone!* filter – the sort without scent but *with* lashings of TLC.

I took Avril her tea. She harrumphed her thanks. That's Mesdames for you. I made a quick exit. I knew I was flushed and I just could not – and call me a coward if you like – face an interrogation from the leading litigation lawyer at Moseley and Lumumbashi. I headed back to the Nirvana Precinct, a lifetime supply of swing-bin liners with no bottoms filling the Hubby Strain-Saver.

Of course, you've guessed it, the salesMrs had gone.

I was close to despair. I wondered about going to Dad's to have a quiet sit and work things through, but I knew late Saturday was Dad's time for *Senior Hubbies' Depilatory and Old-Time Slipper Bath* at the Leisure Centre Annex. I was thinking of ringing the *Harassed Hubby Helpline*, I have to admit, when a Mrs came up to me and asked me if the liners were for sale.

Well, I didn't think. I looked to right and left, and said, "You can have the lot for 30 estuarios."

"All right, darlin'," the Mrs said, "let's see what we've got here. What are those stringy bits all about?"

"They're infallible locking drawstrings patent-pending. A revolutionary leap-forward for swing-bin liners," I said. To my alarm she gave one of them a shake, but it was desultory and if my shake hadn't exposed the fatal flaw in the bin-liners I was d. sure hers wouldn't. Mesdames have lost the knack. If they ever had it. They're hopeless in the household department. My Avril can't cook an egg. I dread to think what'll happen if I shuffle off first. In fact, come to think of it, I should start cooking meals to freeze against the time.

"Done!" she said. "My hubby will be over the moon when he sees them."

I nodded and ran behind her, helping her load them into the boot of her EcoJag, the one that is fuelled by Evening Primrose Oil, the emissions of which not only deodorize the environment it passes through, but also clear hubbies' vulnerable arteries.

Well, fortune smiled on me because they had a three-for-the-price-of-two offer on *Butch Bags Size 3* at Plain Wayne's Hubby Supplies and I still had time to get home before Avril noticed that anything was up.

It was around that time that Avril suggested that I went to the Leisure Centre. It might be the making of me, she said. Then she started whistling "Hubby Keep Your Looks (If You Want To Keep Your Mrs)" in her Power Shower on a daily basis. Well, I took the hint and off I went.

I'd broken a nail on the rowing-machine – I didn't know about *Hard As Nails* then – when I met Les. Les was climbing the step-to-health steps in company with Dave, the nappy-for-quads washer, whose Mrs, Mavis, is Chief Carer at The Distressed Shopper Drop-in in the Nirvana Precinct, that I mentioned before.

"I'll never let the Mrs shop for me again, Dave," Les said.

"They can't do it. Just pick up the first thing that comes to hand," Dave replied. "Hopeless!"

"You'll never guess what mine did. She thought she was doing me a favour, too."

"What?" Dave asked.

"She bought 500 swing-bin liners from this hubby in the Nirvana Precinct. And not one of them was sealed at the bottom. Useless! I told her – 'Barbara,' I said. I didn't mince my words – I said, 'Leave the marketing to me. There's a pet!'"

"Cheapness is often a false economy in my experience," Dave said, all righteous, while I quaked, sucking my nail. I dreaded them finding out who had sold faulty swing-bin liners to Les's Mrs. Two or more hubbies united against an erring one can be real – pardon me – cows. I've seen them in the precinct HubbyBar, nursing their *Export Babychams* and bitching like dockers. Course, I stay well away. I've never been a great one for hubby-chums, if you want to know the truth. Until Les came along, that is.

It took a week before nemesis fell – if that's what nemesis does. Les's Mrs, Barbara, came into the Leisure rattling her car-keys and sizing up the hubbies. I flexed my hamstrings. Like you do. She saw me at once and gave me a straight look. Well, I knew who she was. And vice versa.

Barbara told Les it was definitely me that sold her the swing-bin liners with no bottoms. Of course, I denied it when Les mentioned it. I mean, I'd built it all up in my mind until I had this horrid vision of myself being blackballed from the Leisure Centre, snubbed at Plain Wayne's and, worst of all, losing Les as my best mate (well, he wasn't my best mate then, you understand, but a hubby can hope).

Les nodded and said, "If you say it wasn't you, Harry; it wasn't you."

That made me feel terrible, as you can imagine. I went on a course of *Calm Down Hubby!* straight away. The 10mg ones, so you can see how bad it was. And it might have been the pills that helped me see things clear, at least clear enough to realise that I needed help. I picked up the VideoChat and called *The Harassed Hubby Helpline* to ask for advice.

That call changed my life. Not only did the carer advise me to tell all to Les – the best bit of advice I've ever had – but she nudged me in so many other life-enhancing directions. Still that, as they say, is another Hubbytale. I mustn't run ahead of myself. I've a tendency to do that. Have you noticed? Don't say you have.

it's funny. When I explained to Les how it had ...pened – that I had been terrified of Avril finding out, then terrified of losing my best mate – he understood completely. It was then that we became *real* mates.

The Harassed Hubby Helpline had only been going a few years when I took all my courage – and a handful of *Calm Down Hubby!* in both hands, swallowed them and my pride and punched out the number.

Magenta was my Mrs Counsellor's name. I knew from the very first moment that Magenta could see beneath the VideoChat image of me, right the way down to the real Harry Manley.

"Why are you feeling harassed, hubby?" Magenta asked, straight off.

Well, I told her all about Les and the swing-bin liners.

Magenta, without any hesitation, said that, if I was a hubby worth the name – and she could see from looking at me that I surely was – I must bite back my pride and confess all ... "because you know what will happen when you do, hubby?"

"No," I said, "what?"

"A wave of peace will flow over the furrowed shore of your brow."

"Will it?" I asked.

"It will," Magenta said. "Will you do something for me? Unfurrow your brow right this minute, hubby."

I did my best. It was a bit like trying to get the crinkles out of *HubbyHelp* kitchen foil. I hadn't realised how furrowed my forehead had been.

"That's better. You'll see," Magenta promised, "as soon as you've told your friend the truth almost everything will be back to normal."

I furrowed my brow again. "How do you mean *almost*, Magenta?" I asked.

"Well, hubby, all the counsellors at *The Harassed Hubby Helpline* have been trained to pick up on the peripherals of hubby demeanour on line. You see, quite often an enquiry as to oven-cleaning can be a cry for help about far more important, sometimes quite intimate, matters. We counsellors have to be on the alert for tell-tale hints."

"I don't think I have any problems in my life – apart from the swing-bins," I said. "You see, Magenta, I'm a very fortunate hubby in all areas of life. My Mrs, Avril, is a litigation lawyer of worldwide reputation; Jason is turning out really well – he passed all his assessments, including those hard-to-pass genetic revamping ones, with flying colours – and I pride myself on being a scrupulous shopper. I've got the Nirvana Precinct taped."

Magenta said that it was in the area of shopping that she thought I was in need of some counselling. At first I tried to argue the toss with her, but she nipped my protests in the bud by reminding me of the swing-bin-liners. "Your brand loyalty isn't all it could be, hubby!" she said.

"No, but . . . "

But Magenta interrupted me and what she said really upset me.

"I think your loyalty to the Nirvana Precinct betrays a pre-millennial hubby. Times have moved on, you know . . . "

"Hold it right there, Magenta!" I said, triumphant at finding a crack in her logic. "Before, you were saying that I'd fallen down on brand loyalty and now you're saying I'm too loyal to the Nirvana. That doesn't add up, does it?"

I should have known better, of course, trying to take a Mrs on in arguments. I haven't done it with Avril since the Great Restructure. "It's part and parcel of the same thing, hubby," Magenta said. "The Nirvana Precinct is yesterday's shopping experience. You must have noticed how it's gone down of late. That's because all the Hubbies-Who-Go-Out worth the name have taken the shopping leap past Nirvana."

"I don't hold with home-shopping and all those gadgets," I told Magenta severely. "I'm a hubby who likes to get out, despite the dangers."

"I'm not talking about home-shopping," Magenta said. "There is another path . . . the path less travelled . . . the high path . . . "

"Oh, yes? Well, what are you talking about? What is this higher path?" I asked, all militant. "I frequent the Nirvana Precinct because of Plain Wayne's Hubby Supplies and Hubbies Ah Us. Granted, there are other splendid shops at Nirvana but I am loyal to Plain Wayne's because Plain Wayne himself stuck by us hubbies in the bad old days when we couldn't tell the difference between hypoallergenic and ph-balanced."

Magenta tried to interrupt but she didn't stand a chance against me when I got on to the subject of Plain Wayne.

And I told Magenta. I told her how Plain Wayne and his friend and business partner, Neil, had stood by hubbies during the Decade of Social Readjustment when everything was turning upside down and hubbies were trying to adjust to sperm-free ejaculations, imported gene pools, endless clones of Richard Gere appearing at the crèche, b. all going at the Job Centre . . . and adapt to hubbydom.

Plain Wayne and Neil would hold low-dusting sessions and cookery demonstrations and, when depilation became the thing, show us chapter and verse of waxing. Without Plain Wayne and Neil, I said, there was many a hubby who would have given up and thrown himself into the Estuary. The Hubbies Ah Us people had been poppets too. In short, I concluded, I wouldn't be the efficient hubby she saw on the VideoChat if it wasn't for the Nirvana Precinct and its helpful, hubby-centred shops.

Magenta was looking really sad. She didn't say anything for ever such a long time and then, still looking sad, she said in this really glum voice, "If only you knew the truth, hubby."

"I do know the truth. I'm telling you the truth," I said, though I'd be telling you a lie if I said I wasn't wondering whether I really did.

"Correction, hubby. You *think* you know the truth, but . . . " She stopped. "Will you do something for me, hubby?"

"I don't know," I said. "Like what?"

"Will you give *The Floating Bo$co* a try? I think you'll have your eyes opened."

Well, I told her – and this is hard for me to say, knowing what I know now – that nothing would persuade me to go on board *The Floating Bo$co*. It didn't make any difference to me that it was now a ship that plied back and forth across the Estuary. It was still just a floating version of Bo$co Superstores, and they had been responsible for decimating the small businesses of the country; not to mention the farmers, milkmen, pharmacists, and paper-shops. Hubbies worth the name didn't frequent anything with the name of Bo$co. And that was that – not Bo$co DIY, Bo$co EcoCar Parts, Bo$co Books, Bo$co Airlines, Bo$co Bank – NOTHING. And could I go now please, I had Les to confess to.

"But all that's in the past, hubby," Magenta said. "Now that Lord Bo$co of Upper Bebington has passed away – and he left Bo$co International in complete financial disarray – the reins have passed to Lady Lavinia Bo$co. And she has the needs of hubbies at the very top of her agenda."

"Well, I don't know . . . " I said.

You see, I was remembering how it was when Bo$co International took over. As a nipper, Mum and Dad would take us on an outing to their out-of-town store. We'd pass all the closed up, vandalised, hopeless streets where once – Dad said – families had run these little shops. And people in the area went to them. And the streets were full of people, neighbours, chatting and that. He got quite animated. He did!

"You're having me on!" I'd say to Dad, unable to imagine a time without a Bo$co Superstore.

"No, son, I'm not. And I'll tell you something else . . . "

Mum interrupted him, "Will you stop going on about the old days, Dad. The Bo$co Superstore has been a life-saver as far as I'm concerned."

Mum had already got her BA at the Open University and was working on another degree. Dad, on the other hand, had just lost his job in fruit and veg wholesaling. He never worked again as if you didn't know.

But Magenta hadn't finished with me yet. "Hubby," she said, "I think you owe it to yourself – and your family – to try *The Floating Bo$co*. I'll make you this never-to-be-repeated-offer, shall I?"

"If you like, Magenta," I said.

"If you don't take to *The Floating Bo$co* and take against Plain Wayne's Hubby Supplies after one Morning Cruise around the Estuary, I'll give you 150 estuarios to spend in the Nirvana Precinct. Now I can't say fairer than that, can I?"

"What's the catch?" I asked.

"Hubby!" Magenta exclaimed. "Please don't be cynical. If there's anything more unattractive than a cynical hubby, well, I don't know what it is, I'm sure. Cynicism leads to what?"

"Negativity," I said.

"And you know where negativity leads?"

"I do, Magenta," I said.

"Where does negativity lead, hubby?"

"The Industrial Nostalgia New Town."

Magenta beamed. "Right first time!" she said.

I thought about that. I shuddered. Then an idea came to me, "I tell you what, Magenta," I said.

"What?"

"If Les forgives me and we get back to being best mates, I'll accept your challenge and go with Les on board *The Floating Bo$co*."

"That's wonderful," she said.

"I must warn you, though. I think you're going to lose 300 estuarios."

"300? But I said . . . "

"Yes, but the offer applies to Les too, doesn't it?"

"Very well," Magenta said.

Anyway, I thanked her, rang off and ran around to the Leisure Centre. Everything was patched up with Les, like I told you.

That day I watched as Les finished his round, winking at me drinking *HubbyLite Lite* in the HubbyBar. I wondered if it might be time to bring up the vexed topic of the dinginess of Les's singlets and briefs, but I bit my tongue. We had a good old exercise and, ready for anything, went off comparing prices in the Nirvana Precinct. We both have our strengths. I'm good in the body-care/Environmental Protection/cleanser areas – as you've probably guessed already – and Les is a whiz on fruit and veg, anything with fibre, and tinned fish. Plain Wayne was away that day, but Neil was there and he showered us with attention. I stood there in the middle of the shop, thinking, *I'll be loyal to you and Plain Wayne until my sell-by date is ancient history*.

The following Friday night I told Les what I had in mind. We were at a Hubby-Only night at The Angel Delight Public House. I'd told Avril we were going to ogle strippers. She laughed – thinking we will have our little joke. She's always found it hard to credit that a handful of hubbies off out on our own can really get quite frisky. Actually, to tell you the truth, there was this crockery demonstration in the pub. They showed us the most incredible micro-to-table melamine-ware that was dishwasher-safe, hypoallergenic and available with the photographs of your choice sunk into them to a depth of four microns. Guaranteed non-fade. I couldn't wait to see Avril's face when the order arrived and there was Avril's face on the dinner plates. Like it says on the blurb, "*We marry practicality and aesthetics. We are unbreakable, yet delicate in appearance. A joy to possess!*" A bit like your average hubby, really.

Anyway, all the activity and the stampede to place orders made me keep forgetting to mention the trip to *The Floating Bo$co*. When I did get round to it, Les was really shocked. He knew what I thought about supermarkets. It's what he thought about British Coal.

Still, I explained about the 150 estuarios. "I mean, Les, you and I both know that *The Floating Bo$co* doesn't have a hope in h. of winning our custom away from the Nirvana Precinct and Plain Wayne. All we have to do is go through the motions, have a nice blow on the Estuary and come back to terra firma with all that lovely lolly to spend."

Les was not so sure. "*The Floating Bo$co* has a funny effect on Hubbies-Who-Go-Out, Harry," he said. "I've seen really hard-headed hubbies turn to Bo$co-fodder overnight."

"Well, it won't happen to us," I said. "Not if we stick together."

Les brightened then. "No, I s'pose not. Not if we stick together."

"And we will, won't we?" I said.

"'Til the methane in the mineshaft at Congleton Colliery

breaks through the astroturf pleasure gardens and farts 'Dixie', chuck," Les said.

I didn't exactly get Les's reference, but I knew exactly what he meant.

"We're best mates, aren't we?"

"That we are," Les said. "That we are."

"Do you have any thoughts on which photos you're going to have inserted to a depth of 4 microns on your set of oven-to-table, dishwasher-safe tableware?"

"Wouldn't you like to know?" Les said. But I knew that me and Les at the Leisure Centre, the day I lifted 15 kilos, would have pride of place on his side plates. His Barbara would have to take the lion's share. She'd be on the dinner plates. Still, me and Les on the side plates together is good enough for me.

2

The Black Diaries of Plain Wayne

I don't know why I still get surprised and upset when things don't go according to plan. You'd think I'd have learned to take surprises in my stride by now, wouldn't you? Well, maybe I have a bit but I was still in a shocking state when Les didn't show up in time to go with me aboard *The Floating Bo$co*.

I got down to the quay with twenty minutes to spare. I'd told Les – several times and a few more times for luck – that he was to make sure to be there at least ten minutes before the ten o'clock cruise set off. Any more than that and I'd start worrying and have licked my *Kiss The Wind (Sailor Strength)* lip-salve off before we were even on board.

At five-to I was in a state. And no sign of Les! A stern voice behind me announced "All aboard, hubby! The Mid-morning Cruise of *The Floating Bo$co* is about to depart!"

I looked around, and there was Big Yvette.

"Goodness gracious me!" I said. "It's Big Yvette, isn't it?"

"It is," Big Yvette said.

"Fancy! I haven't seen you since the odd old days when I was Head of Parts at Widdecombe Three-Wheelers!"

"And I was in charge of the Dashboard and Glove-Compartment Department. Small world, Harry!"

"You've never said a truer word, Big Yvette. You don't mind me calling you Big Yvette, do you?"

"Seeing it's you, Harry."

"I just can't get over it," I said. "Did I say what a small world it was?"

"You did, Harry. You did."

"The years have been really kind to you, Big Yvette. You look really well. A credit to your hubby."

"I've been through three since then, Harry."

"You haven't!" I said, though I had heard a bit about it – while trying not to – at the HubbyBar in the Precinct.

"I have," said Big Yvette, twisting apart the skeins of a mooring-rope and leaving it looking like a three-petalled flower with a stem each end. "And I'm not sure the current one is up to snuff. You still with – "

"Avril. Oh, yes," I said. "Avril and me are inseparable, except we don't see that much of one another."

"She was Mrs of the Year again, wasn't she?"

"She was," I said. "Avril's Queen of Litigation. She's really put Moseley and Lumumbashi on the map. To tell you the truth, Big Yvette, all her Mrs of the Year awards are becoming a real b. to dust."

"Still the same old Harry Manley!" Big Yvette said.

I frowned at her and would have said something just a little bit tart in tone. In fact I was having a think about what, but the hooter on the funnel of *The Floating Bo$co* blew, making me jump.

Big Yvette laughed. "If you want to get on board, Harry, you'd better look sharpish. Miss this one and you'll have to wait for the afternoon QuickieCruise and that gets to be a madhouse if the Hairy Hubbies from the Industrial Nostalgia New Town are aboard – and you can bet your bottom-thruster they will be, Harry."

Well, you can imagine – I was in a state. I looked for Les up and down the landing-stage, but could see no sign. "I don't know what to do, Big Yvette," I said. "You see, I'm waiting for Les. He's my mate, and it's our first time on *The Floating Bo$co*. I don't know what's keeping him. I really don't."

"Your first time on *The Floating Bo$co*? Where have you been, Harry?"

"Plain Wayne's Hubby Supplies, Hubbies Ah Us, HubbyCare. I find these shops answer my shopping needs perfectly satisfactorily, Big Yvette."

Big Yvette spat. I pretended not to notice. Spitting is something that Mesdames have got into the habit of doing of late. Don't ask me why; I can't tell you why. It's just one of those fads, I suppose. I think it started when Lucy-Jean Moriarty, the netball superstar, did it at the Astrodome when one of her scores was disallowed. It just caught on. One must live in hope the habit passes. I try never to let any spitters notice I've noticed.

"Get yourself a *LIFE*, Harry!" Big Yvette said, wiping her mouth. "*The Floating Bo$co* is the best thing to happen to hubbies since the GREAT RESTRUCTURE."

Well, that was quite a claim. "Do you think so, Big Yvette?" I asked.

"I do," Big Yvette said. "It's like Lady Lavinia Bo$co says, Harry: *The Floating Bo$co* is everything you want from a store and an ocean more!"

The hooter sounded again. I jumped again. I could have kicked myself for not being ready for it, I really could.

"Come on, Harry! Let's be 'avin' you!" Big Yvette boomed, in the voice that used to reach from one end of the Widdecombe production line to the other.

"But I can't!" I pleaded, "Les . . . !"

The gangway was going up and Big Yvette, without a by-your-leave, picked me up bodily and – there's no other word for it – THREW me on board. Of course I was livid, but you have to admire her. She's got biceps of steel. To tell you the truth, being held by her like that made me come over all funny. "You're as strong as ever you were," I said from aboard the ship, adjusting my pec-organizer.

"A gangplank is nothing!" Big Yvette shouted. "Remember how I was with the dashboard and glove compartments?"

"How could I ever forget, Big Yvette?" I said, "If everyone at Widdecombe Three-Wheelers had been able to come close to your productivity we'd still be world-beaters."

Then I saw Les running along the landing-stage. "There's my mate, Les!" I called.

"Too late now, Les," said Big Yvette. And, do you know, she seemed quite pleased.

"Harry!" Les called to me. The boat was already moving away from the harbour wall. "I'm sorry, chuck! My Barbara took it into her head to give me a training-hour. Are you going to be OK?"

"Course I am, Les!" I called back, though I wasn't so sure. Still, I stopped worrying about myself when I saw Big Yvette put her arm around Les's shoulder, lead him to a capstan and sit him down. "Be good!" I added, but I don't think they heard me. Big Yvette, I thought, up to her old tricks again!

I turned away and had my first real sight of *The Floating Bo$co*. There were lots of hubbies milling about, many holding those electronic list machines that bleep customers towards each item to the tune of *Nearer My God To Thee*. Still, Plain Wayne's had them for years and if you want my opinion, call me conservative if you like, but with Plain Wayne and Neil showering attention on their customers, you don't need electronic list machines when all's said and done.

Then this young Mrs done out in a green-and-red suit, same as the colours on the funnel, came up to me.

"Hubby Harry Manley?" she enquired.

"That's me," I said. "I'm only here for a look round."

"I'm Justine," she said. "Correct me if I'm wrong but am I right in saying that this is your first time on board?"

"It is, Justine," I said. "I'm a devotee of the Nirvana Precinct and I'm not ashamed to admit it."

"Jolly good!" enthused Justine. "I'm all in favour of hubbies having opinions. There are too many hubbies these days who don't think for themselves, but follow their Mrs's opinions in everything."

"Are there?" I asked, all innocence.

To tell you the truth, I'm one of them. Still, I knew I was in for a testing time of it. Here Justine was, knowing all my details. She probably thought I'd fall for *The Floating Bo$co* in no time at all and desert the Nirvana Precinct for good and all. Well, I thought, I'll show you, Justine!

"Now what shall we do first?" Justine asked.

I could have told her straight off; I knew she'd want to take me for a coffee to loosen me up. That's what they always do. I'd kept my ears open, you see. Well, you've got to, don't you?

"How about a coffee at the HubbyCaff? You'd like that, wouldn't you, hubby?"

"You're the boss," I said. "I'd like a coffee very much. Very much I'd like one. It'll be nice to get the weight off my feet."

We walked along this deck. It had lovely polished floors, I have to say. On both sides there were portholes, but instead of windows there were pictures of Hubbies of the Month dating back to the launch of the SS *Lavinia I*.

"What do you think of the ship?" Justine asked.

"Very nice," I said.

"Is that all you can say? 'Very nice'!"

"What would you say, then?" I asked, holding back. You can see me holding back, can't you?

"I'd say it was glorious," Justine said.

"Oh, you would?" I said, in that edgy, mean tone I'd got quite good at of late. A bit like Dad. It was worrying me a bit, to tell you the truth.

"I would," Justine said, unfazed by my tone. Still, they're trained to be, I suppose. She opened a door. "Welcome to the HubbyCaff, hubby!"

Well, to tell you the truth the HubbyCaff was rather lovely. Everything was gingham in every colour you could think of. Each table was in a different colour gingham right down to the serviettes and the crockery. The Mrs waitresses wore gingham in white with the slightest hint of yellow and the thick-piled carpet exactly matched the uniforms.

"I bet that carpet attracts the spots," I said. "Bet you use a ton of *Lady Macbeth for Spots Organic* on that, like."

"Trust a hubby to think of spots!" Justine said. "But there's no need to worry about the carpet, hubby. We treat it daily with aerosol *Bo$cown Brand Eternal Grace*. Spots don't stand a chance. As for *Lady Macbeth*! Well, it's been on our unethical products list for almost a decade."

"How do you mean?"

"I mean," said Justine, "that it's dangerous to health – especially if you leave it on the spot for thirty-six hours."

"I don't believe that for a minute," I said. "Plain Wayne would never have sold it to me if he'd thought it was dangerous."

Justine looked shocked, "You don't shop at Plain Wayne's Hubby Supplies, do you?"

I was ready for her. "Yes, actually I do, actually, Justine.

Actually, Plain Wayne is very popular with all the hubbies of my acquaintance. Why?"

"It's not for me to say," Justine said. "Coffee?"

"Yes, please," I said, with all the briskness at my command.

Justine flashed a menu in front of me. Green gingham. It occurred to me that a bit of gingham would cheer up our kitchen at home. I can't remember if I mentioned it but my Avril went all titanium and black marble some years ago and a touch of gingham would soften it up no end. I opened the menu and studied the coffees.

"There's a choice of thirty-seven blends, hubby. If I might recommend Tanzanian Mountain with a touch of Colombian Black. Both from Lady Lavinia Bo$co's own plantations." She must have seen me looking impressed. "Lady Lavinia travels the globe seeking out the very best for *The Floating Bo$co*."

"Oh, yes?"

"I wonder, does Plain Wayne and his friend – "

"Neil."

Justine smiled unsmilingly, if you get me. "Do they, I wonder, travel the world to find the very best for hubbies? Do they even travel as far as the nearest Cash and Carry or do they wait at the docks for things to FALL OFF LORRIES!"

Justine was getting really aerated. "Why is everyone so anti Plain Wayne?" I asked.

"I'm sorry I mentioned it," Justine said. "Please don't tell anyone what I said, will you?"

"Don't worry about that, Justine."

She took my hand and held it in a clench of iron. "Please don't go back to the Nirvana Precinct, hubby! Believe me, I wouldn't say this if I didn't have your best interest at heart. I know things that you don't know, Harry – you don't mind me calling you Harry, do you? – things that would make you weep. There has been treachery at the Nirvana Precinct, Harry! Treachery!"

"What is your evidence for this?" I asked, like Avril on the VideoChat.

Justine recovered herself. "I'm sorry. I shouldn't have said any of that. It's just that I like you, Harry, and I like the idea of your family. I want to protect you from all the harm that's out there. Do you believe me?"

No, I do not, I thought. "Of course, I do, Justine. But if you'll excuse me, I think I'd like to look around to see what's on offer and everything."

"If I might," Justine said, "might I show you around?"

Well, I didn't really want a tour from Justine. But neither did I want to hurt her feelings. It's not often that a Mrs gets all emotional with a hubby. They just don't like doing it for reasons I can readily relate to. I mean, I can remember how it was. Just. Anyway I said I'd be charmed, and off we went.

All went swimmingly. Each deck did have this amazing range of goods, all very nicely presented. I had to fight hard not to stop and pick things up. The thought of the 150 estuarios held me back. We darted into the HubbyLoos and took a quick look at the changing bays. All pristine. It wasn't until we were alone in the Interdenominational Chapel that things started getting oddish.

We sat down in the front pew looking at this stained-glass window of Lady Lavinia Bo$co launching a ship on some estuary with thousands of multi-racial hubbies all smiling and chirpy.

"It's lovely and peaceful in here, isn't it?" Justine said.

"Very nice," I said – trying to reclaim my word.

"I'm worried about you, Harry."

"For why, Justine? Good heavens, there's no reason to worry about me. I'm having a really lovely time."

"I'm worried that you're resisting *The Floating Bo$co*. It's just a feeling I have, Harry. I know hubbies don't trust Mesdames' feelings. But I'm different, Harry. My hubby is always saying, 'You're different from most Mesdames, Justine. You can really understand how a hubby feels.' That's why I'm a counsellor, I suppose."

"And you think I'm in denial about the benefits of *The Floating Bo$co*?"

Justine leaned back in the pew, looked at her very shapely hands, holding them out in front of her. Then she placed one on each of her knees and said, looking the spitting image of the climax of a play: "Denial?" she said. "Yes, I think you are in denial, Harry. There's a side of you, Harry, that keeps thinking of old loyalties to precinct and neighbourhood. That side makes it difficult for you to take the plunge, to slip the mooring-rope that anchors you – chains you – to Plain Wayne's Hubby Supplies, Hubbies Ah Us and the other shops you frequent. You want to set out on a voyage of discovery with the good people aboard *The Floating Bo$co* – you've seen a little of what we can offer you. But you're afraid, Harry . . . something is holding you back, keeping you marooned on the sandbank of the past."

"There's a lot of truth in what you say, Justine," I said, not believing myself for a minute. "When I was new to Hubbydom I couldn't tell a bar code from a bar stool. I was hopeless, *hopeless*, in the Household Needs department. But Plain Wayne and Neil took me under their wings and taught me everything I know. If it hadn't been for Plain Wayne, well . . . "

"Oh, Harry! I AM sorry!" Justine said.

Well, that did it. Talking about the start of it all always

makes me weepy. I just can't help it. Tears were not like me when I was Head of Parts at Widdecombe Three-Wheelers, though I must have been weeping inside in a dry sort of way all the time.

Then, when the Great Restructure came along I was all fingers and thumbs with my new roles. I growled with frustration. I cursed the heavens! I did! I punched and I kicked and I smoked fags – when all I really wanted was a good weep. The first time in the *Don't You Dare Ask The Price: It's An Estuario* department at Plain Wayne's, I broke down completely. Neil saw me, told me to let it all out. And that's how I've been ever since. It doesn't take much to set me off.

But there in the Interdenominational Chapel with Justine, it was much worse. I was remembering the bad times, feeling sorry for myself and really guilty at the same time that I could ever have thought Justine wasn't being sincere. The coffee was repeating on me. I belched into my hanky as the tears flowed.

"Sorry," I said.

"What for, hubby?" Justine said. "There are very few more attractive things in this world than seeing a lovely hubby having a good old cry."

"That's what my Avril says," I said. "Avril freely admits that she's addicted to tears. And she sees quite a lot of them in her job as a litigation lawyer."

"That wouldn't be Avril Manley Ll.D., the star litigation lawyer with Moseley and Lumumbashi of the Mersey Estuary Enclave, the City Enclave and everywhere on the Pacific Rim, would it?"

I knew Justine was trying to butter me up. I lay on the plate steaming, feeling the emollients penetrating my subcutaneous regions. "It would," I said with pride.

"Do you live in a lovely big house, Harry?" Justine asked.

"No," I said. "I know that Avril is well-paid, but she doesn't discuss money with me. I think most of it gets ploughed back into the company. They're huge on the Pacific Rim, apparently."

"Well," said Justine, "if you're going to be huge there's no better place to be huge, so I hear tell, than the Pacific Rim. Lady Lavinia Bo$co is launching *Floating Bo$cos* in the Pacific Rim at the rate of one a fortnight. The Chinese love the ocean-going Bo$coCruises."

"Don't mention China to me," I said. "I saw a documentary."

"I know!" Justine said. "Shocking really. I don't agree with hubby-to-hubby relationships. Call me old-fashioned if you like but it just doesn't seem what you'd call natural to me."

"There aren't enough Mesdames to go around," I said, "what with them doing what they did to female babies for so long. I think it's very good to have hubby-to-hubby relationships. Especially as they're being given the female babies to bring up. It'll redress the gender imbalance. Things will be as right as rain in no time."

"Ah," Justine said, "but will they?"

"How do you mean, Justine?"

"Young Mesdames brought up only by hubbies with no influence from Mesdames? Do you think that's a good thing? I mean, every child needs a Mrs's stern discipline and that."

"I expect you're right," I said, more for something to say than to say something.

Quite suddenly, Justine stood up. "Are we quite recovered now, Harry?"

"Yes, thank you, Justine," I said.

"Good."

Justine walked over to the statue of Sophie, Queen of

Enterprise – whoever she is – and unlocked a little cupboard in the statue's plinth. She came back to me holding this old-fashioned exercise book, the sort with a shiny red cover with close contour lines etched into it. I used to buy them by the dozen at Plain Wayne's.

"I'll not beat about the bush," Justine said. "Harry, I am holding in my hand a copy of *The Black Diary of Plain Wayne*. It came into the possession of *The Floating Bo$co HubbyCare Department* some years ago. After much deliberation, we at *The Floating Bo$co* have decided it is only right and proper to allow confused acolytes of Plain Wayne to read it. The handwriting has been authenticated by no less than five independent experts."

"I don't under– " I stammered.

"You owe it to yourself, Harry. It won't be easy reading. Just press the buzzer when you've seen enough. I'll be in with a nice hot cup of something and a Hubby-sized portion of *Tender Loving Bo$coCare* if you need it. You may, Harry. You may."

"Justine, I – "

She handed me the notebook and tiptoed out. I looked at the front. On a white label was written. PROPERTY OF PLAIN WAYNE. DO NOT READ! I stared until the notebook swam before my eyes. Then I reached into my pocket and found my *Hubby On The Move* pack of *Calm Down Hubby*! I swallowed the lot, opened the notebook and read:

24th of Thatcher: Had a particularly useless lot of hubbies in today. Completely hopeless. Led them about shop explaining different nappy sizes and the maths of three-for-the-price-of-two offers. Some of them just can't get their daft heads around it. As I said to Neil, "Thank God we're bachelors, Neil! Where would we be now if we'd not had to do everything ourselves?" One particularly daft hubby called Les held up a packet of spaghetti and said it must have gone off because it was hard. I smiled sweetly and had him eating out of my hand in no time. Spent a nostalgic evening listening to all those jumpy Orchestral Oasis CDs and putting up-to-date date stamps on all the out-of-date cheese, bacon and dips. Coining it!

3rd of Cartland: Got some great stuff off the back of a lorry from one more hubby going bust and giving in to his Mrs. Vacuum-packed coffee that looks like the real thing! Tastes crappy, but still. Feel proud. Gave a nappy-changing demo. Wanted to throw up, even though only a dolly. Hubbies wept with gratitude – they'll weep over anything – and ran home to wow the Mesdames when they get back from the pub. The world is going mad. Neil is a great support.

17th McAleese: Meeting of the Precinct Association to discuss tactics. Smile and be nice is the motto. Not easy, but if Neil and me are going to be able to retire to the Bahamas on this side of fifty, it has to be done. The hubbies really make me sick. Hopeless! Bought three sides of beef from the Mad Cow Sanctuary. A mark-up made in heaven.

1st Gorman: Had a philosophical discussion re retail and the best approach. This Mrs was going on about buying cheap and piling high. Low profit and quick turnover. Me and Neil, on the other hand, while we want to buy cheap, we don't think much of selling cheap. Talk about daft! Pile it low and sell it high is more our style. Smile and be nice, of course. That's worth a bundle. We must never forget how vulnerable the hubbies are. They'll pay way over the odds as long as we keep their egos perky. The berks!

It went on page after page. Awful things – really terrible things – about me and many another well-meaning hubby. I couldn't believe what Plain Wayne said about Les. It was just too horrible. I mean, I know he's hopeless in Washday

Requisites but he does his best – and he's not the worst by a long chalk.

I didn't cry, though. I was past tears. Iron had entered my soul. To think that all that time! Anyway, I knew for a fact that I would never again darken the doors of the Nirvana Precinct.

I also knew that I would remember this moment for as long as I lived. I looked around me. The sun shone through the stained-glass windows and the oak pews creaked in the gentle swell of the ship. I put the notebook down on the seat beside me and knew that a new Harry Manley was being born.

Avril's always saying that in her experience hubbies can't get their heads round more than a teaspoon of reality. Well, I thought, I'll prove her wrong. I will come through this strengthened. I may never again be the trusting, even gullible, hubby I once was, but I will survive. And I will survive as a loyal customer of *The Floating Bo$co*. Of course, I could have retreated into the house and become a customer of Home Shopping. But I could not imagine myself giving up on the great outside world. I mean, the Mersey Estuary Enclave is a small world in a way. Estuaries are much larger than they were, of course, due to the rise in sea-level.

It was like conversion. And, wouldn't you know it, at that moment a choir began singing My Hubby's Little Ways which, Justine told me afterwards, is Lady Lavinia Bo$co's favourite song. Avril's too for that matter. It's not often people's favourite songs win The National Anthem Contest three years out of the last five.

There was a gentle tap on the door of the Interdenominational Chapel. And there was Justine, armed with a dainty pack of *Hubby Comfort* tissues. It was the first time I'd seen them then. She held out the very attractive sequined pack to me and I pulled one out. And do you know what happened? (Well, you probably do, seeing as how *Hubby Comfort* tissues have captured 98% of the disposable hanky market.) The BOX started playing *You're Such a Comfort To Me*. Well, I'm not ashamed to admit it, that really set me off and I had a good weep into the tissue. It held up very well under the strain, I have to say. You have to hand it to the Hubby Comfort people. They get 12 on 10 for presentation but have not let this in any way affect the quality of their product. And that's saying something in this day and age when you've got to have eyes and ears in the back of your head.

"Let it all out," Justine said. She pulled another tissue for me and the box played *Comfort Me in the Wee Small Hours* which is Dad's favourite from his time in the trenches during the GREAT RESTRUCTURE. He backed the losers as you've probably guessed. Still the Mesdames were gracious in victory. More than Dad had planned on being. "I can empathise with you, Harry," Justine said. "Believe me, at this moment, there is not one staff member aboard *The Floating Bo$co* who is not reaching out. We all know what you're feeling. It must be very close to bereavement. There's nothing worse than betrayal, is there?"

"Why, Justine? Why?" I sobbed.

She pulled another tissue. *The Comfort of Strangers* played. "I don't know that, Harry," Justine said. "But you and I both know that there are fellow-travellers out there who pretend to support the fruits of the GREAT RESTRUCTURE but who, inside, are completely unreformed. They are a canker in the body politic – I know what I'd do if I had my way. Shoot the lot! But they're on their way to oblivion. Plain Wayne,

Neil and their kind won't happen again. You can rest assured that when your son is ready to come on board, the world will be free of the drones of the Nirvana Precinct."

"Honestly, Justine," I said, "I've never read anything like that diary. To think that all these years Plain Wayne's *Angel Breath Supermoist Toilet Tissue* was just *Forward to Fundamentals Recycled* with tap-water added! I feel such a fool, Justine."

"Don't dwell on the past," Justine said. "Think of strategies for the future."

"What shall I do?" I asked.

"It's up to you to decide that, Harry. I can't do it for you."

"Well," I said, "the first thing to do is patronise *The Floating Bo$co* exclusively. That's the first thing to do."

Justine beamed. "I wonder if you know how proud that makes me, Harry! I feel really privileged to be instrumental in assisting a hubby to take a giant lifestyle-leap forward."

"What else should I do, Justine?"

"Nothing else, Harry. You've done everything."

She led me to the door of the Interdenominational Chapel. "There is one thing, Harry."

"Anything!" I replied.

"Tell your friends."

"I will," I promised.

Justine opened the door and I saw a crowd of smiling Mesdames of *The Floating Bo$co*. They cheered when they saw me. They threw flower petals. Then one came forward and presented me with a shopping-trolley done out like a galleon. "Bon Voyage!" she said.

More cheering; triumphant music on the tannoy.

"If you're quick, Harry," Justine said, "you'll be able to get a good shop in before we land."

"I will, Justine," I said, set fair for my route through Household Requisites, smiling at the welcoming Mesdames. The portrait of Lady Lavinia Bo$co above Fresh Croissants seemed to glow.

I filled my trolley past the plimsoll line, but was pleasantly surprised at how reasonable the bill was. In fact, I queried it. "Are you sure this is right, Mrs?" I asked the checkout assistant. Yes! They have people at checkout. It takes you back and it makes all the difference!

"Quite sure, hubby," the Mrs replied. "This must be your first time on *The Floating Bo$co*. Don't worry, you'll soon get used to the reasonable prices."

"I feel I've come home!" I told her.

"I felt I'd come home!" I told Les the following day after telling him everything that had happened.

We were at the Leisure Centre. Les was in the Jacuzzi because, he reckoned, his areas of private access were playing up.

"Well, you've changed your tune, chuck," Les said, "and there'll be no 150 estuarios for you to spend at the Nirvana Precinct."

"Haven't you been listening to a word I've said, Les!" I said, all exasperated. "I'm never going near the Nirvana Precinct again. I'd have thought I'd made that perfectly plain. I've a good mind to give Plain Wayne and that Neil a good piece of my mind."

"Sorry," Les said, "to tell you the truth, Harry, I'm a bit distracted." He pointed through the bubbles towards his area of private access.

I clucked sympathetically. You see, Les is by nature the hairiest sort of Hairy Hubby. Depilating's been a heavy cross for him to bear. Not that I'm saying for one minute that it's been easy for any hubby. But whereas my problem yielded to *WaxNGo* backed up by liberal applications of *HubbySoothe Medium Strength*, Les's had to get some of his depilatory supplies on prescription and even then he's been a martyr in his areas of private access.

"Do you know what I think, Les?" I said.

"No, what?"

"I think you should come with me to *The Floating Bo$co* and consult one of the counsellors about your on-going martyrdom in the depilating department."

Les came over all bashful. "I've already been on *The Floating Bo$co*, Harry," he said, staring into the Jacuzzi bubbles.

I was taken aback, and a bit let down, too. I'd hoped to be able to show Les the ropes on board and here he was telling me that he's already had a go. "When was that, Les?"

"I went on the QuickieCruise yesterday afternoon."

"You went on the QuickieCruise yesterday afternoon?"

"Yes, Harry, I went on the QuickieCruise yesterday afternoon."

"But," I said, "I left you with Big Yvette and . . . "

The mention of Big Yvette brought all my trepidation at the rail of *The Floating Bo$co* flooding back. There Les was in the Jacuzzi trying to soothe his areas of private access. The truth crashed down upon me like an episode of Hubby Premenstrual Empathy Syndrome, to which I am a martyr. Avril has periods and I suffer. It's only been diagnosed in the last few years, but it's amazing how many hubbies are coming out about it.

Anyway, the truth was a bit like that. "Les," I said, "you didn't give in to Big Yvette, did you?"

Les didn't say anything by way of reply. He nodded,

though to anybody except Yours Knowingly, the nod could have been a glance down at his inflamed areas of private access.

"I blame myself, Les," I said. "I should have warned you. That Big Yvette is a hubby-eater. She always was, Les. The times I had to tip her the wink at Widdecombe Three-Wheelers! She once had everyone in the paint-shop painted into a corner with her overtures, Les!"

Then it all came out. "After *The Floating Bo$co* had disappeared downriver, Harry, Big Yvette asked if I'd like to see her collection of Docker Memorabilia that she kept in the old ferry-ticket office. Well, I didn't think anything of it and off we went. She had a key to this place but when we got in there was this great big bed and a powerful scent of *HubbyArouse*. The rest is a bit of a blur, Harry."

I nodded, not believing Les for a minute. "And that's why you're in the Jacuzzi, isn't it, Les?"

Les dropped his eyes, unable to face me in confrontational mode.

"You're not the first, Les," I said. "Big Yvette has been through more hubbies than she can remember. In the old days when hubbies were still able to do their bit in the reproduction department there were hubbies in the Industrial Nostalgia New Town anchored to their tower blocks bringing up nippers mothered by Big Yvette. She used to ring the bell and leave them there, together with the DNA fingerprinting, stamped in triplicate by the relevant authorities, and that's the last you saw of Big Yvette. At least, that's what I hear, Les. Just thank your lucky stars that we fire blanks the whole time, Les. Nowadays you've only got the Mesdames' Monogamy Imperative to cope with."

Les, through his sniffles, said, "But what will my Barbara

say when she finds out I've fallen? I don't *know* I fire blanks, Harry!"

"Haven't you been tested?"

"No. I'd rather not know."

Les is a born conservative. "Les," I said, "if I know your Barbara like my Avril reckons she does, your Barbara will understand completely. I wouldn't be surprised if she felt guilty. It's about time Mesdames examined their consciences about having Mesdames like Big Yvette in their midst. There are more hubby-eaters about than is wholesome for the future of society, if you want my opinion, Les."

"But I'll never be able to go with you on *The Floating Bo$co* now, Harry!" Les said. "Not with Big Yvette on duty all the time."

"That's where you're wrong, Les. You're coming with me next week for your orientation to, and a really good shop on, *The Floating Bo$co*."

"But – "

"But me no buts, Les," I said. "I'll be with you every inch of the way. Anyway, Big Yvette doesn't return to the same flower twice."

"But when I see her I might melt again," Les said.

"I'll give you a good dose of *Calm Down Hubby!* before we go," I said. "Anyway, you're going to have more important things on your mind than Big Yvette."

"What's that?" Les asked.

"Washday Requisites," I said. "You know how useless you are. Next week I'm going to get you oriented to Washday Requisites on *The Floating Bo$co*. They have this amazing range."

"Don't, Harry!" Les cried, covering his ears. You see, Les's problems in Washday Requisites come very close to the centre of his neurosis. If we can clean that up, we can achieve anything.

"Don't worry, Les, I'll be there," I said.

"Thanks, Harry."

"Think nothing of it, Les," I said. "What's a mate for?"

"Yeah," Les said, "what's a mate for?"

3

Les's Crisis

Well, Les and me's trip to Washday Requisites had to be postponed for a couple of weeks because, after Les confessed about Big Yvette, his Barbara decided to confine him to the house for a while.

Of course I didn't say anything to Les at the time, but I was fretting like mad that Les's Barbara might have taken far sterner action against Les. It has been known for erring hubbies to be packed off bag and no baggage to the Industrial Nostalgia New Town. There's a Safe House there where the hubby is shown how bad it is away from the enclaves. He's taken out on these day trips to stare over the deadly laser-beam borders that are all that stand between the Industrial Nostalgia New Town and the heart of darkness. Still, as far as I can tell it was Les's first offence. Mind you, a little bird who shall be nameless told me that Barbara is notorious at those Estuary Nat West get-togethers. But, Avril went on to say, it's not the same for the Mesdames. It's like she always says: she says, "*Higgamus Hoggamus, hubbies are monogamous; Hoggamus Higgamus, Mesdames are polygamous,*" – whatever that means. If it means anything. Not a lot that rhymes does, I find.

Anyway, when Les's time was up I collected him from home and we walked down to the harbour, pulling our jumbo wheelies.

"If Big Yvette's at the landing stage," I told him, "just be civil. Act as if nothing has happened."

"I don't know – " Les said.

He'd been jumpy from the moment I rang his doorbell. "Look, Les, if anybody's going to feel guilty about this it ought by rights to be Big Yvette. We could," I said, "make a complaint."

"Don't do that," Les said. "Promise me you won't do that. Barbara said she's got it all in hand."

I stopped, and looked hard at Les. "I wouldn't, Les. I'm just saying that we'd be perfectly within our rights."

"Sorry," Les said. "It's all been building up. The incident with Big Yvette. Then having all that time in the house to think about visiting *The Floating Bo$co* and having to cope with Washday Requisites. It's a lot to take on board, Harry."

"I'm here, Les," I said.

Les smiled, then punched my arm. Like he does. Punching arms is not something hubbies generally do. I wouldn't take it from any other hubby apart from Les.

As luck would have it there was no sign of Big Yvette at *The Floating Bo$co* terminal, though there was a rather tasteless tartan wheelie parked ominously outside the old ferry-ticket office.

We got on board in plenty of time for the Morning Cruise and I decided to bite the bullet by exposing Les to the Washday Requisites Deck straight off.

"Les," I said, as we surveyed the washing products swaying off into the distance and Les started sweating. "Les, I'm a great one for learning by doing. You see, when I was Head of Parts at Widdecombe Three-Wheelers it was no good me bleating to counsellors when I couldn't find the *Widdecombe Super Blatch Three-Wheeler* cruise control. No, I had to have it ready and in tip-top condition. Well, that field of endeavour has changed a bit since those heady days but I still like to learn from my mistakes."

Les nodded. "Harry, chuck," he said, "I'm sure I'll be fine everywhere else on *The Floating Bo$co* – it's really lovely, isn't it? – but Washday Requisites still puts me in a proper tizzy, I have to admit. It was bad enough at Plain Wayne's, but here! I'm not sure I can handle it, Harry. You don't mind me telling you that, do you? I mean, you don't think any the less of me?"

I could see the anxiety in his eyes. "Course I don't, Les," I said. "Better out than in."

"Washday Requisites won't stay still," Les said. "At least with a coalface you knew where you were."

"Correction!" I said. "Same as Widdecombe Three-Wheelers, you thought you knew where you were."

"Yes, but here!" Les said. Sweat was once again standing on his brow as he looked down the aisle. I reached into my bumbag and popped open a *Yono-Wash* from its airtight individual envelope, brought home for me, along with a Singapore Airlines comb and toothbrush, by Avril after she attended the World Convention of Litigation Lawyers at the Oriental Hotel in Lawas, Malaysia. Actually, between you and me, every single lawyer except Avril came down with food-poisoning. The Oriental Hotel will never hear the last of it.

"Here you are, Les," I said.

"Cheers," Les said. Like he does. He just can't stop himself.

Course, I could see straight off how the land lay. The *Yono-Wash* wasn't going anywhere near solving Les's perspiration problem. I dreaded to think what was going on in his areas of private access. "I think we'd better adjourn to the HubbyCaff, Les," I said.

We sat down with our coffees at a corner table – purple gingham – with a good view of the river. "I think you'd better get it – you know – off your chest, Les," I said. "You'll see, you'll feel like a new hubby in no time when you do."

And out it came. I would never have thought Les was the sort who could purge himself like that but, as in lots else, I was wrong.

"Washday Requisites make me feel inadequate," Les said.

"And how does that make you feel?" I asked.

Les fiddled with the strap of his pec-organizer – I don't know why he doesn't invest in the ones with *Monovelc* fasteners – he's a born conservative. "Completely hopeless, Harry. I'll tell you how it was the last time I was at Washday Requisites at the Nirvana Precinct, shall I?"

"If it helps," I said. "Take your time. We've all the time in the world – if we look sharpish."

"Well," Les said. "I stood in front of the amazing range and I just couldn't move. I was rooted to the spot and I felt a cold flush coming on. Picture this, Harry: you've got this fabulous range of powders and liquids in front of you. Fair enough. I can handle that. Sort of. I know that the liquids are powders with water in them and the powders are sort of vice-versa – but after that I'm stuck."

"How about the ionising products?" I asked.

"The what?"

"Sorry I spoke," I said.

"It's a worry, Harry."

"Go on," I said.

And he did. "I used to have a bit of an allegiance to the old powders that were on the kitchen window when I was a nipper in Congleton. *Wave, Ama, Fiat* – for soft things – and dear old *Oxylon* – gone now, of course. Now, when I was new to being a hubby, I thought it was going to be a cinch. I bought a packet of *Wave* and shoved a mound of it in the drawer of the Bosch. I don't need to tell you what happened, Harry. Suds all over the shop and back to the ironing-board. Still, I reckoned I had learnt an important lesson, even if it did cost me a bollocking from Barbara. From then on I had to look for powders that had *Automatic* written on them because that meant they didn't produce all those bubbles. Now you'd think that that would have been the end of my problem. No such luck, natch. Barbara started to complain that she was getting jock-itch and she was sure it had to be the washing-powder. Was it 'eco-biological' she asked. Well, to tell you the truth, Harry, I had to look at the packet to find out. And you've guessed it, it was. So back I came to look for automatic non-biological, with Barbara's words ringing in my ears, 'Make sure it's hypoallergenic, too, pet!'"

Les sighed. I nodded, encouragingly. "I never did find one that was what she said, but I did find a powder that kept telling me how 'kind' it was. All went great for yonks, thanks to *You Got It! Automatic Non-Biological*. No complaints apart from the usual about stubborn stains. You see, Barbara would insist on keeping her biro in the top-pocket of her white blouse – even though I'd bought her a pen-case befitting her station at the Estuary Nat-West, a pig-skin job – she was too bone-idle to press the button of the biro so that the nib retracted into the pen. I tried pleading with her, but it did no good at all. Then I taped little signs to her pen collection: PLEASE RETRACT MY POINT AFTER USE! THANKING YOU. But that didn't work either. Barbara said she was too busy banking to read the reminder and anyway wasn't it my job to get rid of stubborn stains like the good and efficient hubbies she saw on the telly? Meekly, I said I'd try harder. I found – and this is an irony for you, Harry – a pen – yes, a pen! – that you uncap and then squeeze in a circular motion on the stain. Out comes the *Stain Fairy* that will eradicate the most stubborn stain. Anyway, with my pinny-pocket full of pens, my automatic non-biological washing-powder and my Bosch, I thought life in the Washday Requisites department would be plain-sailing . . . "

"But?" I asked.

"But, of course, I was wrong. Out from under the work-surfaces came The Environment."

I put my hands over my ears. "Don't, Les! Please!"

Les smiled wanly. "You can see the problem, can't you?" he said.

And I thought I detected that Les was beginning to self-empathize. Like they say.

Les looked over at me. I noticed the circles under his eyes and wondered if I should tell him about *New Zealand Flounder Oil*. I didn't. One thing at a time, I thought. "I bet I'm boring you, aren't I, Harry?" Les said.

"Not at all, Les," I said. "I'm here for you."

"Thanks, Harry," Les said. He frowned. I knew what he was going through because I'd been there myself – only in Tinned Goods. Don't ask me why hubbies have these blanks, because I can't tell you. The number of hubbies of my acquaintance who have just given up going out and being social because of these blocks in one area of shopping or another! They've just told their Mesdames that they've decided to be Hubbies-Who-Stay-In. The Home Shopping Consultant comes round to the house, then you see all this electronic gadgetry going in and that's the last you see of them.

"Anyway," Les went on – and there was nothing I could do to stop him, even if I'd wanted to which, of course, I didn't. "*Washday Grail* is the brand leader in the ecological end of the market and it comes in this glass bottle like a chalice with a gold dove for a stopper. When you come to refill it you present it to the *Mother of the Grail*, which is an oak barrel with a tap on it, and are trusted only to take enough to refill your chalice – which is quite something in this day and age, what with the Hairy Hubbies rampaging around the Nirvana Precinct like they do, and makes you feel good about the *Washday Grail* people. Anyway, to cut a long washing-line down, *Washday Grail* says that all its ingredients actually *feed* the environment, which is quite a claim."

"It is indeed, Les," I said. "It is, indeed. It's a bit like saying that one of the *Widdecombe Three-Wheeler models* helped to build up the road's resistance to irritating pot-holes."

"But the clincher is," continued Les, "if you send the label from the chalice to the manufacturers they donate a tree to the reforestation of the Black Forest."

That gave me a start. "Hold on a tick. Did you say the Black Forest, Les?" I asked.

"Yes. The Black Forest, chuck."

"Well, pull my petals!" I exclaimed. "The Black Forest was where the last model we produced at the Widdecombe Three Wheeler factory came to grief – and if my memory serves me right the place could do with a bit of greenery, I can tell you."

"Anyway," continued Les, "as a conscientious hubby, I should use *Washday Grail* religiously. But it's not as easy as that. You see, though *Washday Grail* may as it says *give back more than it takes out*, it costs the earth and doesn't wash to the high standards demanded by my Barbara. Now either of these failings would be sufficient to damn *Washday Grail* to the Unmentionable Regions in my book, Harry; but there is always that sneaking feeling of guilt when I pass it, knowing that streams, rivers and oceans are going to have to do without my washday residues and the desert of the Black Forest is going to creep towards Capetown – where Barbara's auntie is the leading estate agent on the Robbin Island Enclave – without benefit of my hubby's mite, a tree, that would padlock the desert in place."

I nodded, but didn't say anything. I didn't think it was my place, to tell you the truth. I was there to listen.

We arrived at the Washday Requisites deck. But Les was still in a state. I had to hold on tight to his arm.

"Think of Barbara and the twins!" I counselled.

I held him up with the aid of the trolley and led him along the aisle. Washday Requisites flashed past us, all different, all screaming their virtues but all, as I too knew to my cost, flawed in some way.

We arrived at the crowd of hubbies clustered round a demonstrator. Les held back.

"I can see the two hubbies at the back are a bit shy!" said the demonstrator.

"Er," I said, "begging your pardon, my friend and me have trouble deciding which Washday Requisite to buy."

Les gave me a grateful look. I knew then that we'd be mates until Frozen Foods froze over. You see, I had included myself in the problem. I had shared the responsibility. There's no better bond in my experience.

"That's what I'm here for!" said the demonstrator, rubbing her hands. "It's really a nice change to see two hubbies who can be so honest. Judging from the rest of you . . . " her eyes scanned the rather common-looking Hairy Hubbies who had probably boarded *The Floating Bo$co* at the Industrial Nostalgia New Town landing stage, and they wilted, like trees in the Black Forest, "you're all quite content with a tablet of *Pixie Carbolic* and a washboard!"

The hubbies inhaled a shocked breath at the suggestion.

"Those hubbies at the back, however, are not yesterday's hubbies. They're prepared to be adaptable." She smiled at us. "Now tell me your problem. Remember, there is nothing to fear but fear itself . . . well, almost . . . "

Les looked at me. He was still like wet jelly, so I spoke for him. "We," I said, and I looked at Les, "*we* have to have a washing product that is kind to sensitive skin and to the environment and doesn't cost the earth. You see our Mesdames are careful – quite rightly – with the housekeeping money."

The demonstrator nodded and Les added, right off his own bat, "It needs to be non-biological and automatic too."

I was proud of him. Really proud.

"It's a change to find hubbies who have taken the trouble to know what they want," the demonstrator said. "And I have just the thing for you. *Extra New Washday Grail* with added ecological scrubbers for stains both organic and inorganic in origin. Also – and this is a first – *Extra New Washday Grail* will automatically conform itself to the exact ph-value of your skin. I think it's what you've been looking for, hubbies!"

"It sounds expensive," I said.

"Not at all. I think you'll find that at 40.47 deci-estuarios per 100 ml. it's the most hubby-purse-friendly washing product on *The Floating Bo$co*."

I turned to Les. "What do you think?" I asked him.

By way of reply, Les turned to the demonstrator. "Can *Extra New Washday Grail* be refilled at the *Mother of the Grail Trust Barrels*?"

"Certainly, it can. I am standing in front of one as I speak."

"Then *Extra New Washday Grail's* the one for me!" shouted Les, quite his old self.

The demonstrator held out a 2-litre-capacity glass bottle of Washday Grail and presented it to Les, gratis and for nothing. The other hubbies broke into applause and before we knew where we were they had lifted Les on to their shoulders and were carrying him towards the check-out, while Les held up his chalice as if it was a *Pristine-Lounge-of-the-Month* trophy.

On the way home, Les looked at his *Washday Grail*. "Harry," he said, "we're in trouble. Big trouble."

"How do you mean, Les?" I asked. "It seems to me that *Extra New Washday Grail* fulfils all the criteria you demanded: it's kind to skin, feeds the environment, has added cleaning power, can be refilled, is non-biological, automatic. It's just the ticket."

"There's nothing on the back of the label," Les said, all miserable – so miserable that I started to feel miserable too.

"I don't get you, Les."

"A tree for the Black Forest, Harry. You can't get it with this variety of *Washday Grail*."

I thought of my last model for Widdecombe Three-Wheelers and how it had let me down because of one filter I'd supplied – the wrong one – which had pores large enough to let the sands of the Black Forest through. It was that which, I reckon, got me the push. "You're happy with *Washday Grail* in every other way, are you, Les?" I asked.

"Oh, yes! Very happy!"

"Good," I said, "then the Black Forest!"

"Yes," Les replied, all smiles now, "b. the Black Forest!"

Since then, I've felt bad about what I said but, like I

often say to Les, 40.47 deci-estuarios per 100 ml. doesn't buy perfection. *Extra New Washday Grail* isn't your average hubby, after all's said and done.

P.S. An Important Aside

Before I continue *The Days of Harry Manley, Hubby*, though I'm not sure that will be the final title, I really do think I should pause to thank most warmly and very sincerely Lady Lavinia Bo$co who, knowing that I am her number one fan, presented me with this very tasteful laser-voice diary with integral printer-n-binder at *The Wise Owl Till Receipt Awards* last month, and asked me to put my story into it. The finished opus will be kept for posterity in the Hubby Counselling area in the Interdenominational Chapel aboard our enclave's *Floating Bo$co*!

Of course, I've been all of a tizzy about consigning my "thoughts" to posterity. Lady Lavinia Bo$co is not only the President of *The Floating Bo$co* worldwide, but also the bestselling author of such hubby-novels as: *The Triumph of the Till; The Hubbies Demand Free-Range; The Hubbies Who Go For It By Going Out* and other blockbusters too numerous to mention. Knowing that, I know you'll feel for me when I say that I feel inadequate for such a task, I really do, and I'd be telling you a lie if I said I didn't.

Still, I take heart from the interview I had with the Virtual Reality Lady Lavinia in the state-of-the-art Hubby Consultation Chat-box at the back of the Interdenominational Chapel aboard *The Floating Bo$co*. You see, my Avril had said that Lady Lavinia only wanted me to consign my story to the tasteful laser-voice diary because she wanted me to provide *The Floating Bo$co* worldwide with valuable – and buckshee – market research. Of course deep down I sensed that this wasn't true, but I had to make sure.

I sat in the dark of the Chat-box and there was "Lady Lavinia" sitting opposite me on an antique IKEA armchair in brown corduroy. Of course, I knew it wasn't the real Lady Lavinia. I mean, I knew for a fact from the *World of Bo$co News* that the *real* Lady Lavinia was opening a new ocean-going *Floating Bo$co* on the Pacific Rim. But, and call me daft if you like, as soon as "Lady Lavinia" opened her lovely mouth to welcome me to the chat-box, I completely forgot that I was talking to the Virtual Reality Lady Lavinia (currently available to all customers on *Floating Bo$cos* worldwide in 125 languages and 49 dialects) and, supping the reassuring cup of *HubbyBroth*, told her all my reservations.

"Why do you want me to write down my story, Lady Lavinia?" I asked. "I ask because my Avril thinks you will only use what I have to say for market research. That isn't right, is it?"

There was a pause and Lady Lavinia gave this sort of hiccough. She half-smiled, froze, and then completed the smile. I forgot the momentary glitch in the technology straight off as she replied in that same authoritative voice that always so moves me when she speaks to us over the tannoy on *The Floating Bo$co*.

"Hubby Harry Manley," Lady Lavinia said, "I want you to record your story in your own way. What need have I of market research? *The Floating Bo$co* worldwide already has 97% of the business of the Hubbies-Who-Go-Out in hubby enclaves worldwide. I can peruse till-receipts if I want to know your spending patterns. I hope you're enjoying your *HubbyBroth*, hubby!"

"I am, Lady Lavinia. I am!" I said. "To tell you the truth, I've never liked the lettuce and mango flavour, but I'm really enjoying this. I wonder if the boffins have jigged up the recipe."

"It's extra new and improved, hubby," said Lady Lavinia, "and if you buy three packets of the 10-sachet lettuce and mango *HubbyBroth* you get a free sample of *HubbyLite-Superlite* with Essence of Morning Glory absolutely free, together with three gold stars for the Wise Owl of the Month Till Receipts Award."

"Do you? That's worth remembering," I said.

Lady Lavinia nodded. "It *is* worth remembering, hubby."

I decided to bite the bullet. "But, Lady Lavinia, why do you want me to write down my story? I'm such an average sort of hubby."

"There is no such thing as an average hubby, Harry," Lady Lavinia replied. "I want to keep a record of lots of hubby stories so that, in the future, hubbies not even thought of will be able to use them to look back and learn. There's too much amnesia around. Have you noticed?"

I nodded, though, telling you not a word of a lie, I'm usually much too busy trying to remember what I've forgotten to give much attention to amnesia to tell you the truth.

"I want you to be totally honest, Harry. I don't want any censorship. Censorship is fibbing when all's said and done and I, as a writer of some small reputation, know that you can't fool your readers. If they don't think they're in the hands of a narrator they can trust – well, you've lost them, Harry. No second chances, Harry. And it's just the same in retailing as in literature."

"I'm the number one fan of your Hubby Romances, Lady Lavinia," I said.

"Jolly good!" Lady Lavinia replied. "You don't know how happy that makes me. I've said this before and I'll say it again, I get far more pleasure from being read than I do from *The Floating Bo$cos* worldwide."

"I find that hard to believe, Lady Lavinia!" I said.

"Write your story, Harry, and you'll know what I mean."

"I'll do my best, Lady Lavinia!"

Lady Lavinia smiled and slowly faded.

Tears came to my eyes as the door of the Consultation Chat-Box swung open. I saw the queue of hubbies waiting for their consulations. They saw my tears. I didn't hide them. I wore them like a brooch.

As I went off in search of the *HubbyBroth* offer, I was wondering how to start my story.

Well, I suppose I have started it. This is it and it's gone on for ages already and didn't hurt much. But I'm worried like mad about what to mention next. You'll have to bear with me until I get into the flow. Will you do that for me?

4

The Anti-Depilatory Riots

It's no good. I've got to bite the bullet. There's no way I can give you an inkling of the way we live now without bringing up the vexed – and vexing – topic of Dad.

Dad, if you can call him a hubby at all, was the original Hubby-Who-Stays-In. He started staying in after he lost his job in fruit and vegetable wholesaling. He stayed in even more after the Cambrian Waste Farm went up in smoke back in 2021, turning most of Wales into the first and, it could be argued, the trendsetter among the Unmentionable Regions, areas which are just too depressing to mention. Avril, my Mrs, brought us into the enclave and Dad – playing at being a good Senior Hubby – came along, he said, for the ride.

Well, I'm a Hubby-Who-Goes-Out and I'm not ashamed to admit it. We're in the minority, mind you. My Avril says we're a rump of a rump. I know most hubbies on the Mersey Estuary Enclave stay in with their Home Shopping and those banks of monitors where I like to put my Boots prints of yesteryear and my Franklin Mint *Scenes From Vanished Suburban Life* thimbles in their own thimblerama. Good luck to them, but I just think they're missing out by not going out.

My Avril – when she's home and not off around the

enclaves of the Pacific Rim litigating – is forever sitting me around the kitchen food-bar (did I tell you it's titanium and black marble? Avril shipped it all the way from this really pricey shop in the Mekong Enclave Skylon Center) and telling me the risks I run by being a Hubby-Who-Goes-Out. Avril can rattle off cocktails of chemicals that are bound to do me in before my time.

"I'm sure you're right, dear," I tell Avril. Like you do. "Will you miss me?"

But to tell you the truth, life wouldn't be worth living if I stayed in. For a start, I wouldn't be able to meet my best mate Les on a daily basis in real life. And we wouldn't be able to board *The Floating Bo$co*, the supermarket, hubby counselling centre, cruise ship, fun palace, place of worship and spiritual and physical renewal, that has become the epicentre of this hubby's life.

Of course I'd be telling you a lie if I said that I didn't know that the world outside is full of dangers. I can understand why the Hubbies-Who-Stay-In have been seduced by the inside world and have all their needs delivered. But I feel completely confident that the products in the Environmental Requisites Department aboard *The Floating Bo$co* will keep at bay the worst that the outdoor world has to throw at a hubby.

Dad, like I said, stayed in, but he didn't stay in and buy from Home Shopping like everyone else. No, Dad stayed in and tried to figure out how Hubbydom got started in the first place! I ask you! Talk about obvious! Of course, it's Yours Hubbily who has to keep him supplied with his needs.

And while I ran around after Dad and made myself useful, Dad wasted no opportunity to confide to me his view of the world. As I'm sure you don't need me to tell you, I had no time at all for Dad's theories. When I was round there and he'd be going on about Anita Roddick or Mary Goldring being the start of the rot, I did my best to clean the place up. I zoomed around with my *No Taint! No Odour! Just Pristine!* in its supergun spray dispenser with integral chamois and abrasive (3 settings) surfaces. It costs a little more than *GermDemol*, which used to be my surface-cleaner of preference, but I have found it worth a lot more for what it gives you in the cleansing and peace-of-mind department. It's available on all vessels of *The Floating Bo$co* above 15,000 tonnes, by the way.

Anyway, I'd be shooting the grease, grime, UV rays, Radon gas and the rest to kingdom come and Dad would be going on:

"Look at you! A real little hubby! I don't know how you turned out like this, Harry!"

"Honestly, Dad!" I'd say. "I know perfectly well why I'm a hubby. We had the GREAT RESTRUCTURE after all those years of us mooning about with nothing to do except feel guilty about how we'd brought the world to a pretty pass. It was progress that did it; progress and the see-saw of history. Nothing more; nothing less."

Dad shook his head, looking at the table. I used the opportunity to try out *Extra New Window Frend* – the sort guaranteed not to contain vinegar; though, call me slow, I've never seen the harm in vinegar. I think we should be told!

"It was all a plot!" Dad said. "If you lot hadn't allowed the Mesdames to take over, none of the rest would have happened."

I don't know why I bothered, but bothered I was so bother I did: "Dad! I said. "We were a spent force. The Mesdames didn't need us in the reproductive department – not that we'd have been able to manage much even if we *had* been needed, what with the pathetic sperm-count and everything. They'd stored up the best genetic material the North-West had to offer while we were sitting all flaccid on our backsides. While men were going berserk about footer and darts and spending their redundancy, the Mesdames were beavering away to keep everything ticking over. Remember how Mum went out and worked at that sweatshop above Undo It All when you lost your job? You were too proud to take jobs like that. You spent the whole time mourning for what was gone. And that's not even mentioning the Big Picture. The Big Picture is unmentionable in my book, Dad. Just remember Mum's struggle."

"You leave your poor sainted mother out of this!" Dad said.

"Then she'd come home and make the tea, do the ironing, clean the house AND study her Open University books while you moaned and drank too much Asda cider."

"I wanted a man's job. All that was on offer was women's work."

"You have to adapt to changing circumstances, Dad. I've adapted. I'm happy to be a hubby! I really am! What a relief not to be Head of Parts at The Widdecombe Three-Wheeler factory any more. To tell you the truth, I'm grateful."

"You're a sissy!" Dad said.

Well, I had to laugh. "You're such an old fuddy-duddy, Dad!" I said, applying my *Hubby Saver* lip-salve (Sailor Strength). "By the by, I hope you don't mind me mentioning this, but when did you last . . . you know . . . depilate, Dad?"

"This morning," Dad said, all defensive.

"Not shave, Dad," I said, really stern, determined not to let Dad off the hook. "Depilate."

"Just before the last inspection by the Senior Hubby Home Help."

"Don't let your standards slip, Dad."

"I've lived too long," Dad said.

Well, I suppose he was right in a way. "That's no way to talk," I said, clearing up my cleaning equipment into my bumbag. "Must rush! I'm meeting Les for a QuickieCruise on *The Floating Bo$co* at three. There's an old-time dancing session. It's 'House' this week. We'll all be dancing round our bumbags while you're searching through the entrails . . . keeping an eye on our trolleys, too, of course!"

Dad couldn't summon up the energy to say goodbye. I popped a lo-cal, vitaminized *Your Breath is DEFINITELY Like the Ocean Breeze, Hubby!* (with UV and dioxin protection) into my mouth, and left Dad to all his hopeless yesterdays, my mind fixed on meeting my best mate Les at the Bo$coQuay. Mind you, I'd be telling a lie if I said that what Dad had said didn't prey on my mind.

Still, back to sanity . . .

The next time me and Les went on board *The Floating Bo$co*, we stayed all day. We shopped energetically for the home on the morning cruise and then, after the very reasonably priced lunch in the Hubbycaff, set sail again on the afternoon MiniCruise for a good sniff around on the Furnishing Deck.

On the morning cruise, Les got his own back by making me go through Tinned Goods, my blank spot. I was a bundle of nerves, I don't mind admitting.

We spent a whole hour there with Les panicking me into decision by threatening all these really dire penalties. That night I dreamed my Avril had lost her job because I hadn't managed to find a tin of dolphin-friendly tuna in dolphin juice with a ring-pull, child-n-tamper-proof top fast enough . . . and we'd been bundled off to the Unmentionable Regions.

Anyway, after we'd finished our morning shop, we placed our purchases – paid for – in the purser's office and went to eat lunch. Both of us had the *Lithe Little Hubby Lunch* and we sat at the blue-and-white gingham table with this really lovely view out over the Estuary.

"This is lovely, isn't it, Les?"

"It is," Les replied.

"You're not feeling nostalgic for the Nirvana Precinct, are you?"

"Not in the least," Les said.

I looked hard at Les. "Are you happy, Les?" I asked.

"Why do you ask?" Les asked. I could feel his tension.

"Well – and call me daft if you like – sometimes it seems to me that there's a shadow of sadness behind your smile." I laughed, then, a bit nervous about what I'd said. "I'm probably wrong, though. I usually am," I said.

"No," Les said, "you're spot on, Harry. It's true; I'm not what you would call happy."

Well, that made me feel really terrible as you can imagine. "Do you want to talk about it?" I asked.

"Not at the moment, Harry," Les said. "Not at the moment. How's your dad?"

Les mentioning my dad rang alarm bells. Don't ask me why. "Why do you ask, Les?"

"I don't know," Les said. "It's just that from what I hear you tell about your dad, he sounds like a good sort."

"My dad," I said, "is a Neanderthal."

"Steady on, Harry . . . "

"No, I'm sorry, Les, I don't feel like steadying on. Do you know how much time I have to spend running after Dad because he refuses to avail himself of the facilities on offer for Hubbies-Who-Stay-In? A lot of time, Les. And do I get any thanks for it? I do not. He looks at me the whole time, shakes his head and calls me a sissy. Now do you call that fair, Les? Do you call that being 'a good sort'?"

"Sorry I spoke," Les said. "It's just – "

"Just me no justs, Les."

"Right you are, Harry," Les said. "You're the boss."

In order to distract ourselves from the vexed topic of Dad, we looked around at new hubbies being oriented to *The Floating Bo$co*. Some I knew from the Nirvana Precinct and I reckoned they'd also heard the shocking news about Plain Wayne. But there were others I'd never clapped eyes on before.

I mentioned this to Les by way of changing the subject and dusting away the gloom as he was tucking into his full-fat calorie-free dessert.

"They're Hubbies-Who-Stay-In. Look at how bowed over they are. That's what comes from sitting about all the time."

"It's good to see that *The Floating Bo$co* is helping the hubbies to be all they can be," Les said with this odd smile on his face.

I decided to take Les's words at face value. I hoped he meant it. I hoped against hope that I had not detected a first sign of negativity. "It is," I said. "You know that the Hubbies-Who-Stay-In never go out, don't you?"

"I had heard," Les said.

We shook our heads.

"Half our road is made up of Hubbies-Who-Stay-In. You never see them," Les said.

"Same here," I said. "There's Kevin Earnshaw just next door. He used to be a solicitor, according to my Avril. Now he just stays at home. He never even opens his curtains."

"There's nowt as queer as . . . " Les said.

"You never said a truer word, Les," I said.

Just then a voice came over the tannoy inviting us to the on-board cinema to watch a bio-pic about Lady Lavinia Bo$co.

"Can we go, Les?" I asked.

"If you want, Harry. We will have time to go around Furnishings, though, won't we?"

"I'm sure we will," I said.

Anyway, the film about Lady Lavinia's life started with Lady Lavinia appearing from behind a curtain – on film, not in real life – and saying as how she hoped we would enjoy the film and learn a little about the philosophy of *The Floating Bo$co*.

There was this great surge of music and then this lovely little girl sailing a boat on a boating lake. She was as happy as anything. There was this big house in the background. Then a horrible old Hairy Hubby (the film was set long before the GREAT RESTRUCTURE) came up behind the little girl. "LAVINIA!" he shouted, "HOW MANY TIMES HAVE I TOLD YOU NOT TO PLAY WITH BOATS?"

And do you know what the horrid old man did? He whacked Lavinia and made her cry. The audience – including me and Les – let out an involuntary collective scream; I mean, we just couldn't help it. Then he whacked Lavinia's boat and made it sink. Close-up on Lavinia's tear-drenched face, looking at the water where her dear little boat had been.

Cut to Lavinia in the big house. She is being tutored by another hairy man. There is a map of the world and a model of a Bo$co Superstore. The old chap – Lavinia's teacher – goes on and on about distribution centres and buying low and selling high and never giving the public an even break and restructuring to get out all the dead wood. Les gave me a dig; he knows we can both identify with restructuring. And we weren't alone. A hubby somewhere in the dark booed and a Mrs with a torch came and gave him a stern talking-to.

Lavinia takes all this for a while. "Any questions?" the teacher asks.

"Yes," says Lavinia, "I want to know why there isn't any fun in Bo$co Superstores!"

"Fun!" shrieks the teacher. The cane is raised in the air and falls with a sickening crack. The screen goes dark. Lights up on a young woman approaching the same house. It must be many years later. The place is all overgrown. Tumbleweed tumbles. Ivy creeps. In she goes through the creaking front door. There is Lord Bo$co of Bebington – I know because his name is on his coffin – lying in state. A solicitor comes up, "The Bo$co Empire is yours, Lady Lavinia, but I must inform you that the company is in terrible debt." Close-up on Lady Lavinia looking determined.

Newsreel films of the GREAT RESTRUCTURE. Nuclear leaks, cars choking the roads, road rage, shopping rage, pollution rage, age rage, sperm-depletion rage, anti-depilatory rage, animals-in-cages rage. Rage was all the rage, I can remember that well enough. The Night of the Mesdames. The Retreat of the Underclass. The setting up, after the trench wars, of hubby enclaves by concerned Mesdames in work . . . it all passed in front of us in a few short minutes with the face of Lady Lavinia as a shadow, looking angry, worried, concerned. Fade out. Then Lady Lavinia is jogging through the empty streets of various hubby enclaves. All the curtains in the houses are drawn. All the hubbies are staying in. Home Shopping has won. Lady Lavinia is thoughtful as she jogs. She comes to the estuary and runs along the sand. The music (from *The Triumph of the Till* unless I'm very much mistaken) is played. Lady Lavinia sees a ship leaving the estuary. She stops, panting. Then she speaks directly to the camera. "It was then that I had my idea. A ship that would fulfil the inner needs of hubbies. *A store, yes, but an ocean more.*"

The camera pulls away. It must have been on a helicopter all the time. It climbs away, high above the estuary as Lady Lavinia spins her Eureka dance. She becomes a pin-prick and then the music reaches a crescendo and we have shot after shot of *The Floating Bo$cos* of the world with waving hubbies. The Verazzano Broads, the Shannon, the Congo, the Malacca Straits, the Persian Gulf, the River Plate, the Thames, the Severn . . . all *The Floating Bo$cos* of the world pass, hoot and wave. Then the camera pulls away, high, high into the air, until there is only sea and sky. Lady Lavinia's voice is heard, "You buy my care; my care can't be bought!"

THE END.

"That was good, wasn't it, Les?"

"Very moving," Les said.

I stopped. "Is that all you can say, 'very moving'?"

"Well, I can't quite say exactly what I mean," Les said. "It was great. Really good."

"That Lady Lavinia Bo$co is a hero in my book," I said.

"You never said a truer word," Les said.

We made our way through Skincare Products trying to find the way to the Furnishing Deck.

It was Les who noticed. I missed it, still in a world of my own like you get after a really good film. "They're demonstrating a new variety of *Hubby-Soothe*, chuck."

"They're not!" I exclaimed. "Where?"

Les pointed. It was true. They were. We looked at one another. We didn't need to speak. Deciding to go and inspect Furnishings on our next trip aboard *The Floating Bo$co*, we went instead to learn about the new variety of *Hubby-Soothe*. I mean, first things first when all's said and done. Like Les says.

And by the time we'd listened, sampled, asked questions

and made our purchase – wouldn't you know it? – it was time to disembark.

You see, I don't know if you're like me, but there are some things I never like to be without, certain icons among products. And one of those icons is – you've guessed it – *Hubby-Soothe*, a post-depilatory balm. It's by appointment by the way – not sure who to – and has been my balm of preference ever since the Anti-Depilatory Riots were at their height and I first had urgent need for a balm.

To tell you the truth, I've been having this little battle with my conscience about whether I ought to go into controversial topics like the Anti-Depilatory Riots. I mean, so much has been written about them and how they brought about the split among hubbies that even to this day has failed to heal. It's all a bit hard for me. There's no agreement on the topic, you see. Pick up any Mrs writing about it and she'll say the Depilatory Imperative was the icing on the cake, the "pivotal moment" when hubbies had to face the fact that not only were they a spent force economically but would also have to do something tangible to show the Mesdames that hubbies knew that Mesdames had, in the nicest possible way, the whip hand.

You see, after the setting up of the hubby enclaves everything on the back patio was lovely – for those who'd managed to get in, that is. All the unpleasant part of the Decade of Readjustment was well and truly behind us. If my memory serves me right the Depilatory Imperative was the one and only time the Mesdames really laid down the law and got imperious. Normally the hubbies just went along with everything in a moony, don't-care sort of way. After all, the Mesdames were getting such a buzz from taking over all our old roles. We'd been struggling for an age, what with restructuring, retooling, the looming Pacific Rim, the sperm count going down the tubes, genetic choice, rogue genetic mutations in the plant and animal world and everything, that when it became clear that the Mesdames could do a better job than we could – and actually enjoyed doing it – we all just sighed, dropped our heavy loads and said, "Over to you, precious!"

It was all very informal at first. A lot of hubbies would stay at home all day without doing a stroke and then expect their hard-pressed Mesdames to come home and do all the work there as well. Well, that couldn't go on and there was this campaign against "Home Drones" which worked a treat. I can still remember the ad. A cartoon Mrs done up like a worker bee brings home nectar in a briefcase to this fat slug of a HubbyDrone who would be sitting in an armchair in the corner of the hive smoking a fag by the fire. When the worker Mrs asks – politely – for her tea, state of the nippers, etc., the HubbyDrone buzzes angrily and the poor worker Mrs gets this torrent of abuse as the HubbyDrone strides up and down the hive pulling his braces and droning on about his masculinity and what he'd like to do to the powers-that-bee. The camera leaves the unfortunate couple to their problems and a slogan appears: IT TAKES TWO TO FILL A HOME WITH HONEY!

Well, it was surprisingly effective. Of course, it never worried Harry Manley because I'd taken to the home like a bee to clover and was producing lovely little meals for Avril on her return from Moseley's (there was no Lumumbashi then). And in those days she was grateful, she really was. That was before her career really took off.

But when the Depilatory Imperative came along, the gloves were off and the hair flew. All the organs of Mrs

Management plc (the government) were spurting out the message that hubby-hair did not, despite all our preconceived notions, appeal to Mesdames. It was time to depilate or get out. As a popular song of the time said,

> "Hubbies, I'm tellin' yu straight
> If yu wanna get 'n' keep a mate
> Yu'd berrer depilate!"

Hubbies were driven hairless with worry by the Depilatory Imperative. Previously docile hubbies who had got their act together after the "Home Drone" campaign started buzzing angrily about their rights. Graffiti started appearing: IF HUBBIES WERE MEANT TO BE HAIRLESS, WHY DO WE HAVE HAIR? To which some Mrs added: SAME REASON YOU GOT NIPPLES AND FIRE BLANKS.

It makes me go all funny writing that sort of crudity, but you need to know how bad it was.

And give the Mesdames their due, they gave hubbies time. For three or four years there was Hubby Depilatory Day, with all sorts of events on Home Shopping and Worldwide Rupert. Plain Wayne and Neil – may they rot in the Unmentionable Regions! – no, I don't mean that – organized free depilatory workshops. I went, but I'd never seen the Nirvana Precinct emptier. In short, hubbies did not want to depilate, and that was that.

"Remember the bad old days, Les?" I said.

"Don't remind me, chuck," Les said.

"It all happened so fast," I said. "There was no time to, you know, work ourselves into the idea. It seemed like one week the Mesdames couldn't get enough of Hairy Hubbies and the next week they were laying down the law saying it all had to go."

"Can you remember where you were when it struck you that we were going to have to depilate?" Les asked.

I thought about that. "I reckon it was that report from the Shannon Estuary Enclave Pharmacological Association that brought it home to me, Les," I said. "Once news was out about the dangers of the hubby-hair-mite, I knew the game was up. These pictures of the hubby-hair-mite on the nine o'clock news were horrific. I could see my Avril stiffening."

"The Mesdames completely went off hubby-hair overnight," Les said. "And not only that. The depilatory product manufacturers saw an alternative market, didn't they? They were really sore about Mesdames' body-hair being suddenly all wholesome."

"You're right, Les," I said. "Never righter."

"Call me cynical, Harry," Les said, bold as Big Yvette, "but I reckon it was all a conspiracy."

"Steady on, Les," I said.

"It's too late now," Les said. "I just wish we could have our time over again. If we did, I know I'd embark on a rewarding regime of depilatory action. As it was we were panicked up many a blind alley, depilatory-wise."

"And all the support services completely broke down. The Harassed Hubby Helpline was hopeless . . . hopeless!"

"They ordered a razor in a hot-oil bath for me," Les said. "They lulled me into a false sense of security. You see, it worked like a charm but the hair grew back tougher every time. As I used to be quite hairy in my areas of private access it got so's I had to walk with my legs apart. Of course, all the Mesdames knew. They'd laugh like anything when they saw me in the precinct."

"If we'd been mates then," I said, "things would have been different."

Les winked. I smiled. Then I shuddered, thinking back. "It makes you shudder, thinking back," I said.

"It certainly does!" Les said.

I told Les that if I'd known then what I know now, I'd have fought tooth and nail against the Depilatory Imperative.

Les knew I was just kidding, of course, but it got him going all nostalgic about the past. "Harry," he said, "do you remember where you were during the Anti-Depilatory Riots?"

"That's easy," I said. "I was locked up in the guest bedroom with a tub of *Red Hot Wax*. My Avril sent Jason to the 24-hour crèche and wouldn't let me out until I'd done the necessary."

"At least you were able to depilate in the privacy of your own home," Les said bitterly. "My Barbara pushed me out to *Plain Wayne's Hubby Supplies* – of accursed memory – and the Hubby Depilatory Department. She wouldn't render any assistance as to choice of products. She said she'd never had any help in the bad old days and it was up to hubbies to learn by doing, same as she'd had to. And wouldn't you know it, I walked bang straight into a demonstration by the Angry Hubby Brigade. Well, they just panicked me. All my carefully acquired consumer priorities just went straight out of the window and I picked up an armful of depilatories at random – the Angry Hubbies scoffing away – and ran away, with them chasing after me and calling me names. I tell you, Harry, it was worse than my initiation at Congleton Colliery – and that's saying something, believe me. I haven't been able to give a high-pressure hose a straight look since."

I thought about that time as I counselled Les. The Anti-Depilatory Riots had been the last gasp of Hubby-power. Of course, in those days lots of hubbies were still holding out. A few still thought that Hubbydom was something that was just a way of showing willing until the upturn came, We hadn't thought it was the Final Wave.

But when the history of hubbies comes to be written,

they're going to say that the Anti-Depilatory Riots were the beginning of the end for hubbies – or the beginning of the beginning, depending on your point-of-view. Hubbies who tried to hold on to their body-hair would come home from a hard day's jeering at the good hubbies loading up on depilatory products in the Nirvana Precinct only to watch commercials which really struck at the heart of the anxieties of hubbies. You see, for yonks Virtual Hubbies had become available. These Virtual Hubbies, conjured up by the Mesdames using computer technology and fashion sun-glasses, were posing a real threat to real-life hubbies. Virtual Hubbies, you see, were everything the Mesdames wanted in hubbies. It was always a wise move for hubbies to borrow the Mesdames' sunglasses and run the programs, just to see what appealed to them – and then go off and get into shape. Luckily, Virtual Hubbies never managed to knock real hubbies off our perches. For a start Virtual Hubbies were so perfect both physically and psychologically that they weren't challenging enough for the Mesdames. Also, as if you didn't know, they couldn't shop to save their lives.

Still, back then the very sight of a Virtual Hubby was enough to turn the real ones really twitchy. In this advert, Hairy Hubbies had sand kicked in their faces, their car keys thrown into ravines by Mesdames who were busy ogling hairless Virtual Hubbies who bowled up along the freeway wheeling their powerful prams and simpering in time to Light Polythene music. And the errant Mesdames would run their hands over the arms and smooth chests of the hairless Virtual Hubbies and run off, leaving the Hairy Hubby alone and unloved surrounded by buttes in the Montana Desert.

And it didn't take long for the daily soaps to take up the theme. Meryl, the leader of the Mesdames in *The Hubbies of Jamaica Lodge*, actually walked out on her hubby because he was refusing to depilate, and all the good hairless hubbies were 100% behind Meryl. Even *The Archers* divided the hubbies along class lines. The middle-class hubbies, starting with the hubby who owns Grey Gables, depilated from Day Zero – ably assisted by much sage advice from Peggy; whereas Eddie Grundy and his ilk fought it tooth and nail. Still, no prizes for guessing who won in the end. *The Archers* even took to mentioning "A Depilatory Expert" in its credits. So it was all a set-up from the start.

Well, I reckon we could have survived all that but then the government stepped in with their health warnings about the hubby-hair-mite. The Prime Mrs appeared on the telly. Did hubbies not realise, she said, that their kiddies were 90% more likely to suffer from respiratory ailments due to the dung of the hubby-hair-mite. They showed a time bomb ticking next to a baby's cot and then closed in on a dithering Hairy Hubby. The bomb was about to go off and then the hubby makes the decision and depilates like he ought. The bomb turns into a friendly kiddies' alarm-clock with a smile on its face.

That did it. All but the most stubborn rump of hubbies caved in. And those who didn't cave in found themselves deserted by their Mesdames and, alone with their kids, down at the bottom of the housing list or sent off to live in the Industrial Nostalgia New Town. This was too much for their Mesdames, who left them in droves. And we won't go into the shocking blight visited upon the Industrial Nostalgia New Town and similar sorts of places up and down the country since. I'd be telling you not a word of a lie to say that it's awash with single Hairy Hubbies; the whole place gets sprayed from a council helicopter with Anti-Hubby-Hair-Mite preparations on a daily basis. It's really too depressing for a hubby like me, who tries at all times to be positive.

Well, you've got to, don't you? I'm a hubby who can't, who doesn't feel it's his place to say no. The Mesdames know lots of things that we don't. That's my Desiderata, you might say. Of course we know lots of things that they don't have an inkling of. It's a two-way street. But in the end it's the Mesdames that bring home the housekeeping. That's the bottom line, as my Avril would say.

I think I've said quite enough on that vexed topic. Mind you, it still goes on. Any time now I'm expecting a total ban on Hairy Hubbies aboard *The Floating Bo$co*. You see, from what I hear tell from Big Yvette and some of the counsellors on board, a close scrutiny of the till-receipts of the Hairy Hubbies shows that the items they purchase would fit comfortably into the cabin of a decommissioned fishing-boat. So that might be what gets laid on for the Hairy Hubbies.

Still, until that day comes, Hairy Hubbies on board *The Floating Bo$co* are a cross we just have to bear. Thank goodness, security is top-notch. Also each and every hubby who boards the vessel has to go through a Hubby-Hair-Mite Detector and, if the buzzer goes, he must go through Bo$co's own decontamination check-in. It's not an ideal solution, but it will have to do until complete segregation is achieved, as it has been in education, housing zones and places of hubby recreation.

I mean, if you're going to be a Neanderthal, you're going to have to expect to be treated like a Neanderthal.

And that, I promise, is all I have to say on the subject. For further reading, I refer you to the seminal work on the subject *The Depilatory Imperative* by Mrs Diane Fern (Yale University Press) or – a much better read in my book – *The Hubbies Take the Silk Route* by – you've guessed it – Lady Lavinia Bo$co (Bo$co Check-It-Out Press).

5

Scruples

According to the *Why Not Write, Hubby?* instructions manual on creative writing that I've been using to get ideas for my opus, I should never introduce characters and then drop them like hot baguettes straight out of the Electronic Bread-Maker. It causes, according to *Why Not Write, Hubby?*, this terrible reader dissatisfaction and may be instrumental in making the reader erase the Story Chip.

Now Jason – remember Jason? – might be one such suspended character. He's me and Avril's son, though he's not actually mine, as you may have guessed already. Avril did the necessary by mail-order from this flash clinic in the LA Estuary Enclave. I don't know if the lawyers at Moseley and Lumumbashi got a special three-for-the-price-of-two bargain, but there are three nippers at Jason's school who are the spitting image of Jason, and they're all the spitting image of Charles Bronson. Don't ask me what goes on. I can't tell you. I like to stand aside from all that sort of thing. It's completely the province of the Mesdames.

Jason is all right. He will, as I've mentioned before, make a great little hubby. The thing is, he only enters my life occasionally. It's the old story. We blamed the teachers and the teachers blamed the parents for this really shocking indiscipline around the millennium. The argument was never settled, of course. They never are, are they? Still, when the Mesdames took over, they decided that one or the other – teachers or parents – should take over responsibility for the nippers, seeing as they were the enclaves' greatest resource and that. There was a lot of argy-bargy for *ages*, but then it was decided that the teachers should do the rearing and the parents should pay.

So, from the age of two onwards, the nippers stay at school with only occasional R and R at home IF TWO PARENTS ARE ON SITE. Now, seeing as I am married to a litigation lawyer of worldwide renown, it doesn't happen that often that we are given time with Jason. So, when Avril is away I'm as good as a single hubby – 'cept I have Avril behind me in the finance department. A b. good job my Avril's got, a b. good job.

Anyway, I hope that satisfies you. You probably knew the score anyway, but I thought I'd mention it in case you were feeling dissatisfied.

Of course, you might be asking yourself, "If Harry's Mrs is a litigation lawyer of worldwide reputation, why doesn't she see to it that her Jason gets a proper home life?" A good question. Back in the mists of antiquity, when I still asked Avril questions of pith and moment, I asked that question myself. "I mean, Av," I said, "I really like having Jason around. He's company for me when you're not here."

"No way," Avril said. "If the Boarding Initiative hadn't been initiated by a concerned cadre of teachers I'd have initiated it myself, Harry. We don't want Jason to inherit a scintilla of death-dealing laddish ways, do we, Harry?"

"Of course not, dear," I said. "But I'm not in the least laddish, am I?"

"No," Avril conceded. "*You're* definitely not. But I'm not sure I can say that about one or two of your hubby chums."

"But I've only got one or two hubby chums, Av."

"That's correct, Harry. Need I say more?" Avril said in a tone that suggested strongly that if she did have to say more she would reduce me to tears.

"I expect you're right, Av," I said. Like you do.

And that was the end of it and pretty much the end of Jason as a character in this hubby's life.

Another thing they say in *Why Not Write, Hubby?* is that the narrative thrust should be kept up throughout to help the readers turn the page or press the button on the *AutoBook*. The writers of *Why Not Write, Hubby?* compare a good read to a long scarf. A plain scarf keeps you warm – and that's what a good, well-told tale does apparently. A heavily-embroidered scarf, though it may look nice, might irritate the neck. It might also, of course, be so garish as to make you scared to go out wearing that particular scarf. Too many asides, according to *Why Not Write, Hubby?*, are like those irritating embroideries.

And while I'm on the subject of "irritating" . . .

Before Dad became a peculiar sort of Hubby-Who-Stays-In, he put this notorious advert in *The Mersey Estuary Enclave Sunday Times*, whose motto was, until it shut shortly after – WE ARE THE SUNDAY PAPERS. Well, that all depends what you want from the Sunday Papers. If you want a lot of rubbish to line a cat-box or donate to the Industrial Nostalgia New Town *Fire-Lighter Appeal* then I suppose they were the Sunday Papers. If, however, you wanted a decent read, you were out of luck.

Of course, like I've said, I'd stopped getting that sort of paper by that time. Dad would insist on getting *The Mersey Estuary Enclave Sunday Times* because, back in the mists of antiquity – the times where Dad's head is – that paper had poured scorn on the GREAT RESTRUCTURE and had run a campaign pouring more scorn on separation of the Unmentionable Regions from the enclaves.

Dad had been in full agreement with them on that. You see, Dad, despite the shocking dangers in the Unmentionable Regions, had contradicted the whole Desiderata of the Hubbies-Who-Stay-In by rubbing himself all over with Dettol and venturing over for a day trip on his bike. He always came back to me full of stories of how folk in the Unmentionable Regions were "salt of the earth".

I, through my mask and spraying Dad with *Instant Quarantine*, tried arguing with him. "Dad," I'd say, "salt of the earth the inhabitants of the Unmentionable Regions may once have been. But they've lost their savour, Dad. And, to continue the salt metaphor, they can cause you a great deal of harm, what with the high radioactive count, the dioxins, the asbestos dust, the TB, the rogue genetic spores, and the rest."

"I had a cup of tea from this chap in a caravan at the side of the road!" Dad said, really chuffed. "We'll really lose something if we retreat into so-called Hubby Enclaves."

"You're such an old romantic, Dad!" I said. "We can't afford to be romantic these days. My Avril says that unless we align ourselves with the Pacific Rim sharpish and sell them our services, we'll go down the tubes. They've been ruthless with their pockets of poverty, though 'pockets' is probably the wrong word to describe 95% of the Pacific Rim. Wiring off the Unmentionable Regions is an idea whose time has come, Dad!"

"The Chinese are killing off their old folk," Dad said. "They've imported all these Hara-Kiri slot machines from Hatishoo Inc."

"Where did you read that, Dad?"

"In *The Mersey Estuary Sunday Times*."

Well, of course, the Unmentionable Regions were left to their own devices and wired shut. The GREAT RESTRUCTURE came and went, but the wretched *Mersey Estuary Enclave Sunday Times* continued publication against all the odds. And that's where Dad placed this advert which caused such a fuss and almost turned me into a Hubby-Who-Stays-In. I mean, I was really embarrassed to go to the Nirvana Precinct after it appeared, knowing that all the hubbies were pointing at me, knowing that it was my dad who had placed it.

The advert read:

WANTED BY MATURE GENTLEMAN:
SWEET AND OBEDIENT LADY
FOR HELP AROUND THE HOUSE
GOOD CONVERSATION
AND ROMANCE ESSENTIAL.
APPLY
ARTHUR MANLEY
BOX 823

Well, I'm sure you don't need me to tell you that the advert caused a real scandal. Avril ordered me "to do something about your father" at once.

"Yes, dear," I said, though I wasn't sure what.

Of course there were no takers for the ad. What Dad had requested was everything the Mesdames had absolutely no interest in at all. It was a measure of how out-of-touch Dad had become that he could think it might work.

I remember Dad had just attended – all on his ownsome – the ceremony for the 110th Anniversary for the Battle of the Somme and had asked my advice on cleaning up the memorial. (It was demolished a few months afterwards – and not before time!) I said that I'd help him as long as he'd let me take over in the Household Needs department.

"I'm getting a woman!" Dad said.

"Oh," I said, "you've had lots of replies to that shameful ad, have you, Dad?"

Well, he didn't have any answer to that. He agreed, with much bad grace, that I should go in and help out in the house.

I remember that first time I took Dad around *Plain Wayne's* – this was long before *The Floating Bo$co* or Les sailed into this hubby's life. Dad wandered off and I came upon him holding a bottle of *Double Duck* lavatory cleanser. And, do you know what, he was looking all disapproving!

"What's all this about?' he asked.

"It's *Double Duck*, Dad. No home worthy of the name should be without it."

"It cleans the bog, does it?"

The teaching starts here, I thought. "Dad," I said, "*Double Duck* not only cleans the lavatory, it also deodorizes and reodorizes the area. As you can see, Dad, there are two bottles, both with duck-shaped apertures. The split-second time-lag in application, followed by the combining of *Double Duck*'s unique formulation, not only deodorizes, reodorizes and kills all known germs and harmful pollutants (including dioxin and rogue genetic spores) but also gives the user a burst of DD-Energy (patent pending) that helps the user through the domestic tasks that still lie ahead."

"Funny you should say that, son," Dad said. "That's exactly what it says on the label."

"I have read the label of *Double Duck* many times, Dad. You know – or maybe you don't – that reading labels is an essential part of good housekeeping."

I made Dad buy a *Double Duck*, telling him to watch carefully as I placed it at the far right of the trolley. "Dad," I said, "imagine the bottom of this trolley is local geography.

The big section up here is the Unmentionable Regions. Here you put all the possibly harmful things, well away from foodstuffs."

"I want Baked Beans," Dad said.

"Tinned goods you may regard as the clear blue water that lies between the Unmentionable Regions and the Estuary Enclave," I continued. "They might, if you get a lot of them, also inhabit the Industrial Nostalgia New Town area . . . " I pointed out the part of the trolley I had in mind.

"Beans, son," Dad said.

We pushed our trolley to Plain Wayne's Baked Bean display. The range, need I say, was nothing compared to that on board *The Floating Bo$co*, but it seemed impressive – and alarming – then.

"The question is, Dad," I said, "which beans? I would tend to go for the *Georgia Amalfi Hydroponically-Grown Designer Baked Beans – With guaranteed Protection against irritating flatulance*. True, they're a bit on the pricey side, but experience has taught me that *Georgia Amalfi Hydroponically-Grown Designer Baked Beans* are, quite simply, a better product. You might also consider *Plain Wayne's Old Reliable Baked Beans*. They're excellent in the taste department and if you buy their Wind Factor 1, you'll find that, for deci-estuarios more, you'll experience a fine product without side-effects."

"Give me half a dozen of the cheapest," Dad said.

"Dad," I said, "haven't you been listening to a word I've been saying? I'm here trying to educate you into healthy eating options."

Still, there was no telling Dad. He trolleyed six dented cans with "BEANS" written on them in biro. I was already going red with embarrassment at the prospect of having to confront Plain Wayne or Neil at check-out.

Dad said he wanted bottled water. I left him to graze the range and was knocked sideways when he bought a six-pack of *H2OH!* You see, *H2OH!* is bottled water from a remote lake in the Hoogley Estuary Enclave world-renowned for the erotic properties of its water. This didn't seem to be the sort of bottled water Dad should have been going for at all. Still, after the experience with the beans, I didn't say anything.

"I'd like to buy your Jason something nice," Dad said.

"That's very thoughtful of you, Dad," I said. "We're trying to get him weaned on to educational snacks. *Fascinating Fact Crisps* are not only delicious and nutritious snacks; they also come in ten flavours and ten categories. A useful and educational fact is printed on every crisp using harmless colourants of vegetable origin."

"You used to like Mars Bars," Dad said.

I looked around again. "Dad," I said, "Mars Bars are something that Jason will never ever even hear about, let alone taste. *Plain Wayne*'s doesn't stock them. You'd have to go to some horrid corner-shop on the Industrial Nostalgia New Town for a what-you-said. No, I think a few packets of *Fascinating Fact Crisps* will do Jason very nicely. If I might recommend the *Enclave Curriculum 3+ pack, Barbequed Salmon Flavour*. Jason loves those, and they've definitely helped improve his averages."

Dad shrugged. Dad's shrug indicated consent in my book. It took him ages to sort out the *Fascinating Fact Crisps Handy Combination Chart*. Of course, I had to forgive him for that. Ten flavours and ten categories of facts adds up to a headache in the Stacking Department. Well, you can imagine.

Anyway, that was the start of Yours Filially taking on responsibility for Dad. Mind you, I don't think I could manage without the HomeHubby-Helps who manage to get Dad to do all the things I can never get him to do. Without them the situation would be hopeless. Hopeless!

Trouble is, when I'm there, I always get the same old negative chat about how everything's gone to the bad. From the moment I arrive until the moment I leave, Dad goes on and on. It's a monologue because I just won't enter it. Generally, I just go off on my own monologue, partly to tune him out.

This is typical. You'll have to imagine this going on all at the same time, which is generally how it is. Dad first:

DAD: *Well, I don't know, I really don't. I just can't see why you don't rise up and take control again! You could do it, Harry. A strike in the household department and your Avril would soon see the error of her ways. You see, Harry, this is only the start. If it goes on much longer men will no longer exist, Harry. They won't! I mean, what use are they? What? The Mesdames are already pleasuring themselves with gadgetry from the Pacific Rim. They don't need you for reproduction. What are you all except good little shoppers? I don't understand how you can sit there and take it.*

ME: *I've probably mentioned vacuuming skirting boards to you before, Dad? They're worth installing, they really are. You just nail them around the wall, switch on and all the dust disappears into them and is collected in a central bag. We've had ours for years and it really is trouble-free, Dad. Also, with the new type you can reverse the flow and odourize the home by adding a sachet of Home Accent in five perfumes. All hypoallergenic and with neutral ph factor.*

And so it goes. And father and son end up as poles apart as ever. It was ever thus: I believe Lady Lavinia Bo$co asserts in her *History of The Hubby Enclaves* that the very first thing written on the Graffiti Board in the Hubby Comfort Station on the very first maiden cruise of the very first *Floating Bo$co* was: *What are we going to do about the older generation?* A pithy answer came there none. Sometimes, in my darker moods, I think the Chinese got it right with the importation of the Auto Hara-Kiri machines.

I don't know where it's all going to end, I really don't.

Anyway, back to the scarf.

In the weeks and months that followed me and Les's introduction to *The Floating Bo$co*, we were seldom off the ship. It didn't take long for us to find the Clothing Department on the bilge deck. And I have to say that it was a real revelation. No expense had been spared. Designer Mesdames worldwide had lent their services to kit out hubbies in an appropriate manner that would both fit in with our busy lifestyles and please the hard-to-please eye of the Mesdames.

Everything was up to the minute on a clock that's streets ahead of its time. You went into this lovely area where they have the catalogues showing all those glamorous hubbies dressed in the latest fashions. You choose what you fancy and this really interesting thing happens. You see, all the items have a code. You mark it down and it goes into this computer. Of course, you've put all your size details on the card. This is compared with a *Size Up Hubby* read-out which was taken by a camera when you enter the department for both security and size-verification purposes.

So a hubby trying to disguise bulges and cellulite problems doesn't stand a chance.

Anyway, after the measuring up comes the really good bit. You go on a few paces into a darkened room with comfy chairs all around and a cat-walk going down the centre. Then a voice announces, "The Fashion Choices of Hubby Harry Manley!" and out walks a virtual reality Harry Manley – or should I say "Harry Manley" done in lasers and magic and wearing the outfits I've got thoughts on. Streets ahead of the Nirvana Precinct where, in the bad old days, we'd rummage along the hangers and then change behind saloon-swing-doors that only came down to your knees and wouldn't lock and then parade yourself for Plain Wayne and Neil's approval.

Of course, we're used to the Clothing Department of *The Floating Bo$co* these days. But that first time it really was quite a fright for both me and Les. "I" came on first wearing a house-hubby coverall made of breathable, water-and-spill-proof material. In green. Well, to tell you the truth, I was so taken aback to see "me" up there on the cat-walk that I just couldn't concentrate. I hadn't realised I walked like that. And my bum was definitely bigger than it is in real life. And I'm not just saying that; Les said it wasn't a bit like me. Well, I returned the compliment when "Les" came on. "He" was wearing this really lovely kitchen-to-table one-piece suit in blue and grey check and was absolutely appalled by the way he "strutted" – Les's word, not mine – along the cat-walk. "I don't walk like that, do I, chuck?" he said.

"No, of course you don't!" I said, though to tell you the truth the laser "Les Chumley" was exactly like the real thing in my book – and I'd be telling a lie if I said it wasn't.

Well, I've often thought how odd it is that *The Floating Bo$co* hubby-simulation machine manages to capture Les to a tee but misses me completely. I suppose there are bound to be glitches in the technology. The trollies still have wonky wheels, even in these state-of-the-art times. Work that one out!

Anyway, that first time, we just nodded dumbly when the Fashion Counsellor asked if we wanted to purchase the items demonstrated. We both made mistakes that day. Since then we've really come on. We're very choosy about our purchases and I've got my Wise Owl of the Month awards to prove it.

It must have been around then that I had my little ethical crisis. Yes, it was then because I was wearing my new ensemble and the counsellor who sorted me out complimented me on my excellent taste.

As if you didn't know already, not every hubby is fortunate enough in the manner that me and, say, Les are. Of course, we know that just across the river from us live hubbies in a right mess. But we usually put down their plight to some form of delinquency, be it failure to depilate, dependency on dole or the last three of the Five Dreadful Ds – Drink, Drugs and Drudgery.

Of course, putting it mildly, I wouldn't fancy living in one of those tower-blocks that litter the Industrial Nostalgia New Town. They do say that there are hubbies up there whose feet don't touch terra-firma for weeks on end. It's not surprising that they seize on their excursions on *The Floating Bo$co* to indulge in anti-social behaviour. Anything that's in the least bit social, those poor hubbies will be after like a shot.

My Avril, of course, won't give my sage ideas house-room. "They've made their beds," she says – though probably they haven't – "and now they must lie on them." I can sympathise with Avril's point of view, of course. She's had a hard job reaching the top of the greasy pole in Moseley and Lumumbashi and, as she never tires of telling me, she's worked so that we can have all those little extras that make our lives so comfy.

A part of me really admires Avril's attitude to life. She's never in the least bit dithery. For Avril the world is very simple. People are innocent or guilty. They should either be employing her to litigate on their behalf or be brought to book.

The trouble is that I can't stop thinking about everything that's going on over the horizon. When I'm sitting in the

HubbyCaff on *The Floating Bo$co*, all on my ownsome, with my trolley at my side, I often look out of the window, along the brown estuary towards the sea and think, *That just goes on and on. Every drop of water is connected to every other drop of water in the whole world! It's all connected!* I'm not sure how many hubbies on *The Floating Bo$co* are thinking this thought. When I told Les about what I'd been thinking he said it would be better if I just concentrated on my own back-patio. Still, Les has had more counselling than Yours Truly. No idea why; he's the best-adjusted hubby I know.

Anyway, it's easier said than done. Listening to *Hubby Hour* every day, reading *Hubby Matters* every week, fills me full of really worrying information from the wide world of hubbies. I think about the hubbies in the Industrial Nostalgia New Town who are having a devil's own job making ends meet; the problem in Saudi Arabia about veils and driving – the Mesdames there are for the former but against the latter – well, it just goes on and on.

Now, wouldn't you think that shopping at *The Floating Bo$co* would give me a break from worrying about the great world? Well, I'm sorry but it doesn't. You see, the shelves on *The Floating Bo$co* groan with produce from the whole groaning world and every single item has a tale of distress to tell – or so it sometimes seems.

In some ways, I know, it's like the crisis that Les had in Washday Requisites, but these days – knowing what I know – it's just about everywhere on the ship. I pick up coffee and think of the hubbies who aren't being given a fair price for their beans by Cafecoco International; the mangetout, the baby sweetcorn, the tropical fruits . . . there's no end to it. Every product tells a story and every story upsets me.

Some time ago, just after me and Les started boarding

The Floating Bo$co on a regular basis, a Hubby-counsellor caught me having a little weep next to the *Thaithong Tips* display.

"What's the problem here, young hubby?" she asked me.

"Nothing," I said. "An eyelash is . . . well . . . you know . . ."

The counsellor had heard that one before, of course. But if she did know she wasn't letting on. "Come on, love," she said, "out with it."

"I don't like to . . ." I said. "I mean, it doesn't seem right."

The Hubby-counsellor led me discreetly away to the Hubby-Counselling Area and sat me down with a cup of hot *HubbyBroth Low Fat Instant*. To tell you the truth I think they were trying to shift it by giving it away in the Hubby Counselling Area. It's never caught on. Now I'm not sure why this is. The flavours make it through the *low fat* and the *instant*, but there's a queer sort of after-burn that the *HubbyBroth* people would do well to iron out. Anyway, I sat there sipping my *HubbyBroth*.

"Take your time," said the Hubby-counsellor.

Well, I did. To tell you the truth, I was interested to hear what the hubby at the next counselling-module was saying to his counsellor. Apparently, he was having trouble realigning his Mrs to a healthy eating style and it was worrying him sick, he said.

I got distracted from my own problem – well, you do, don't you? – hearing this hubby's problem. I thought to myself that if me and Les could have got him to ourselves for ten minutes in the changing-room at the Leisure we'd have sorted him out in no time.

"Are you ready to share?" the Hubby-counsellor said, looking nervously towards the surveillance cameras.

I nodded, took a sip from the *HubbyBroth*. Actually it improves the colder it gets. You should write that down. It's worth remembering. I took a tissue and held it against my mouth. "Well, it's like this . . . " I began.

"Yes?"

"I read this article about the hubbies who pick *Thaithong Tips*. They're kept in special hostels; not allowed to see their Mesdames for months on end and are sacked if they don't bring in their quota. I know I should think of *Thaithong Tips* as a refreshing cuppa, but I can't. It makes me cry to think about those poor hubbies."

"Well," said the Hubby-counsellor, "you're not the first hubby who has come to me with this problem. All I can say is that you really mustn't bother your pretty little head about how the produce arrives at *The Floating Bo$co*. It'll give you wrinkles. But believe me, Harry – you don't mind me calling you Harry, do you? – believe me, we at *The Floating Bo$co* do all we can to be certain that our produce comes from ethically-assured sources."

"So everything I've read in *Hubby Matters* is less than the truth, is it?"

She nodded sadly. "I hate to say it, but you are putting it mildly, Harry. I do wish you hubbies wouldn't worry yourselves sick with all this nonsense. *The Floating Bo$co* won't sell *Hubby Matters* for that very reason. We have learnt over the years that it is the cause of more angst among hubbies than any other organ and contributed greatly towards causing hubbies to fall victim to *Consumer Stress Disorder* which, as we all know, can very easily lead to complete consumer breakdown. Harry, if you'll take my advice, you won't read *Hubby Matters* ever again. For your own good, Harry, restrict yourself to *The Bo$co Monthly* and the Hubby Romance novels of Lady Lavinia Bo$co. I tell you, Harry, you'll be a happier and, dare I say it, a more lovable hubby, if you do."

I nodded. I wanted to be more lovable. Who doesn't?

"The bottom line is," said the counsellor, "you are a hubby with a valuable contribution to make to the smooth running of your family. We at *The Floating Bo$co* are your friendly partners in that enterprise. Don't worry about things outside your immediate concern. Leave that to the Mesdames. They know, Harry."

"I'm sure you're right," I said.

Anyway, the counsellor gave me a token that gave me a free subscription to *The Bo$co Monthly* and then, just as I was standing up to leave, she forced into my hand a copy of *Hubbies of the Floating Bo$co*, the first of Lady Lavinia Bo$co's hubby romances.

I really got hooked on Lady Lavinia's hubby romances after *Hubbies of the Floating Bo$co* and I'm not much of a reader. *Hubbies of The Floating Bo$co* was what you might call a cautionary tale. It's about these two hubbies, Scott and Terry. Now, Scott recycles his Bo$co plastic bags, always places his trolley neatly in the trolley-bay on the quayside, makes sure to shop with care and discrimination. Terry, on the other hand, is slovenly, never remembers to bring his plastic bags back and rampages around *The Floating Bo$co* in a great tizzy pushing anything that takes his fancy into his trolley having no mind to the golden rule of trolley-loading: *Hard on the bottom; soft on the top; chemical and medicinal at a separation of at least nine inches*.

I forgot to mention that neither Scott nor Terry is married. I should have put that in first. It's typical of me to tell the story all back-to-front. Anyway, both Scott and Terry are very desirable hubbies. They depilate routinely and Lady Lavinia Bo$co used twenty pages to describe their depilatory routine. It was really quite erotic the way she described it. Lady Lavinia definitely has the knack with words as well as floating supermarket empires. Anyway, in comes this gorgeous available Ms called Lara – into *The Floating Bo$co*, that is. Now, Lara has everything: yacht, houses in the major enclaves, time-shares by the bucketful. She's beautiful too. But Lara has spent so much time wheeling and dealing in the Thames City Enclave that somehow love has passed her by. A friend asks her – they're having cocktails in the Astrocaff – what she wants from Hubby Right.

Well, you've guessed it, she wants above all else a hubby who depilates efficiently – naturally – and is a good little shopper. The friend tells her to go to *The Floating Bo$co* and size up the talent. Off Lara goes and her eyes light straight away on Scott – loading his trolley as the Bo$co Desiderata dictates – and she falls for him right off.

But here's the twist: Scott is completely indifferent, whereas Terry falls overboard – not literally – for Lara. But Lara, having seen the slovenly shopping habits of Terry, naturally doesn't give him a second glance.

That's where the friendly Hubby-counsellor comes in. She's been the narrative voice all along, though it comes as a surprise to the reader. She's been sussing out the situation as she walks up and down the aisles and later it emerges that she was Lara's friend in the Astrocaff.

Anyway, she takes Terry aside – just like my counsellor took me aside – and counsels Terry in the complex art of careful, sensitive, shopping. *Hubbies of The Floating Bo$co* changes from then on. It becomes a rites of passage book, with the counsellor having one hell of a battle trying to get Terry to mend his ways. There's a wonderfully moving scene where Terry completely breaks down in Yogurts and Spreads. They have to bring the doctor and the manager in. That really almost moved me to tears because I'd been there. I knew how Terry felt; I almost felt that I was Terry.

Anyway, you've guessed it, Terry improves. He, like me, had trouble with Ethical Shopping, but the counsellor sees him through it. Lara returns, watches Terry being put through his paces, and pops the question in the Trolley-Bay.

Now you'd think that would be it, but no! There's another twist to the tale. Apparently, all this time the counsellor-stroke-narrator has been in love with Scott! She pops the question to Scott who all this time has secretly admired the counsellor-stroke-narrator!

The book ends with a double wedding in *The Floating Bo$co's* Interdenominational Chapel – which has that remarkable cross/star/crescent-moon/mandala as its centrepiece, sculpted out of aluminium cans. It took 70,000 to make it, apparently, all donated by devout customers – and the happy couples go off on a Bo$coCruise around the world.

And, like they say, end of story.

Pushing me towards the novels of Lady Lavinia Bo$co was the best thing the counsellor could have done. It distracted me from all those negative thoughts that hubbies get from time to time. I've read everything she's written. And I always keep an anxious look-out for the next one, while appreciating that it must be hard to write while running *The Floating Bo$cos* worldwide.

It's rumoured that Lady Lavinia will be doing a signing when her latest book, *The Hubbies Demand Free-Range*, hits the bookshelves. I'll be there at the head of the queue. And I'll make sure that my full trolley will be beautifully-stacked, with *Thaithong Tips* at the top. I'm sure I won't be able to get words out to tell her how I feel. But I have the feeling she'll understand. I mean, you couldn't write books like Lady Lavinia writes and not understand, now could you?

6

Friday the Thirteenth

Not many people know this, but Lady Lavinia Bo$co can't get enough of Friday the Thirteenth. She wishes they happened every week. They represent transcendent leaps forward in lateral thinking, she reckons, if only we could see the possibilities.

As she says so eloquently and movingly in a sort of postscript to her best-selling novel, *The Hubbies Demand Free-Range* – and I quote from memory which, I reckon, is saying something in this day and age – *I used to be like just about everyone else in the world. The approach of Friday the Thirteenth absolutely terrified me. What cured me? I'll tell you, hubbies. On Friday the Thirteenth of January 2020 my application for a Bo$co Super Round-the-Clock Shoperama on what is now an Unmentionable Region was turned down flat.*

Now I can guess what you're thinking and I don't blame you at all: how could Lady Lavinia have a soft spot for Friday the Thirteenth after her application for a Super Shoperama had been rejected on that inauspicious date? Well, she goes on in her own inimitable style to say how this reversal gave her the idea for the *Floating Bo$cos*. She had been jogging by the Estuary and noticed how empty of shipping it was. Why not, thought Lady Lavinia, kit out a redundant ship as a Bo$co supermarket and see what happened?

And the rest is history in the making. Before a couple of years had passed, the *Floating Bo$cos* were floated on the Stock Exchange and now *Floating Bo$cos* are to be found on river estuaries worldwide. They're a gold-chip stock. My Avril has lots and always gives *Floating Bo$co* shares to our Jason for Christmas and birthdays. When she's in the country and not off litigating worldwide. When she remembers.

And so it was that Lady Lavinia Bo$co took to launching not only *Floating Bo$cos* but also some of her most forward-looking initiatives in the realm of social engineering on Friday the Thirteenths. It was on Friday the Thirteenth that she managed to clear out the end-of-the-road Hairy Hubbies and their hopeless Mesdames from the Millennium Mansion tower-blocks in the Industrial Nostalgia New Town.

This initiative was received with much baying at the time. Reactionary elements (and Les) thought it a bit thick that families should be fooled into collecting wrappers from *Econospam* to go towards a holiday in the mountains of the Unmentionable Regions which, Lady Lavinia assured everyone, had been newly cleaned up and made chipper by the waste-management arm of Bo$co International.

Of course, lots of the dole-dependent in Millennium Mansions jumped at the chance for a change of scene. They sent in their labels and found themselves transported by luxury eco-lorries – picked up from their very doorsteps apparently – and taken for a refreshing holiday, away from the dingy drudgery of their lives, in the Industrial Nostalgia New Town.

They never looked back . . . or came back.

It was Les who told me what had happened. "Harry," he said, producing a copy of the *Industrial Nostalgia New Town*

Natterer from the back pocket of his denim (denim!) bumbag, "Harry, have you read this?"

"No, I have not," I replied. "There's no faster way in my experience to imbibe the virus of negativity than to read that rag."

"Harry, it says that all the empty flats in the Millennium Mansions have been done up by Bo$co International and rented out to Hairy Hubbies whose till receipts are up to snuff."

"Jolly good!" I said. "That should help the area come up a bit."

"But don't you smell a rat, Harry?" Les asked.

"I smell the gorgeous aroma of good government, Les. That's what I smell. I smell rough Hairy Hubbies being pulled up by their boot-straps. I smell justice being done to the hopeless lot who brought the Millennium Mansions to the very brink of collapse. I hear they never picked up their litter, Les!"

"But Lady Lavinia has shipped off innocent people to the Unmentionable Regions, that's what she's done."

"They've been spring-cleaned!" I said.

"They have *bugger* been spring-cleaned!" Les said.

"Les," I said, "I never thought I'd hear you use the b. word."

"Never mind the bloody b. word, Harry. This is important."

"Look, Les," I said. "Lady Lavinia Bo$co has often said as how when she dies "Industrial Nostalgia New Town" will be carved on her heart. The Industrial Nostalgia New Town is one of Lady Lavinia's special causes.'

Les made to protest, but I went straight on, "Les," I said, "Lady Lavinia has always allowed the inhabitants of the Industrial Nostalgia New Town to shop aboard *The Floating Bo$co*. She's always had hope for them, Les. Despite ample evidence to the contrary. Now she has decided that there is an element there who simply cannot be saved. Hence, they are to be confined to a nicely spring-cleaned area of the Unmentionable Regions. It's an idea whose time has come, Les, and will go some way to reducing the terrible problem of theft aboard *The Floating Bo$co* and that will, in the fullness of time, trickle down to lighten the load for decent hubbies both of the enclave and the Industrial Nostalgia New Town. Every little helps, Les."

Les gave me this look, I remember, and turned away. I gave him some time on his own for my sage advice to sink in. He never brought the subject up again. I felt really proud of myself, to tell you the truth. I suspect it was my sage advice to Les that was instrumental in earning me one more Wise Owl of the Month award.

And, probably following Lady Lavinia's lead, the Mesdames have stopped being worried by Friday the Thirteenth. I know my Avril positively attempts to take a long-haul flight on Friday the Thirteenths. When I tackled her about it – though tackled isn't the right word for what I do to Avril – when I stroked it into the conversation one evening, Avril said that it was true she did like to travel on Friday the Thirteenths because the sort of passengers who *didn't* travel on that date made Super Executive Numero Uno Upper Class almost tolerable. Almost.

Of course, me being a hubby who knows his path in life and knows that in all probability it does not wind upwards to the sun-bathed skyscapes that my Avril flicks down the blinds to avoid could barely imagine what Avril meant. Still, before Lady Lavinia Bo$co wrote that she was unafraid of Friday the Thirteenth for reasons I mentioned before, I could not understand Avril's devil-may-care attitude. And neither could Les.

Both of us were bad, but Les was worse than me. You see, Les, having been a miner before becoming a hubby, had had all kinds of superstitions bred into him. He could name chapter and verse and casualty list of every accident in the mining industry worldwide that had occurred on Friday the Thirteenth. I was able to contribute my pessimistic pennyworth by mentioning that every *Widdecombe Three-Wheeler Model* I'd been involved with that was produced on Friday the Thirteenth broke its big-end before the warranty was over – and in those days the warranty period wasn't anything to hold your breath about. Or your big end for that matter.

"Yea," Les said. "If we heard a bird singing on our way to the pit head on Friday the Thirteenth, we wouldn't go down."

"Really, Les?" I asked. "Why was that?"

"Well, chuck," Les replied, "it all dates back to Alf Wakefield's granddad's canary. You see – "

"Excuse me for interrupting, Les," I said, "but Lady Lavinia says in her blockbuster, *The Hubbies Who Sailed That Extra Mile For Air-Flown Parsnips*, that there never was any reason to worry about Friday the Thirteenth. It was all, she realised in hindsight, in the mind."

"Try telling that to Alf Wakefield's granddad. His canary, too, come to that," said Les.

Now, much as I love and respect Les – to tell you the truth I'd be lost without him and I don't care who knows it – there is no denying, as I might have mentioned before, that he is a born conservative. He seems to want to hold on to the old ways long after the rest of the hubbies have tossed them out. For example, it took him ages to follow my example and desert the corner-shop at the end of his street. I'd tell him until I was blue in the face, "Les," I'd say, "one of these days you'll catch something from the rubbish you buy at inflated prices from that corner-shop. It's like Lady Lavinia says in *The Hubbies Who Couldn't Float,* "Only losers stand – or shop – on corners."

Well, it took much repetition to get Les to take that bit of sage advice to heart and in the superstition department he was hopeless. Hopeless! Friday the Thirteenth would find Les locked in his bedroom with *Hubby Hour,* a hot-water bottle and the nets tight shut. And there was nothing I could do to make him see the error of his ways. Not one thing!

Then peculiar occurrences started to happen aboard our local *Floating Bo$co.* I flatter myself that I was the very first person to notice these untoward and highly immoral events. In a way I feel badly about mentioning them even now for fear that it might put bad ideas into the heads of otherwise good people . . .

It was Thursday the Twelfth of something or other. I was having a bit of a crisis in Shampoos, I remember. To tell you the truth it had been a day of crises. I was fresh through a crisis with bottled water. Well, I don't need to tell you that a hubby is often judged on his acumen in the Bottled Water department. They've got this amazing range. There's water that suits tea, water that suits coffee, water that suits herbal infusions, water for washing the face. Well, you'd expect all that. But it's become even more complicated of late what with the bottled-water manufacturers becoming even more specific about the uses to which their water should be put. I nearly died when I saw, for example, that there was one water for Kenyan coffee-making and quite another for Colombian. Then you've got to watch the ingredients label like a hawk to make sure they're vitaminized and contain dioxin protection.

Anyway, I got out of my crisis in Bottled Water through an escape hatch thoughtfully provided by the bottled-water consultant of *The Floating Bo$co*. She had, with much care and market research, compiled a mixed carton of waters to cover most eventualities. The bottles were colour-coded, so you wouldn't find yourself making tea with water meant for washing areas of private access. Phew, I say.

The crisis in Shampoos was simpler than the one in Bottled Water, but it still got me all in a tangle. I was wondering whether I wanted a *Prewash-'n'-Wash-'n'-Gogo* for flyaway hair that required frequent washing but infrequent conditioning, or the one for hair that is damaged and flies away because it has been too infrequently washed and overfrequently conditioned. It's a subtle distinction, granted, but good shopping comes down to subtle decisions in my experience. And if you didn't know that, perhaps you should write it down while you think about it.

In the middle of all this it happened. I smelled this hubby before I saw him. He made the aisle reek of *Northern Birch*, and no hubby with an ounce of self-respect was wearing *Northern Birch*, even then. I looked round and sight confirmed smell, as is so often the case. The hubby just did not belong on *The Floating Bo$co*. He was undepilated and badly turned out. I would have had him down as a member of the Angry Hubby Brigade except that his trolley was full. And not full of any old thing either; he had taken time and trouble to shop at the extensive range on offer at *The Floating Bo$co*'s Delicatessen and *MrsTreat* Department. There were little packets of cheese, pâtés, sliced salamis, the lot.

Anyway this hubby got to the end of the aisle and left his trolley next to the collection barrel for the Lady Lavinia Save The Estuaries of the World Campaign – my favourite charity. Now I'd thought the chap had popped into the next aisle to pick up the week's special offer. It was hard to resist. I was so impressed that I kept a note of it in my diary. If you bought a

450g jar of Bo$co's freeze-dried tomato-paste with basil, plus a packet of *Hubby-be-Lovely* defoliant crystals, you got a token towards the purchase of Lady Lavinia's forthcoming blockbuster, *The Triumph of the Till*, which only became a novel after it had been produced as a television film. Only five tokens were required in order to get the book for nothing. Anyway, that's by the by. To cut a long story short, the Hairy Hubby did not come back. The trolley was left unattended!

Well, and looking back I feel really daft and dithery – everything Avril is always accusing me and the other hubbies of being – I turned back to the Shampoo display, though I have to admit it was hard to concentrate on wise hair-care choices with this full trolley nearby. While I wondered about split ends bonding through hypoallergenic hot oil, the thought that *The Floating Bo$co* was about to land at the Industrial Nostalgia New Town Landing-Stage kept flashing through my head and leaving my nerve endings really split. It was as plain as the nose on Plain Wayne that the common hubby wearing *Northern Birch* had got on *The Floating Bo$co* there and would undoubtedly be getting off there too. I had that sinking feeling that as a crowd of common hubbies got off another crowd would get on and I wished, though I felt guilty about it – don't ask me why – that Lady Lavinia would bring in her two-class *Floating Bo$cos* as she has on the Hoogly River in Calcutta, the River Congo and at other problem locations. I also thought how there was bound to be some deterioration in the products in the trolley. I hate waste and I think it was the thought of all the food going off – and if you've ever experienced hummus that's past its best you'll know what I mean – which sent me to consult with one of the hubby counsellors.

"Mrs," I asked, "I hope you don't think I'm over-reacting but there's a trolley over there that's just been left!"

"Been left, young hubby?" the counsellor asked.

"Yes," I said. "Left. I wouldn't have worried except that it's full of really wonderful stuff from the incomparable delicatessen and was driven by a common-looking hubby of the type who only like products with E numbers coming out of their ears as a rule."

"You mustn't stereotype the valued customers of *The Floating Bo$co*," said the counsellor, slipping me a wink.

I hung my head, only half meaning it. "No, I'm terribly sorry," I said.

"Can you show me where the trolley is?"

I took the counsellor to where the abandoned trolley was. It was exactly where I had last seen it. And no sign of the hubby in charge. I looked at the counsellor and the counsellor looked at me.

Well, that was the start of a rash of senseless and disturbing lawlessness aboard *the Floating Bo$co*. And the incidents always occurred on Thursday the Twelfths so that the wasted produce – for much of it had to be thrown away – always showed up on Lady Lavinia's computer screen on Friday the Thirteenth in order to ruin her day.

And not only were phantom trolleys filled on my local branch of *The Floating Bo$co*. There seemed to be a country-wide conspiracy to spoil Lady Lavinia's Fridays. The Tyne and Weir Estuary *Floating Bo$co* was especially afflicted.

Of course, it took a while for everyone to realise what was happening. Lady Lavinia announced to the press that these filled and discarded trolleys, occurring as they did on Thursday the Twelfth, were a way for disgruntled and disturbed members of the Angry Hubby Brigade to make her eat her sage words which I quoted before.

Now I, even now, find it almost impossible to understand how even the angriest hubby could have anything but the greatest respect for the achievements of Lady Lavinia. She has, after all, broken all the rules of retailing and come up smiling and adored, like Aphrodite on that plate Les's Mrs, Barbara, brought back for me from her trip to Cyprus. Why anyone would want to prove her wrong I have no idea. I don't know about such things.

But the incidents went on. Despite surveillance, angry hubbies managed to fill their trolleys on Thursday the Twelfths and then disappear without trace, leaving their valuable purchases unpaid for.

A fax was sent by *the Floating Bo$co* Care Department to all the loyal hubbies who frequent *The Floating Bo$cos*. In order that all valued clients should be able to shop in complete security, the fax stated, we were to be tagged. A microscopic chip would be injected into our fatty tissue.

There was a lot of worried chat in the HubbyCaff after that announcement. Hubbies were really scared that the injection of the surveillance chip might leave an unsightly scar on the hubby's anatomy. This got back to the powers-that-be on *The Floating Bo$co* and the whole PR machine went into overdrive to convince hubbies that there was absolutely no danger of scarring.

Of course, after that, we all submitted to the injection-gun without a word. And I have to say that things improved overnight. A great many of the rougher hubbies from the Industrial Nostalgia New Town stopped coming aboard. Needless to say they are not missed by the good and law-abiding hubbies, the quiet majority who wear their GLAD TO BE TAGGED buttons with pride.

The next book of Lady Lavinia was renamed *The Hubbies Who Put Yesterday Behind Them*. It was – need I say – a wonderful read, right up there with *The Hubbies Demand Free-Range* in my book. I was especially moved by the passage where Lady Lavinia reiterated her determination to see Friday the Thirteenth as a lucky day for her and so, by extension, for all her loyal customers. It was, she wrote, the wicked trolley-abandoners who, determined to prove her wrong, resorted to the most heinous tactics to rob her of fair profit and make her believe that Friday the Thirteenth was an unlucky day. But had the wicked plot worked? Of course not! The scam had given Lady Lavinia Bo$co her idea for customer-tagging. Now, at the flick of a button she could monitor the spending patterns of each and every one of her hubbies worldwide. She could, like a Guardian Angel, follow them wheresoever they went and protect them from all harm. Tagging, an idea that had occurred to her on Friday the Thirteenth, would make sure that *The Floating Bo$co* Company was everything a hubby could want from a store – and an ocean more.

And I can vouch for that. The other week I got locked in one of those portable loos on the Estuary landing-stage. Couldn't get out and I thought if I heard *My Oklahoma Hubby* once more I'd – well, I don't know . . . But within minutes there was Big Yvette prising the door open with her truncheon.

"Thank you, Mrs Yvette!" I gasped. "You saved me!"

"Thank Lady Lavinia Bo$co, hubby. She told us where you were," growled Big Yvette in that gruff way she has that you know she doesn't mean. Deep down.

"I will. I will! Oh, I will!" I said.

And I did. And I will. Forever and ever.

And wouldn't you know it? I got stuck in that toilet on Friday the Thirteenth – a lucky day you see; the day on which I proved to my own satisfaction that Lady Lavinia Bo$co is divine – simply divine!

7

The Sparkling Adventures of Shirley Surfactant

I've probably already told you about the Angry Hubby Brigade. Mind you, consider yourselves forgiven if you've forgotten them. If you have, I'm very glad you have. I should probably ask to be forgiven for even mentioning them.

You see, I've glossed over their activities on purpose. It's like I say to Les, "It isn't right to give them the oxygen of publicity".

Les agrees with me wholeheartedly, even though some of his mates from the Congleton Xed-Colliery are active members of the Angry Hubby Brigade and have been holed up in the mountains and mineshafts of the Unmentionable Region for years. Nevertheless, he really despises AHAB, to give them their pet-name – though where they get the second "A" from is completely beyond me – and says they're the scum of the earth and are determined to destroy family life as we know it.

There's supposed to be an "acceptable" and an "unacceptable" face to AHAB, though call me thick if you like, I've never been able to see the difference. Still, the media will insist that there's "regular AHAB" and "revised AHAB".

Regular AHAB puts up candidates for parliament if you please, and loses its deposit; publishes a newspaper and goes around without pec-organizers. It's all pretty harmless, as harmful and detestable goes. But "revised AHAB" make up for it. They try to picket *The Floating Bo$co*. I know for a fact they cut electrical power to the Rational Parenthood Sperm Bank – thereby really muddying the Mersey Estuary Enclave gene pool, have conducted an ongoing campaign against depilatory products for years and were rumoured to have been involved in the assassination attempt on Lady Lavinia Bo$co some years ago – though they never admitted responsibility for the outrage which, luckily, failed to harm a hair of Lady Lavinia's head. It was a close thing, mind. They had put a bomb in one of Lady Lavinia's books. She was doing a book-signing on board the Dart Estuary *Floating Bo$co* and, fortunately, demand was not so great as to cause her to open the book with the bomb in it – though to tell you the truth I was as shocked at the shocking lack of good taste by the Dart Estuary Enclave hubbies in failing to buy up Lady Lavinia's whole supply as I was by the dastardly bombs. The book was put back onto the shelves after Lady Lavinia had left and blew up during the night. They had to send the ship to the Pacific Rim for a refit.

Anyway, I haven't any time for AHAB, either regular or revised, and I am sure you can see why. Occasionally a copy of their newspaper will come through our front door. I use it to wrap up vegetable matter.

Les, though, will insist on reading it. I've tried to warn him of the pollution he risks by this, but there's no telling him. He's got this shocking independent streak, has Les. Anyway, we were nattering in the HubbyCaff after having had a good shop the other day. Our trollies were beside us, padlocked together with this lock I got at *Plain Wayne's* back in the innocent days before Wayne's *Black Diaries* came to light.

I padlock the trollies because – even though we haven't paid for them while we're at the HubbyCaff stage – when you think about it, a trolley-load of shopping is an investment in time. And time, as Avril is always telling – and VideoChatting – me, is money. If you spend upwards of an hour of quality time picking the best, only to have it nicked, then the cost is considerable. There's no guarantee that "the Shopping Muse" – to borrow Lady Lavinia's phrase for it – will come back. Also, it has been known for a common hubby to steal a full trolley and march off to the check-out to pay for the contents and take full credit for the wise-purchasing decisions of a conscientious hubby – who is probably being driven distraught searching for his trolley up and down every deck of *The Floating Bo$co*. It happened to Les, just as he was just two Lady Lavinia Stars away from receiving the Wise Owl of the Month award. Well, I'm not going to risk it happening again, either to me or my best mate. You'd be well advised to invest in one of those locks. They'll pay for themselves in no time with the feeling of security you get.

Anyway, Les out of the blue came out and said, "I'm worried about surfactants, chuck."

"Anionic, nonionic or amphoteric?" I asked. Like you do.

"All of them, Harry. I'm not sure there's anything to choose between them with regards the possible harm they've done to hubbies."

To tell you the truth I was really split. One part of me wanted to give Les a hug. He's really come on in Household Products, Washday Requisites and BodyCare. There was a time when he couldn't tell his surfactants from his zeolite perborate combo.

But whistles of alarm were blowing in the other part of my head. How could Les be worried about surfactants? After all, Lady Lavinia Bo$co had made Shirley Surfactant into the hero of a whole display case of children's stories. I'd bought Jason the gorgeous limited edition of the laser-discs of the cartoons in their own slip case for his birthday. To tell you the truth, I doubt I've ever made a better purchase than that limited edition of the complete Shirley Surfactant stories. According to Avril, the Japanese have fallen for them in a big way and, like she says, they'll pay "megabucks" for that limited edition. I VideoChat Jason on a daily basis that he must take care of them. And he does. When he's home he's forever taking the set out of the double-plastic bag with dust-defying press-lock fastening, and polishing them. They're pristine. Long after I shuffle off, that limited edition will spell security for Jason. He'll probably be having to fend off Japanese would-be purchasers on a daily basis.

Avril says that the Japanese have taken Shirley Surfactant to their hearts in a way that makes the HubbyDoll craze of a few years back seem really tame. They dress up as Shirley, have Shirley Surfactant parties. And Lady Lavinia has stopped going to Japan – even when there's a Japanese *Floating Bo$co* to open – because she gets mobbed by Shirley Surfactant look-alikes.

You see, Shirley Surfactant is definitely the most lovable and enduring of all Lady Lavinia's lovable and enduring children's characters. Shirley Surfactant is named after Lady Lavinia's youngest, so you can see why she would have a special place in her – and her adoring public's – affections. In the series of feature-length cartoon films, Shirley is this lovely little blonde. Not human exactly – neither Hubby nor Mrs – more an angel from above. Shirley goes around doing good. Wherever there is grease or dirt or dry flaky skin or ring-around-the-collar or washday red, Shirley Surfactant is there with her little wand and her starry glitter of surfactants which she uses to save the day.

Of course, I was first introduced to Shirley through the series of children's stories that graced the check-out of *The Floating Bo$co*. And, call me an old fashioned hubby if you like, I built up a mental picture of what Shirley was like. As you know already, Lady Lavinia has wonderful descriptive powers and they had stroked their way into me. I pictured Shirley as being just like Lady Lavinia, except she could squeeze herself up really tight to get into and out of bottles and pump-action dispensers, cakes of cleansing-bars and tubes of creams. And Lady Lavinia is a brunette, so when the series was turned into a cartoon and there was Shirley as a blonde, well, it sort of knocked me sideways. I can't tell you the times we've watched the cartoons but, whenever I reach for a cleaner or a cosmetics product, I always imagine Shirley as a brunette, popping out to make my life better, to wipe away household sin with her grace.

So, I'm sure you can see why a part of me was really worried that Les was worried about surfactants. If it had been any hubby but Les I might well have stood up, uncoupled our trolleys and walked off away from temptation.

Still, seeing as it *was* Les, and I could not imagine life without Les, I looked around the HubbyCaff and whispered, "Whatever makes you say that, Les?" And, as I watched Les, I had this vision of Shirley Surfactant, sitting on the flip-top of Bo$co's Hubby-Only brand of Washing-Up Liquid. And Shirley was weeping.

"I read this story in a newspaper, Harry," he said.

"Les," I said, "you know I've tried to steer you away from newspapers. Why can't you be content with *Bo$co Monthly*?

It contains everything you need to know. All the rest is, as I recall telling you many a time, at best a distraction. Which newspaper were you reading, Les? It wasn't *The Industrial Nostalgia New Town Natterer*, was it?"

Les hung his head. "Worse," he said.

"Not *The Unmentionable Region War Cry*?"

Les played with the packets of *HubbySweet* aspartame substitute. He could not look me in the eye. A bad sign.

"Les," I said. "And don't play with the *HubbySweet*. Some poor hubby's going to fret if he sees the envelopes all crumpled. Tell me, what was it you read? I'm not going to pollute my brain any farther trying to think of the titles of those rags!"

You can see I was being stern. But I felt stern. There are times when it's kinder to be stern.

"It was *The Angry Hubby Brigade Tablet*," Les said.

I went hot and cold. Still, I tried to contain myself. "Regular or revised?" I asked.

"What do you take me for, Harry?" Les asked. "Regular."

I shuddered. "And that newspaper has made you worry about surfactants, has it?"

Les confessed that it had. Well, I didn't know what to say. I wondered if there was anything *to* say. I had to have time to think. I went and bought us both another *DecaffDoubleRecaff*. On the way back to Les, I noticed one of the common hubbies from the Industrial Nostalgia New Town nosing about an unlocked trolley belonging to Lionel, a hubby who lives two doors down from Les, whose Mrs is something big in genetic de-profiling. Now I know for a fact that Lionel is a wonderful little shopper. I've seen him stand for at least twenty minutes in front of Yogurts and Spreads and in my book that spells a trolley-load of careful investments. I didn't say anything to Lionel. I just walked straight up to a security Mrs and told her that perhaps she should keep a weather eye out for the common hubby, who was still eying up Lionel's trolley.

"I wish all the hubbies would use padlocks in the HubbyCaff," she said, and gave me a wink, "and were as quick to inform the staff as you were, hubby. May I have your name for our Golden Book?"

Well, I was as pleased as anything. The Golden Book lies in a glass case in the Interdenominational Chapel, a new page turned every day. I'm there seven times. I went back to Les feeling much better about everything though, to tell you the truth, I hadn't sorted out what I was going to say to Les.

Still, I needn't have worried. Les was ready for me. "I'll just tell you what my worry is – I know it's daft – and then we'll talk no more about it, Harry," he said.

A side of me rose up and shouted "No!" inside my head. "Take your time, Les," I said. I had this feeling that here was a time when I was going to be tested. Now was my chance to show that I could be all I could be. I would listen and I would not be changed or corrupted in any way.

"*The Angry Hubby Brigade Tablet* came through my door, dropped on the mat with this headline, "SURFACTANTS RESPONSIBLE FOR UNSEXING HUBBIES!" Well, Harry, I couldn't help myself. I had to read on."

"Go on," I said.

"Well, the article said that surfactants mimic female oestrogens. They've been doing it for years, but it's been hushed up. It said that hubbies have been robbed of their masculinity by these surfactants and that's the reason why the birth-rate's gone down and why we're so happy being hubbies."

"Is that what they said?" I asked.

"In a nutshell, yes," Les said. "They took longer about it, though."

"Look at us," I said, looking hard at Les. "Here am I sitting with you in the HubbyCaff, my trolley filled with thought next to your trolley filled with thought – and let me say here and now how much I admire your having chosen the guava-flavour in the three-for-the-price-of-two offer on any of the range of Del Monaco's 30% real squeezed fruit-juice (from concentrate). You're cunning, that's what you are, Les. You know that the Guava is 11 deci-estuarios per hundred centilitres more expensive than the others and you bagged *three*! So, not only have you got one for free but you have saved a further sizeable sum. That'll get you a star in the Wise Owl competition or my name isn't Harry Manley."

Les beamed. I think. "Thanks, Harry," he said.

I went straight on. "Les, I'm looking at you now and what I see before me is a real hubby's hubby. No, straight up. A real hubby's hubby is what you are, Les. If surfactants were in the least harmful, don't you think I'd have been the first to notice and pass on my knowledge?"

"I suppose you're right – "

"And," I continued, looking up at the portrait of Lady Lavinia hanging above the Salad-Servery, "do you really think that *that* Mrs could have stocked hundreds of products containing between 5% and 25% surfactants if she had even suspected that they might be anything other than Hubby Friendly grade 10? Think about it, Les."

Les thought about it. "Yes, I'm sure you're right but – "

"Lady Lavinia has invested hundreds of hours of her spare time – and she doesn't get much you know, Les – in writing her wonderful children's books for the edification, improvement and entertainment of our nippers. And what is the name of her most popular character, Les?"

"Shirley Surfactant," said Les.

"QED," I said.

"But," said Les.

"But what, Les?" I said, a tad tart in my tone.

"But if what I read about surfactants is true, Harry," Les said, all worked up, "they might be the cause of us . . . " He looked round, and I knew what was coming. "Of us being so, you know, *hubbyish*. I mean, Harry, look at it this way: what was the first thing the Mesdames got us to do to show willing in the household department?"

"Washing-up?" I hazarded, wondering what Les was driving at.

"Exactly, chuck! Washing up. And what do you use when washing up?"

"Washing-up liquid," I said.

"And what does washing-up liquid contain? Yes! Surfactants. In great quantitities. Now maybe the Mesdames knew what they were doing. Maybe they knew that washing up was eventually going to . . . " Les looked to right and left, then whispered in my ear, "unman us."

It was my turn to look round, hoping against hope that the surveillance cameras and mikes were not pointing at us. They're supposed to be on board *The Floating Bo$co* to find out hubby-preferences in consumer products, but you never know. I could see my entries being struck off the Golden Book. "Les," I said, "we are what we are because we have adapted to changing circumstances. You can't say the Great Adjustment was caused by surfactants; it was pure economics and the determination of the Mesdames to pull themselves up by their boot-straps."

"But couldn't it have been that we lost our grip on the

slippery pole because of surfactants?" Les said. "You see, I read something else, Chuck."

"Reading doesn't suit everyone, Les," I said, even tarter in my tone. "In the knowledge department enough is as good as a feast in my experience."

"Are you going to let me get this off my chest or aren't you?" Les said.

"Better out than in," I replied automatically. Like you do. To tell you the truth, Les's revelations were really drenching my day in despond.

"Well, according to what I was reading, the writer reckoned that in the old days before the GREAT RESTRUCTURE – I'm talking a long time ago – hubbies, though we weren't hubbies then, had a little bit of oestrogen in their bodies. It was just enough to keep us tense all the time, a sort of perpetual pre-menstrual tension. It made us all pushy and insensitive and warlike and that. Then, when surfactants started getting into the atmosphere with the coming of detergents the British Empire went for a burton; industry contracted and hubbies lost all vim and vigour. And that's why the GREAT RESTRUCTURE came in. And that's why we are where we are. It all comes down to chemicals in the end."

"That's complete rubbish, Les," I said. "You've got a smudge on your nose by the way." I took out a hanky and Les spat on it. Then I rubbed at the smudge. Lo-tech but hi-bonding.

"Thanks, Harry," Les said.

"I think you've got to be more careful about what you read, Les," I said. "It's complete rubbish all this. I mean, if what you're saying is true, why is Hubbydom in other parts of the world so slow in getting going? Africa's taking its time, you have to admit. And what about the Unmentionable Regions – pardon me for mentioning them."

But quick as a flash, Les was back. "Fewer surfactants in the atmosphere, Harry." Les said.

"Look, Les," I said, "are you happy being a hubby?"

"Yes, but – "

"Yes. Would you have your life any other way?"

"No, but – "

"No. So, if surfactants are responsible – and I'm not for one moment saying that they are – but IF they are, aren't you pleased? Doesn't it make you want to celebrate? I mean, if you were still digging coal and I was Head of Parts at Widdecombe Three-Wheelers, we might never have met, might we?"

"No – but – "

"But me no buts, Les," I said. "Look, I tell you what, let you and me go to the Counselling Centre."

"What? Now?"

"Yes. Now. It's obvious you're working yourself up into a state. The Counsellors will know exactly what you need. That's what they're here for, after all."

You see, apart from wanting a bit of Mrs input into all this, I was really worried that my name would be erased from the Golden Book, the Wise Owl of the Month Club and goodness knows what else if it was found out that I'd been letting Les rabbit on without asking for counselling.

"It's no good," Les said. "They're never going to admit that surfactants are messing me about, are they? They're employed by *The Floating Bo$co*. They know which side their bread is spread."

I looked round. "Don't even think that, Les," I said. "I don't know how many times Lady Lavinia has asserted that the counselling service on *The Floating Bo$cos* worldwide is an independent arm."

"Pull the other one," Les said. "Where did you find that out?"

"The *Bo$co Monthly*," I said. "You know it's the only paper I read."

"There you are then."

"Give it a try, Les. I'll come with you. If you're not satisfied after your counselling session, we'll think again."

Well, Les took some persuading but eventually I was able to get him to the Counselling Section on deck five. A Mrs in a white coat met us with a clipboard: "Do you hubbies require counselling in products, budgeting, health strategies or 'any other business'?" she asked, all efficient.

"Any other business," I said, as Les had gone all silent.

We were shown into the waiting area where several hubbies sat looking self-conscious below a sign which read: *We're all in the same beautiful boat*.

Still, in no time at all Les and me were called in to see the counsellor. Les, after some prodding from Yours Interrogatively, explained the problem. The counsellor nodded, and made some notes.

"You're not the only hubby who has come to me about surfactants, Les – you don't mind me calling you Les? – and Harry is right to tell you that the so-called news story in that so-called newspaper is a lie from start to finish. And I'll tell you why it is a lie, shall I?"

Les nodded.

"It is a lie because, if surfactants in any way harmed a hair of one hubby's head, Lady Lavinia would not let a millilitre within a mile of a *Floating Bo$co*. The research and quality-control laboratories of *The Floating Bo$co* are state of the art institutions. They test and test and retest and only when the boffin Mesdames are 110% certain of the purity, beneficial effects and lack of toxicity of every ingredient that goes into every product aboard *The Floating Bo$co* worldwide will they be passed for inclusion on our shelves. Now does that set your mind at rest?"

We nodded.

"Regarding the source of this defamation of surfactants, I have a number of photographs in this book of the people who write the dangerous garbage in – " her lips curled – "*the AHAB Tablet*. I think this will back up what I have just told you rather well."

The counsellor handed across the photo album for me and Les to look at. We turned the pages with mounting horror. Bearded men in singlets sat smoking cigarettes in the kitchen while their nippers played about. There was even a cat on the table. Dishes piled up in the sink. And everything looked filthy. We turned over and there was a picture of a completely un-depilated man, stripped to the waist, with a beard. He was sitting behind a typewriter and his unexercised pecs drooped without – you've guessed it – benefit of a pec-organizer. Below the photograph it said, THE EDITOR OF THE AHAB TABLET.

It was me who cracked first. "I don't think I can look at any more, thank you very much, Mrs Counsellor. I realise completely that we've been mistaken. We are curling up just imagining ourselves believing anything those awful people could possibly produce."

The counsellor smiled, took the album and pushed it into the bottom drawer of her desk. Then she locked it. "Most hubbies can't get past page one," she said. "The cat on the table and those stacks of dishes are more than they can stand."

"I feel much better now," Les said.

When we got back to the HubbyCaff it was time for us to pay for our purchases. Les would insist on running back to the household cleaner department to stock up on the whole range of his favourite products. I helped him out so's we could get through check-out and off *The Floating Bo$co* before it set sail again.

"I know why you're doing this, Les," I said. "It's seeing those horrid Angry Hubbies with all that hair and all that dirty crockery and stains all over the shop. They've obviously not seen surfactants in their lives! And all those kids! They ought to be ashamed, so hairy, with all those nippers – "

Les looked at me and I looked at Les. I wanted to bite my tongue. I knew what he was thinking. For a moment there I was thinking the same myself. Then *The Floating Bo$co* turned, causing Soft Drinks to tinkle, preparing to tie up at the Estuary Enclave landing-stage. The sun came through the stained-glass windows of the Atrium-Check-out area and caught the huge plaque of Lady Lavinia done in rose granite and presented to her by grateful Thai hubbies. She looked gorgeous, so gorgeous a hubby with only a loose grip on his trolley could fall to his knees without thinking.

"Look, Les!" I said.

He looked. We looked. Lady Lavinia looked at us.

"Read the motto, Les."

Les read, "*'You buy my care. My care can't be bought.'" Lady Lavinia Bo$co, the fourth world convention of the Floating Bo$co, the Verrazano Broads, 19Boadicea 2027.*"

"Feeling better, Les?" I asked.

Les looked at me. "I've been a fool, Harry. Thank heavens you were here to see me through it."

"Till Frozen Foods freeze over, Les. Till Frozen Foods freeze over," I replied.

We walked, arm in arm, meditatively, to the check-out,

where Les won the last two stars he needed to become Wise Owl of the Month.

I felt proud of myself. A job well done.

To reward myself I bought the latest adventures of Shirley Surfactant, *Shirley's Big Clean-Up*. I read it out loud to Les on the way home.

I think even the robotic rickshaw-puller was moved.

8

The Cult

When the Leisure Centre closed, all the hubbies – led by Les – were up in arms. Not that it did any good. The Councillor Mesdames had, in their wisdom, decided that the Leisure was a place that corrupted hubbies, distracted them from the real purpose of their lives. I thought, and still think, it was a bit thick. I mean the only case they had to go on was Dave's.

It all started innocently enough. A poster went up on the noticeboard of the Leisure announcing the visit of a dietary expert from the Catalina Island Enclave who had a proven and unique way to not only make hubbies fit and healthy but actually build up the body's resistance to all sorts of diseases. It was our duty as good hubbies to see what the expert had to say.

Now I was all set to go, but Les reminded me that I had promised to accompany him on the monthly day-trip to the Post-Cambrian Hubby Enclave and Freeport aboard *The Floating Bosco*. There were to be classes in advanced freezer arranging and demonstrations of a new product called *You Never Managed To Get It ALL Out!* which promised to remove dust from the most intricate crevices of one's ornaments and knick-knacks.

Now Les, being an inveterate collector of model locomotives of yesteryear over the years – he has a hubby-tall stack of the monthly magazine which includes a free example each month, ready to slot together and paint – felt he had need of a product that would get at dust in the crevices.

"This does sound intriguing," I said to Les, looking at the poster for *The Overindulgence Way To Perfect Health Inc.*

"Maybe it does, chuck," Les replied. "Of course, you'll have to make up your own mind. I won't think the less of you if you decide to let me down, but did you know that Lady Lavinia Bo$co will be reading and signing her new book, *The Hubbies Who Shone The Stars And Pasteurised The Moon?*"

"I didn't know that," I said.

"It's to be a surprise. Big Yvette told me," Les winked. "I thought you ought to know."

"Thank you, Les," I said. "There really isn't any competition in my book. I wouldn't pass up an opportunity to meet Lady Lavinia. Do you think she'll recognize me?"

"I'm sure she will, Harry. She didn't get where she is today by forgetting her most adoring fans. Anyway, I hear that watching hubbies shopping over the surveillance cameras is Lady Lavinia's only form of recreation. She's bound to know all about you."

"Do you think so, Les?" I asked, going all hot and cold in a nice warm sort of way.

"Definitely," Les said.

Anyway, me and Les had a great time that day and didn't give a thought to what was going on back at the Leisure. We bought our sets of *You Never Managed to Get It ALL Out!* and, though the complete stock of *The Hubbies Who Shone The Stars and Pasteurised the Moon* was sold out before I managed to get through the scrum to the bookshop, I got to see Lady

Lavinia in the flesh. I think. By the time we got back to the harbour that evening – the sun was setting purple and gorgeous over the Unmentionable Regions – the harm was already done and Dave was an acolyte in this disgusting cult.

Of course neither Les nor me knew what was happening for a couple of days: we had our time cut out trying out our new *You Never Managed To Get It ALL Out!* on all the dust traps in our respective homes. Naturally, we'd have done this anyway but were encouraged into getting going by getting home only to see a succession of wonderful telly ads for *You Never Managed To Get It ALL Out!* in which the hard-to-reach, never-before-reached dust was portrayed as a huge ugly family living in the crevice of a picture frame. The camera approached closer and closer until you were actually inside this great baronial manor house with cobwebs on the chandeliers and horrid things sitting on the settee. All these horrid things are watching an ad on this greasy telly for *You Never Managed To Get It ALL Out!* in which this yellow dust-cloth is sucking out people-germs similar to the ones watching the ad on the telly. The disgusting dust family are laughing at the ad as they slurp down cups of bubbling soup with flies in it when suddenly a high treble voice is heard, which grows into a great choir like the Hubbyfield Pick-of-the-Enclaves Choral and rays of celestial light enter the dark, disgusting lounge of the dust family.

At first, the disgusting Dusts are not sure what is happening, but when the fat one covered in – pardon me – snot, sitting in the middle of the settee, is sucked bodily out of his comfy seat and impaled on the duster which appears out of nowhere like a spaceship in the ether, terror engulfs the Dust family and all the horrible little pets they keep all about. Then with a whoosh and a climax from the Hubbyfield Pick-of-the-Enclaves Choral Society off they all go on to the duster. The horrid room is transformed into a glittering tasteful lounge and stars glitter from all the surfaces. The camera draws back and we see a hubby looking pleased in front of the pristine picture-frame. A cleanliness star glitters and is gone. Then the hubby wraps the dust-cloth in a press-lock plastic bag and drops it into the swing bin.

A voice tells us that *You Never Managed To Get It ALL Out!* can be obtained from larger branches of Hubbies-Ah-Us and ships of *The Floating Bo$co* above 10,000 tonnes.

Les looked at me and I looked at Les.

"We're ahead of the pack!" I said.

"Been there! Done that!" Les said.

Well, that set both me and Les off, as you can imagine. Les ran off to try out his *You Never Managed to Get It ALL Out!* I unpacked one of my sets, plugged in the magno-ioniser and read the instructions. I had to place the dust-cloth into it for charging. That took half an hour so I had time to go back to the television. Up popped another advert for *You Never Managed To Get It ALL Out!* This one couldn't have been more different. It showed a Mrs about to leave for work. Suddenly she notices some difficult-of-access dust in her briefcase lock. She imagines all the Mesdames at the office pointing out her lapse, making comments about lazy hubbies, etc. Then her hubby comes up and tells his distraught Mrs not to worry. Off he goes and we get that high voice and the Hubbyfield Choral and back the hubby comes with this glowing, golden dust-cloth. This he sweeps in front of the briefcase and it shines and sparkles. Off the Mrs goes up the road, her briefcase lock shooting out stars that impress the neighbours no end.

I saw that there was a report on a confrontation between the police and the Angry Hubby Brigade coming up next. I switched off the television straight away.

Still, I had some time to kill so I parcelled up a little parcel of goodies to send to Jason. He's a great fan of *Chococleans*, the sugar-free sweetmeat which cleans the teeth, so I put in several packets, along with a couple of new outfits for his *Busy Hubby* doll.

Then the magno-ioniser bleeped that all was ready. Straight away I started on Avril's Indian carved desk and in a trice it was cleaner than I'd ever seen it. Cleaner than the Indian carver of yesteryear had ever seen it, I'll be bound.

I happened to look at my hands after cleaning the Indian carving and – do you know – I found that my nails were the cleanest I'd ever seen them! Yes, as an extra bonus, a by-product of its sterling work in the dusting department, the magno-ionised duster had removed all debris from under my nails. My wedding ring was more glittery than usual, too, even under the white-gold heart and around the little petals of the roses. I felt really touched that I had been the recipient of a benefit of *You Never Managed to Get It ALL Out!* that the manufacturers had not even mentioned!

Next, I turned my attention to other fiddly things in Avril's office until, just like it said in the instructions, the little red strip on one side of the dust-cloth had disappeared. This informed me that the dust-cloth had lived its short but useful life and was ready to shuffle off into the plastic bag (provided) and be discarded with care.

I was recharging a second dust-cloth when Dave rang up.

To tell you the truth I was surprised to hear from him. I thought that he would have been preparing something to tickle his Mrs's taste-buds after her strenuous day at the Drop In Centre.

"You don't know what you missed!" Dave said.

Now, that surprised me too. I'd have thought that Dave was the one who'd missed the great events of that day.

"What did I miss, Dave?" I asked.

"The meeting at the Leisure," said Dave. "Well, it was more of a one-to-one seminar, if you get me. Just me and Lurleen – she's the facilitator. Harry, it was absolutely bloody fantastic!"

There was something un-Dave about the way Dave was talking. "You haven't been at the drink, have you, Dave?" I asked him.

"Yes, I have!" said Dave. "It's part of the therapy. I've got to get myself paralytic. And I'm eating *TofuTiffin Full-Fat*."

"You're not!" I said. "Do you know how many empty calories there are in 100 grams of *TofuTiffin Full-Fat*?"

"I don't care!" Dave said. "I've never felt better!"

"What's come over you? Where are the quads?"

"They're at the 24-hour crèche. I can't wait for Mavis to come home so's I can tell her the good news!"

I closed my eyes, but I didn't need to to imagine how Mavis would react if she came home and found Dave drunk and going on. "Dave, what happened at the Leisure?"

"Lurleen opened my eyes, Harry. And I'm going to open yours. When you see the brand-new me you'll know. This is definitely it!"

"This Lurleen. What did she tell you to do?"

"She told me to do what I want, Harry. Exactly what I want. I've got to test myself, push my self-indulgence as far as I possibly can. You see, Harry, only then will I strengthen every organ in my body. I have to push my body and like an army tested by ordeals, my body will come through for me. I have to self-indulge in order to strengthen my body. And that's what I've been doing, Harry, and it feels wonderful. Bloody wonderful!"

"Moderation in all things, Dave," I said.

To tell you the truth, I wanted to say a lot more than that: I wanted to tell Dave that, while I hadn't been there, what he had experienced at this Lurleen's hands sounded like nonsense. And that was putting it kindly. From the brief account I'd just had from Dave I could tell that it flew right in the face of everything the Hubby Counsellors at *The Floating Bo$co* had been teaching us. Moderation in all things was their clarion call. Of course, even *The Floating Bo$co* people had made mistakes. They had, for instance, pushed the hubbies towards oat-bran for years until the findings came out that it caused all sorts of problems.

I told Dave that he should go to bed at once and that me and Les would meet him at the Nirvana Precinct the next morning and have a good talk about it. On no account was he to tell his Mavis.

Dave said he wouldn't but I wasn't convinced he wouldn't. And in the morning when we arrived at the Nirvana there was no sign of Dave. We were about to leave when Mavis drove up in their EcoLandcruiser Transporter. No sign of Dave – and Mavis got out and marched into Nirvana with a face of thunder.

A hubby I didn't know nudged me. "That's Dave's Mavis," he said.

"Yes," I said.

"Dave's Mavis has taken a job on *The Floating Bo$co*," the hubby said.

"You mean she's left the Nirvana Precinct?" I asked, quite shocked but somehow cheered at the same time. No one had been more anti *The Floating Bo$co* than Mavis.

"That's interesting, isn't it, Les?" I said as we walked down the road.

"What?" said Les.

"About Dave's Mavis's new job."

"It's Dave I'm worried about, chuck," Les said.

"What do you think we should do, Les?" I asked.

"Leave them to it," Les said. "If Dave really has fallen for a load of nonsense, I'm sure his Mavis will bring him round."

"Let's just call at the house. There's nothing wrong in that, is there?"

Les seemed unsure. He said he was charging a dust-cloth to embark on his new dusting regimen.

"You'll enjoy that, Les," I said. "You've got a treat in store. But ask yourself whether you'll be able to dust with peace of mind if you're worried about Dave. If I know you – which I do – I think you'll be distracted."

Les thought for a moment, then nodded. We walked off towards Dave's house.

We rang the chimes on the front door. Dave had recently invested in *Random Rotating Mood Chimes* which came with a mood-pad. You got up in the morning and put your palm on the mood-pad and the *Random Rotating Mood Chimes* automatically programme themselves to play a selection of tunes that mirrored the pulse-points of your mood. Not only that, the tunes changed throughout the course of the day, following exactly the slight changes of mood that might be expected. Dave saw it in the window of Plain Wayne's Hubby Supplies – yes I know – and just had to have it and nothing I could say could persuade him different. That should have rung warning-bells then and there, I suppose, but it didn't.

However, when I pressed the door-bell and heard *Nobody Comes Near Me (In the Love Race)* coming from inside, my worries increased. *Nobody Comes Near Me (In The Love Race)* was not a song I could associate with Dave, who is the most Mrs-dependent hubby of my acquaintance. I just could not imagine Dave's palm on the *Random Rotating Mood Chimes* pad being able to produce that song.

There was no answer.

"Ring again, chuck," Les said.

I rang again. The chimes played *Yesterday, Today, Tomorrow (I Want It All and I Want It Now!)* a song that was definitely aimed at the Mrs market, and sounded distinctly tasteless coming from a hubby's chimes – especially when the Mrs is out.

"Les," I said, "I was right to have reservations about Dave's purchase of those *Random Rotating Mood Chimes*."

"Why? They beat *Ding-Dong* in my book," Les said.

"Well, maybe you're right, Les. But they also give the person at the door a clear hint as to the mood of the occupants. If a rep calls, for instance, and hears what we've just heard, she'll know she's on to a winner. She'll probably sell her complete stock to someone who wants it all and wants it now. One thing you can say about *Ding-Dong* is that it doesn't give the game away."

"He isn't answering," said Les. "Try again."

"I don't like to, Les. I worry about what I might hear."

Les gave me a look and reached out to press the door-bell. As he lifted his arm I could smell a different perfume. I tried to think what it was. It was definitely not *Maine In Fall*. There were flower and mineral accents there, but the main theme was definitely the seashore.

We heard *That's How I Do It* coming from the inside of Dave's house.

We waited.

"What's that you're wearing, Les?" I asked.

"I thought you'd never ask. It's *Seascape for Hubbies*, Harry. I bought it yesterday on *The Floating Bo$co*. Just for a change, you know. What do you think?"

To tell you the truth, I was in two minds. A part of me was a bit hurt that Les should have taken flight in the BodyCare department. That had always been my area of expertise. Still, Les had chosen well and I felt a shiver of elation at the thought that all my little homilies on skin chemistry and perfume themes and accents and secondary harmonics were bearing fruit. I just hoped and prayed for the happy day when I would be as independent in the Tinned Goods department. I mean, I'm efficient; I can manage. But I'm not, as you might say, *fluent*. "It's really lovely," I said.

"Do you think so. Really?" Les asked.

I nodded. We stood on Dave's doorstep and looked into one another's eyes. That moment was the biggest bonding occurrence we'd had for ages.

"He's not in, is he?" Les said, pulling his eyes from me to the front of Dave's house.

"Your eyebrows could do with a shape," I told him.

"And your lashes could do with a comb out. You've got a few too many crossovers."

"Touché!" I said. Then I felt guilty about forgetting Dave. "I'm going to have a look round the back."

Les counselled caution, saying that he was pretty sure Dave had been going to install a *Buried Rottweiler Underground Burglar-Alarm System* which, when you stepped on the side passage, automatically sounded an alarm in a discreet brooch. I imagined Mavis being alarmed if she came home and found us..

"We owe it to Dave," I said.

"Yes," Les said. "We owe it to Dave."

We tiptoed round the back of the house. I must say that Dave kept his side-passage pristine. The bin smelled of pine-trees which is something for a Monday, which is the day before Tuesday when the bin-Mesdames come. The bin-Mesdames coming to Dave's house were in for a treat.

The window of the upstairs back bedroom was wide open. From it hung a couple of rather nice peach-and-white bedsheets, knotted together. "You know what this means, Les?" I said.

"I'm trying to think," Les said.

"It means that Dave's been shopping at Immaculate Linens," I said. "It also means that he may have run off!"

Les nodded. "What do we do?"

"We tell Dave's Mrs, Les!" I said. " There's nothing else for it!"

I did not mention it to Les, but I knew there was no alternative to telling Mavis as soon as we reached the back of Dave's house. I'd forgotten about the great big *Sound-n-Vision Watchdog* that Dave had had installed in case the *Buried Rottweiler* system went on the blink.

Anyway, I knew that the *Sound-n-Vision Watchdog* would have recorded our every movement and remark. Then I thought that, if it had recorded us, it would also have recorded Dave's escape. From the little I knew of what had come over Dave since his meeting with Lurleen, the Catalina Island dietitian, I knew that there was going to be hell to pay and I did not want Yours Affectionately to have to be the fall-hubby. It would be bound to get back to Avril. Summary divorce and exile sans Jason to the Industrial Nostalgia New Town High-Rises nightmared itself into my consciousness, like they say in the insurance ads.

We arrived at the landing-stage in plenty of time. We could see *The Floating Bo$co* nosing across the Estuary towards us. I had time to notice that there was a new exhibition coming to the Mrs Tate Gallery NNW. When all the trouble had been sorted out I made a resolution to pop in to see *Feathery Delicacy – The Traditional Hubby Arts of The Masai*.

The Floating Bo$co docked and me and Les were the first on. My heart was in my mouth as I asked Big Yvette if I could see Dave's Mrs, Mavis, on a matter of some urgency.

"I don't know," said Big Yvette. "She's up to her eyes in restructuring."

"It concerns her hubby, Dave, Mrs Yvette," I said.

Big Yvette twiddled her nose-ring, giving Les one of those up-and-down looks. I could scent Les's *Seascape for Hubbies* go into overdrive. It made me wonder, and worry the more. Still, I thought, one problem at a time. "It really is important, Mrs Yvette. We wouldn't have come if it wasn't, would we, Les?"

Big Yvette, still looking at Les, said, "Well, seeing it's you . . . this way."

I made sure to walk between Les and Big Yvette as she guided us up to the bridge of *The Floating Bo$co*. There, behind a big desk covered with pictures of Lady Lavinia, sat Mavis.

I told her everything that had happened.

"You think he escaped out of the back window, do you?"

"That's where the knotted sheets were, Mrs," I said. "They were peach and white."

"Well, the camera will pick up the exact time and circumstances," Mavis said. Then she looked hard at me. "Did you have any inkling about what was happening?"

Well, there was no use lying. I told Mavis that I had heard from Dave the night before and knew he was really pleased with his day at the Leisure with Lurleen. I didn't go into details.

Still, as usual, the Mesdames can suss us out. They've got this uncanny knack. "And that's why you went to the house to check, was it?"

"Yes," I said.

Then, quick as a flash, Mavis said, "So you were worried?"

I confessed that I had been.

"And you were also worried last night?"

Again, I nodded.

"But you didn't think to tell me? You could have done it anonymously through the *Hubby Helpline Liaison Line* – confidentiality assured. You knew that Dave was going off the rails and yet you did nothing?"

I hung my head.

Les stepped in. "Look, Mrs," he said. "We're here now. It isn't everyone who would have gone to check, you know."

Mavis nodded. "I'll be speaking to your Avril about this," she said. "Where is she, by the way? I received her fax-card from the Puget Estuary Enclave this morning."

"She's on her way to the Pacific Rim as we speak," I said.

"Well, Hubbies," Mavis said, "you've done the right thing, albeit a little late. I suppose that is the best we can expect. I'll alert *The Floating Bo$co's* Security Service. We'll find Dave and that rogue Mrs, Lurleen."

We stood abjectly while Mavis strode over to her console and buttoned in the monitor to play back her *Sound-N-Vision Watchdog* tape. Instantaneously we saw a cat slink past. A blank. Then this Mrs with huge hair came into view, whistling up at Dave's window. The window opened and the peach-and-white sheets were lowered, followed by Dave, wearing a weekend bumbag. Blank. Then me and Les were seen. I looked at myself and worried about my hips, though I know it was out of place. Mavis turned up the volume and listened to everything that had passed between us. I looked at Les. He looked back but do you know what? I could not read his expression. I just couldn't.

Mavis turned off the monitor and called Big Yvette into her office. "I want an all-points alert put out on *The Floating Bo$co* Security Network," she said. Then she pressed a button on the monitor and a picture of Dave and Lurleen emerged. "Fax this through the network," Mavis said. Big Yvette saluted and went off, giving Les a look.

Mavis turned to us and smiled. Yes! Smiled! I wish I'd had a camera of my own to catch the moment. "Things being what they are," she said, "I suppose you behaved with more presence-of-mind than most hubbies would've in a similar situation." She reached into a drawer and produced two tokens. "Go and treat yourself to a slap-up snack at the HubbyCaff, Hubbies. As you see, we have set off across the river again so you are marooned for an hour."

"Do you think we'll get Dave before any harm is done?" I asked.

Well, they did and they didn't. They caught Dave and Lurleen at a Leisure Centre in the Tyne and Weir Hubby Enclave, where Lurleen was scheduled to give her next "seminar". But catching Dave and bringing him home was not the end of the story by a long chalk. Whatever Lurleen had done to him at the Leisure may never be known. Anyway she had filled his head with the most diabolical nonsense about health-enhancement procedures. And, it was like Dave had told me on the VideoChat, Lurleen believed that only by giving way to all one's appetites could the body be strengthened to resist the onset of ailments. Livers had to be immersed in wines and spirits and fats so that they would strengthen themselves; stomachs had to be filled past bursting-point. It was a bit like saying that filling a Widdecombe Three-Wheeler's oil tank to the top and not just to the top of the marking on the dipstick would enhance the car's performance. It just doesn't add up. At least I don't think it does.

But you'd be amazed how many hubbies up and down the enclaves were taken in by it. The cry went up, *"One over the eight – for your liver's sake!"* *"Feast for fitness!"* *"Immoderation in all things!"* *"Take it past the limit!"*

Dave was sent to The Lady Lavinia Home for Fallen Hubbies for several months. He was joined there by many another unfortunate victim of Lurleen's cult. To tell you the truth, he was lucky to get off so lightly. Hubbies have been sent to The Industrial Nostalgia New Town for less.

Then, when Avril got back from the Mishima Estuary Enclave, where she had won a landmark case on behalf of the Ystwyth Enclave Mesdames' Laverbread Cooperative against the Sayonara Seaweed Cartel, she got into a huddle with Mavis and Les's Barbara. I didn't get much about what they discussed – well, you don't get more than the gist taking the tea-tray in – but I did hear enough. It can be summed up in "Leisure", "Disgusting", "Ought not to be allowed" . . . and I knew the Leisure's number was up. I warned Les and we cleared our lockers to be prepared for the forthcoming lock-out.

And none too soon, either. Avril slapped an injunction on the Leisure the day after for spreading sedition. Many a hubby lost his PE kit through being slow to empty his locker, I can tell you. We hoped it might just be a slap on the wrist, that the Leisure would be allowed to open again after a suitable punishment period. But I sensed it wouldn't. For a start they started expanding the Hubby Leisure Deck on *The Floating Bo$co* and Lady Lavinia Bo$co came out with her new opus, *The Hubbies Float At Leisure*. To tell you the truth, it was not her best effort, though still a page-turner-and-a-half in my book.

But I have a slight anxiety that Dave still hankers for Lurleen's excesses. I sometimes wish I could charge a dust-cloth and hold it over Dave's brain and pull out all memory of that disgusting cult. But *You Never Managed To Get It ALL Out!* doesn't work on hubbies' brains, more's the pity. The price of hubby-inner-cleanliness is eternal vigilance.

P.S. Don't ask me what happened to Lurleen. However, Big Yvette went missing for a few days and came back with a black eye but looking pleased with herself and telling Les that all would be well and all manner of things would be well . . . starting now.

Well, we'll see . . .

9

Hubby Island

I'm not sure if I mentioned it, but I won a free weekend for one to *Hubby Island* recently. Thinking on, I'm pretty sure I kept it to myself. You see, what with all the fuss over Dave, I wasn't sure Avril would give the trip the *nihil obstat*, even though she's the one who'll get the benefit in the long run.

The competition was organised by the *Washday Grail* people. I was walking round *The Floating Bo$co* one afternoon and came upon a display of *New Washday Grail Washing-up Liquid*. Now, I was a little taken aback by the display at first, to tell you the truth. You see, the *Washday Grail* people had forsaken their glass bottle in favour of recyclable plastic – this after me and Les's perfect moment in Washday Requisites back in the mists of antiquity – which really disappointed me.

Normally I would have passed by *New Washday Grail Washing-up Liquid* on the other side of the aisle, except for this flash on the containers: *Is there a weekend for one on Hubby Island inside this container?* No, there isn't, I told the display, and I walked on to mug up on Tinned Goods for the next time Les took it into his head to ofsted me.

You see, I haven't had any luck in the competition department. I can't tell you the hundreds of times I've been disappointed by not finding a *You've won!* under the tabs of *OlaCola* cans. The *OlaCola* people have stopped doing that now because the common Hairy Hubbies from the Industrial Nostalgia New Town would do the rounds, opening hundreds of cans trying to find winning ones. Well, as is often the way, the anti-social element spoilt it for the rest of us.

Still, the idea of going to Hubby Island for a weekend kept coming back to haunt and taunt me as I tried to sort out the tuna in brine, tuna in spring water, tuna in vegetable oil, tuna in olive oil, tuna in its own oil, dolphin-friendly tuna in . . . well, back to square one in the tuna department – and then compute the price/weight ratio, label aesthetics, tin design, materials used, opening gizmo – I kept seeing myself launching away from my humdrum hubby routine, being pampered and primped and exercised and indulged and I thought to myself, "Harry," I thought, "Harry, you deserve it!"

Back I went to the *Washday Grail* display. Quick as a flash I picked six bottles of *New Washday Grail Washing-up Liquid* and made for the check-out.

As luck would have it, I wasn't able to get off *The Floating Bo$co* for another half-hour, so I went into the Interdenominational Chapel for a bit of a sit-down. And when I was sitting down I said a prayer that there might be a holiday for one on Hubby Island in one of the bottles.

Call me a daft hubby if you like, but I came out of the chapel feeling all peaceful and there was something in my head as hard as a piece of nutmeg that believed – *me! believed!* – there would be a holiday in the bottle. I went straight home.

I took my six bottles of washing-up liquid to the garage. I put a *Ground CoverUp* down on the ground, fetched a filter funnel and a plastic petrol-can. I then started pouring the contents of the bottles into the can.

I didn't find my holiday until the fifth bottle of washing-up liquid was being poured into the petrol-can. Of course, wouldn't you know it, the little gold token fell into the half-full petrol-can and I had to fish it out. I won't tell you how I did it but I was a wet rag by the finish. That's what comes of being an impatient hubby, I suppose.

I didn't let my excitement show. I took the petrol-can indoors and labelled it *Washing-up Liquid*. I put it in the pantry and stood the sixth unopened bottle next to the sink. Then I washed the little token and popped it in my bumbag.

I find it hard to recall exactly how I felt. I was happy about winning, of course, but I seem to recall a feeling of unease, of guilt almost, that here I was about to walk down a long road of lies and deception. If only I'd known . . .

It took me three days before I rang the *Washday Grail* people to tell them of my good fortune. They told me to send the winning token to them and state the preferred dates for my weekend.

Well, it suddenly hit me that I'd really have to think carefully about that. Avril would have to be away and I'd have to find a discreet and caring hubby to look after Jason, who was between boarding establishments – and you spell discreet and caring L-E-S in my book. There was also the worry of how to keep Jason's mouth shut once Avril got back. Still, I thought, that's the least of my worries. I'd bribe him senseless.

As luck would have it, a weekend turned up three weeks later when Avril was to be away. I was to be deprived of my better half for a full four days while she inputted on the *Hawaiian Sun Oil* scandal. Then Les told me that his Barbara was also going to be away that same weekend at a Estuary Nat West Client Awareness do, in the Colne Estuary Enclave.

Naturally, I let Les in on what was afoot and asked him to

Jason-sit for me. On no account was he to tell on me. I would, of course, return the favour for him one day if, for example, he had a Miners' Nostalgia or Wind-Turbine Spotting Weekend to attend.

"What are you going to do on Hubby Island?" Les asked.

"That's a bit up in the air at the moment, Les," I replied. "I may let them run me through a battery of diagnostic tests. I've been worried about my cellulite density and they may think I could do with a top-up of collagen. I also want to know what it is about my hips that makes them distort on the electronic media. I know I need some professional advice about the usual."

Les nodded, knowing I was talking about hubby-stubble. "I'm a martyr, as you know. *Hubby Soothe* just can't deal with the stubble. If the Hubby Island people can come up with a decent treatment that isn't too pricey, I'd like to know about it."

I told Les that I'd keep my eyes open – when I didn't have cucumbers over them, of course – and he was quite happy to look after Jason. I informed the Hubby Island people about my dates and they sent me details of time of launch at the Estuary Quay to Pleasure, together with a long questionnaire regarding my dietary requirements and a full run-down of my depilatory routine, etc.

I told them – I didn't mince my words – that tough stubble in areas of friction and private access were my main problem. They fired back a reply that I was to allow problem areas to grow for at least four days prior to my arrival at Hubby Island. They needed something to go on in order to be able to make an accurate diagnosis. That got me in a tizzy, to tell you the truth, because I thought Avril would be bound to notice. A day, or even two, I can usually get away with, but four was pushing it.

Avril was in residence when the message arrived and she

usually pounces on faxes, reading them as they emerge and shouting, "YES!" with fist punching the air to celebrate one more victory in the litigation department. But, as luck would have it, she had the home tattooist in that morning who was completing a magnum opus on Avril's back, a long quotation from *Lager with Roger*, a book which Avril has always been partial to. Anyway, she always gets tattooed in the rumpus room and did not hear the drone of the fax over the tattooist's non-stop monologue. The tattooist talks so much she fogs up the windows of the rumpus room and lets me in for half an hour of target-practice with my *DeMist-n-Clean* pump-action liquid – which, you've guessed it, is vinegar-free.

And I needn't have worried about my undepilated spots being noticed either. The *Hawaiian Sun Oil* case was really worrying Avril. She had to deliver some keynote address to the group of lawyers involved and somehow, she felt, it just wasn't coming right. I know if I was Avril's keynote address I'd come right straight away. I'd know better than to get Avril mad. Anyway, Avril kept videoing herself making the address. Then she'd run back to the word-processor to insert directions that were meant to improve her body-language. I had no function at all and the five-o'clock-shadow in my areas of private access grew into great prairies of burning stubble. I itched to depilate but, of course, I couldn't. I must have used a bottle and a half of *Hubby-Soothe, Factor 4*!

Anyway, I saw Avril off at the Airport on their evening feeder flight, hightailed it back home to snuggle Jason under Les's kindly feathers and ran off to the Estuary Quay To Pleasure to wait for the launch to take me to Hubby Island.

There were several hubbies waiting for the launch, though at the time I thought they were all trying to look as if they were not waiting for the Hubby Island launch. I hung about, reading the operating instructions on a fire-extinguisher. And while I read I was wondering about the condition of the smoke-alarms at home. There hadn't been a peep out of any of them for ages. That was odd in itself and for a while I got a bit jittery and wondered if I should run home to check. But then I remembered that the lack of action from the smoke-alarms was due to me having purchased a computer-assisted toaster which runs a scanner down the toast five hundred times a second and highlights any untoward unevenness in cooking on a digital display and cuts out the heat-sensor to that section, and that section alone.

A long way round the houses to tell you that burnt toast is a thing of the past in our house and, as the sounding of the smoke-alarm had been our cast-iron signal both that the toast was done and the smoke-alarm in fire-brigade-preferred condition, you never had to worry. But now it is different and unless you have a schedule of inspection – something I was always telling the powers-that-were at Widdecombe Three-Wheeler would be a good idea – I had never fully implemented it in the household department.

Anyway, I knew I was having a panic attack of the sort that Dad has as soon as he's on the bus on his way to the Nirvana Precinct (I haven't managed to get him on board *The Floating Bo$co*, but I'm working on it). He was always wondering about the gas. Had he left it on? Well, in Dad's case, his worries were usually well-founded. I can't tell you the times HubbyMuggins – that's me in case you didn't know – has been called in to use all my secret knowledge and elbow-grease to remove pressure-cooker and chicken-bones from every surface of his kitchen. I just put him in the lounge with the telly on and tell him to let me get on with it.

I decided to put all mundanity behind me, breathed deeply, scratched my areas of private access and turned my attention to the magic of the present moment – what there was of it.

I knew why I didn't want to be seen but I couldn't figure out what was going on with the other hubbies. After all, there was nothing wrong in trying to make oneself more delectable for the Mesdames, was there? The hubbies hanging about all looked very presentable. If I'd been any of their Mesdames I'd have been happy to be seen out with any of them on my arm. Still, I thought, they're probably looking at me and thinking the same thing, not realising that I'd got a four-day growth of hubby-hair in my areas of private access.

The launch arrived promptly at ten and it was then I got my first real shock – the first of many I'm sorry to have to report. Leaning over the gunswails to throw the rope onto the jetty was Big Yvette!

"Well, if it isn't Harry Manley!" shouted Big Yvette in that gruff way she has that sets you all atingle.

"Good evening, Mrs Yvette," I replied. "I didn't know you were working on the Hubby Island ferry."

"The powers-that-be decided I was sending the wrong sort of signals for a place that was supposed to be hubby-friendly," Big Yvette said. She seemed quite pleased.

I didn't let on, of course. "Goodness, Mrs Yvette! Whatever made them think that?"

"Can't you guess?" Big Yvette asked, adjusting the gangway with one hand.

"To tell you the truth, Mrs Yvette," I said, lying through my teeth, "I always thought you were *The Floating Bo$co's* biggest asset."

Big Yvette seemed pleased. She took my hold-all and tried

to take my bumbag too. "No, Mrs Yvette," I said. "The bumbag is attached."

"That's a shame, Harry! It's covering up that nice pert bum of yours. I always thought your bum was the best of all the hubbies on *The Floating Bo$co*. Have you sorted out your pec-organizer problem yet?"

"Mrs Yvette, *pleassse!*" I said, looking around. Still I was really pleased that Big Yvette had thought enough of my hips to remark about them. To tell you the truth I've been really worried about them ever since that afternoon in the Clothing Department on *The Floating Bo$co*, and I'd be telling a lie if I said I hadn't. Big Yvette laughed gruffly like she does and lifted me aboard. I noticed she had beaded and plaited her underarm hair. It looked wonderful, I have to admit. Not exactly attractive, more impressive. And her touch made me go all weak. Of course, Big Yvette knows her own animal magnetism. There's many a hubby – apart from dear Les – who has fallen away from the path of rectitude because of Big Yvette. It was said that when Big Yvette was Numera Una on the landing-stage at *The Floating Bo$co* she put notches on the flagpole to denote her hubby-conquests. In the end the notches so weakened the flagpole that it broke off during a gale. Anyway, that's the story.

I resisted, though I had to call the Hubby Helpline every day for a week when temptation got really bad. But Big Yvette, while pinching me and whispering threats of what she'd do to me if she ever got me alone behind the trolley-maintenance-area Portabungalow, never really took serious advantage of me. I think this was because she knew that my Avril was a litigation lawyer without pity. Well, I like to think that. I hope it wasn't because she found me unattractive. But – and don't tell a soul – I think when Les fell and told his Barbara, his Barbara complained. Big Yvette's sudden career move might well have something to do with Les's fall from grace. It's only a theory, mind. It's not something I'd ever broach with Les. Least said and all that.

Anyway, Big Yvette parked me in a starboard seat and went off to assist the other hubbies. Some, judging from their luggage, looked as if they were coming for a long stay. They came aboard, worrying about scuffing shoes on capstans, and I could see them one by one melting before Big Yvette's gruff attentions. They were placed equally on the port and starboard sides. Big Yvette shouted to the captain and cast off, jumping back on to the launch with an agility that made all the hubbies gasp.

We set off down the river towards Hubby Island and my appointment with destiny, watching Big Yvette smoking her pipe, flexing her muscles in the bow. I looked down demurely at my bumbag, now covering my front.

Hubby Island is located on what used to be a little hill three miles from the shore of the old estuary. When the water rose and turned it into an island, the RSPB bought it with Lottery money. Trouble was, no birds came there and a developer bought the Island from the RSPB in that asset-stripping operation they had a decade or so back. The developer – Mary Telford and Daughters – at once started building what turned into The Positive Health and Hubby Recharging Centre to service all the confused hubbies in the enclaves. It's been very successful by all accounts, though I have heard that it does have a reputation for being a sort of last chance saloon for hubbies about to surrender to various forms of unattractiveness, both in body and retail attitudes. Or a combination. The two often go together in my experience.

Of course, I didn't feel I was anywhere near that stage myself and I was encouraged in believing that the reputation was ill-founded by the sight of the hubbies on the launch, all of whom looked on the glamorous side. Diamond rings, gold hubby-bracelets, the lot. But then I got talking to Ernest, who was next to me on the starboard side.

Ernest came out and said straight off that he had been sent for a month's R and R at Hubby Island by his Mrs, who is a Big Wheel in the conglomerate that manufacture *Hubby-Soothe*.

"Is that right, Ernest?" I said. "Well, isn't it a small world?"

"Don't talk to me about small worlds," Ernest said. "My Iris is never still. She's always packing me off to Hubby Island because she knows I'll be out of harm's way while she's away."

"It's my first time," I said. "You know, when I come to think of it, it's probably me and other hubbies of my acquaintance that are paying for your trip to Hubby Island. *Hubby-Soothe* is really popular round here."

Ernest didn't laugh or anything. He just nodded, then he put his hand out and said, "My name's Ernest, by the way."

I already knew that of course. "I'm Harry," I said.

We shook hands. Ernest's handshake was really limp, the sort of handshake that Les is always saying is wet-fish. To tell you the truth I was a bit shocked because one thing hubbies have held tight on to is the good firm handshake. It's one of those secret signs between us that we still possess an inner strength; that under the mountains of creams, potions, washday-red, nippers and groceries there beat hearts of solid oak-veneer. A firm handshake I've heard described as a gender memory. It's worth holding on to. A limp handshake is a sign that a hubby has given up in all departments. Les often says, "Death rather than a limp handshake, Harry!" And I've come to agree with him. Not sure why.

"What's the matter, Ernest?" I asked.

"You can tell, can you?"

I made a discreet sign with my hand so's Big Yvette or any of the other crew-members she was joshing with in the bow wouldn't notice.

Ernest shook his head sadly. "To tell you the truth, er – Harry, I haven't bothered with bonding for years," he said. "If you want to know it's been beaten out of me."

He must have seen me looking shocked. "You don't mean . . . ?"

"No, nothing like that. It's just that I was a slow learner in the hubby department. I'd been a salesman at British Aerospace and managed to hold on to my work longer than most hubbies. When the time came and I became a full-time hubby I just couldn't get my head round things in the household department. There was so much to think about and the world had moved on. All the courses and TV programmes had finished. I was a beginner in an advanced world of hubbies."

I nodded. "You're a Hubby-Who-Stays-In, aren't you?"

"Yes, I am," Ernest said. "I'm sure I'd have got the hang of it given time. But my Iris got this big job with De Vere's and said she'd rather hire help to take care of everything. She bought me a poodle and I sit by the heated pool eating *Hubby-Treats* in front of a bank of monitors."

"I've never got on with *Hubby-Treats*," I said, because I was too speechless to say anything else.

"The mango flavour with bran and no added sugar are yummy when you get used to them. And, believe me, Harry, I got used to them."

Ernest beckoned me closer, looking around as he did so. "By the by," he said, "don't let it slip to any of the other hubbies on Hubby Island that you won your trip to Hubby Island in a competition. There are several I know on this very launch who could really turn on you if they suss out that you're not a Hubby Island habitué."

"Get away!" I said – and I thought of Les. "That's hard to believe, Ernest. I mean, they all look so *nice*!"

Ernest surveyed the hubbies on the launch, which was tossing about on the estuary in the wake thrown up by *The Floating Bo$co*. Ernest looked at it wistfully. "That's a floating supermarket, isn't it?"

"Yes," I said. "And it's the original one too. The first bread cast on the waters by Lady Lavinia Bo$co. Course, there's one in every estuary with an enclave now – plying the oceans too – but that's the original, and many hubbies believe, the finest."

"I've never been on one," Ernest said.

"What? Never?" I had to really fight hard to keep my voice from dropping to the lower common hairy-hubby register. My heart went out to him. "Ernest, you don't know what you've been missing."

"My Iris says I shouldn't soil my hands. She says that Home Shopping is the cutting-edge. And she worries what I might pick up."

"*The Floating Bo$co* is pristine," I said. "True, some rather dubious hubbies tend to get on at the Industrial Nostalgia New Town landing-stage, but it takes all sorts. Security on board is top notch."

Ernest nodded and gave the retreating supermarket one last long sad glance. "Remember what I told you," he said, "about the other hubbies. Don't trust them an inch, Harry. Will you promise me that? It's lucky that you and I met up. They'll turn really nasty if they find you're on Hubby Island because of that competition and that you go out, and *shop*. That's what they're like. They're hubbies of leisure and all they have to think about is being glamour-Toms and what they can get the Mesdames to buy them from Y Samuel. They're unhappy, unfulfilled hubbies, Harry. Like me, 'cept I know it."

I looked at *The Floating Bo$co* retreating into the mist and wished – oh, how I wished! – that I was on her then, contentedly driving my trolley up and down the aisles, feeling the delicious heave of the swell beneath my feet, listening to the quiet drone of the subliminal special-offer announcements, the murmurings of hubbies coming to wise consumer decisions for their families. On board *The Floating Bo$co* I knew where I was. I felt secure. Why, I thought, even if the most common Hairy Hubbies that the Industrial Nostalgia New Town could produce got on in droves on their way to the *No Bake Superbake Soda Bread Premium League Netball Finals* at the Astrodome, I would be content. There I would have felt a part of everything. But a weekend on Hubby Island looked like a quite different matter altogether.

And I didn't feel any better when the launch arrived at the Hubby-Island jetty. To tell you the truth I was completely taken aback – shocked would not be too strong a word – by the reception committee, which consisted of several Mesdames dressed as chambermaids. I whispered my worries to Ernest but he whispered softly back, "Say nothing. Survival is the name of the game, Harry."

Well, I couldn't have said anything. To tell you the truth I was in shock. Any more shocked and I'd have keeled over there and then. The idea of Mesdames dressed in that inappropriate fashion – black nylons, garter belts, skimpy skirts in silly fabrics – really upset me.

Anyway, Big Yvette trundled our luggage off the launch after us. As she passed me on her way back to the launch, she said to me, "I want to hear all about it, Harry Manley". Then, quick as a flash, she jumped back on to the launch and it sped off, leaving us to our fate.

What really galled me was that the other hubbies seemed

to think that everything that was happening was the most natural thing in the world and not the very peak of perversity. My chambermaid carried my luggage to a cabin with a lovely view over the Nuclear Nostalgia Safari Park and Lido that didn't cheer me up at all. I kept thinking of the disgusting way the chambermaid wiggled as she walked, making the ends on the black bow go suggestively from side to side. She opened the door of my room, holding my key out with one hand while the other waited for a tip. A tip!

I found an estuario in my pocket – don't ask me how – and gave it to her. She wished me an interesting stay, wrinkled her nose and left.

Inside, the cabin was done out all in pine with animal heads on shields covering the walls. There was a narrow bed with a quilt that had that brown masculine aura of yesteryear, and racing-cars, pipes, yachts, shotguns, flying geese, fishing-tackle, shaving mugs and golf clubs all over it. I never saw the point of those things even then. I'd look at my birthday cards covered in such items and think, *There is not among the whole paraphernalia one item that Harry Manley has the least attachment to*. Now, well it didn't seem appropriate, and that's putting it mildly.

I wandered morosely into the bathroom, trying to make sense of it all. But the bathroom didn't help. It was sort of Spartan, a bit like a clean version of the executive washroom at Widdecombe Three-Wheelers.

I looked at myself in the mirror, wishing like mad I hadn't fallen for *New Washday Grail Washing-up Liquid* and the siren-call on the container. I felt all at sea. Even the free samples of *Hubby-Soothe* products on the pine (pine!) shelf over the basin – and there were some new ones that I hadn't seen before – failed to buck me up. Frankly I was depressed, and that's not like me.

Anyway, I was just beginning to wonder if I could go home early when there was a call on the really old-fashioned phone next to the bed. You've guessed it, it was Ernest. Was I ready for a quick pre-dinner drink at The Cock and Bull?

Noting that there was at least a month's worth of dust on the telephone cradle and making a resolution to check the rest of the room, I told him I'd love to have a drink with him, but would he collect me as I didn't fancy going out by myself after what I'd seen, and was what I'd seen merely an unfortunate first impression?

"You haven't seen nothing yet!" said Ernest in a big deep voice.

Well, I gave him my room number and he said he'd come. I put the phone down and sat on the dreadful bed-cover, trying to remember what I'd forgotten. But I kept thinking, *The Cock and Bull! Surely I must have misheard!* But then I thought *DUST!* and filled in the time very productively on one of my dust-hunts. I knew that seeing I'd seen dust at eye-level on the phone, there was bound to be lots in areas of difficult access. Well, the antlers of those poor animals were thick with it. Ditto the odd shield carvings round the bed. I lifted the bed-cover and looked under it. Enough dust to grow tomatoes in. Even Dad would have been shocked; Dad who at eighty-eight forgets to do the necessary. I sat down in the rocking-chair with a sort of stretched-gut backing. Hubby Island, I decided, was not as advertised.

"What's wrong, Harry?" Ernest asked when he came to collect me.

"What's your room like, Ernest?" I asked.

Ernest poked his head round the door of my room, re-emerged and said, "Like yours."

"But that shocking decor, Ernest! Even the hubbies of the Industrial Nostalgia New Town would have a fit."

"The Hubby Island people have updated it since I was last here," Ernest said, matter-of-factly. "Before it was all done up like a mediaeval castle with swords and lances and four-poster beds. And before that – "

"Stop it, Ernest!" I said. "And what about those awful chambermaids?"

Ernest laughed. I didn't take kindly to that to tell you the truth. "You're going through Hubby Island Shock Syndrome. Everyone does, though for most hubbies it's not so much a shock as a *frisson*, if you get me. But promise me, Harry; promise me you won't show the other hubbies what you're going through. They might try to initiate you. Be cool and stick close to me."

"I want to go home, Ernest. There's something – something – evil about this place," I said.

"It's not as bad as that, Harry," Ernest said. "Just some hubbies out for a bit of nostalgia. Go with the flow. You'll see. You might even enjoy it."

"But," I said, "I'm supposed to be here to improve myself. I want to refine my knowledge of depilatory techniques, to check out my cellulite levels, top up on collagen, maybe have a complete Hubby Health Check."

"You've come to the wrong place, Harry," Ernest said. "Well, the right place at the wrong time. The Hubby Island people have filled a gap in the market. Normally, it would suit you down to the ground. But this weekend isn't about hubby-maintenance. It's about something else."

"And what precisely is it about, Ernest?" I asked.

"You'll see, Harry. You'll see," Ernest said.

We arrived at the door of The Cock and Bull. Ernest opened it and gestured me to enter ahead of him. And I felt myself turning into a pillar of salt at the sight confronting me.

To tell you the truth I've been wrestling with my conscience about whether to go into all the shocking goings-on at Hubby Island. If I'd known that writing was going to be so very hurtful and embarrassing – well – I don't think I would have accepted Lady Lavinia's magnanimous offer. You can imagine how my adulation for her has gone up and up when I confronted the blank mike of the laser-voice-diary.

Also, there was the question of corrupting my readers. This worried me for ages, until it struck me that all the hubbies who will read what I am saying are probably still in the future. They will be totally in tune and comfortable with their roles and will probably not remember the bad old days – bad old days which, I suppose, me and Les are living through when everything is at sixes and sevens.

Still, for those of my readers who are easily shocked, the next few pages should be skipped. I'll put a huge FINISHED when the dubious bit is over.

"What's yours?" Ernest asked, as I tried to adjust to the gloom and the smoke.

"I'd love a Babycham," I said. (*Are you quite sure you ought to be reading this?*)

Suddenly, I was aware that all conversation had ceased. Ernest pulled me roughly by the arm while shouting in this deep put-on voice, "He's a real joker, is Harry!" Then he pushed me down on to this stool. "Two pints of *Dockers' Undoing Export*."

"Ernest," I said, "is that beer? I don't like beer. It bloats me and I'm supposed to be here to get myself in tip-top condition."

Ernest sat down opposite me. He seemed really livid. "Shut up, Harry!" he said.

Well, I told him – I didn't mince my words – I said that nobody – well *almost* nobody – *ever* told me to shut up and I wasn't going to start being told now.

"Look, Harry," Ernest said, "if you want to get off Hubby Island in one piece, just do as I say. OK?"

"How do you mean, Ernest?"

"I mean that you've got to role-play for the weekend. You know what 'role-play' means, I suppose?"

"No, Ernest, I don't. I try to be myself at all times."

"Does you credit, Harry," Ernest said, a trifle tart in his tone, even through the bass organ he was putting on.

We went silent then because this Mrs wearing hardly anything came and banged these two frothing glasses down. I wouldn't be surprised if she chipped the table. Then Ernest pushed a five-estuario note into her knickers! She thanked him and turned to go. Ernest made a lunge for the Mrs's posterior. He missed. A sound I can only describe as a low growl came from the other drinkers in the bar and Ernest said, still in that horrible voice, "My aim gets better after I'm outside a few!" And he turned back to the table, seized his pint and drank half of it back in what seemed like one swallow. A beer-mat skimmed between us. I gave the still-invisible hubbies – I couldn't see them at all because my eyes were smarting – a stern look. Then, still stern – I had lots left over – I turned to Ernest.

"Talking about role-playing," I said, "it's you who's role-playing, Ernest! You weren't a bit like this on the boat and don't try telling me you were! Something's happened to you since you came to Hubby Island."

"Drink up, Harry!" Ernest said.

Well I took a sip of the beer to please Ernest. Disgusting!

"Harry," Ernest said, "I'm not role-playing. This is me. On the boat I was acting. This is the real me." He gestured to the bar. "It's the real them too. Every so-called 'hubby' is a wild man underneath and any who say they're not are liars."

"Well, I'm not," I said.

"You honestly mean to tell me that you're a hundred per-cent happy with the way things are?"

"One hundred per cent," I said. "Well, not quite one-hundred. I wish my Avril wasn't so wrapped up in her work. I'd like to gain added fluency in Tinned Goods on *The Floating Bo$co*, too."

"But there must be a side of you that wants what Hubby Island has to offer: manly sports, cheeky girls and male bonding."

"A great big zero per-cent," I said. "It's like I said before, it all seems – I don't know – so *unnatural* to me."

Ernest stood up. "Harry," he said, "I'm not going to waste my weekend with you. It's nothing personal, you understand, just that I don't manage a trip that often and I'd hate to waste it with a *queer*."

And with that he picked up what remained of his pint and sidled off into the smoky gloom. I was left all on my ownsome looking at my pointless pint and worrying like mad about what Ernest had said. Could it be, I wondered, that it was only me who was quite comfy as a hubby while all the others in the Estuary Enclave – and all the other enclaves worldwide – were just pretending to be good hubbies because that is what the economic realities of life dictated? Were they all hankering after jobs with power and prestige, after – God help us – weekends on Hubby Island? Was I the only one who was left cold by all the goings-on? And, if that was true, what about Les?

I went straight back to my room and locked the door.

Well, thank heavens for Les is all I can say. When I got back to collect Jason on Sunday night I was in a shocking state. And Les being Les could see it straight away.

"It's funny," he said, "all weekend I've been having these feelings. You don't have to say a word, Harry. Up those stairs with you. There are towels laid out. You have a good depilate and shower. Take as long as you like. Jason's dead to the world."

"Les, I – " I said.

"No. Not another word. Up those stairs."

I nodded and did exactly as Les had told me. In the round mirror at the top of the stairs I caught sight of my face. Stubble all over it, dark circles under my eyes. Still, I felt worse than I looked, I have to admit. Anyway, trying my best to empty my mind of the horrors of the last two days I went into the bathroom, where I depilated and re-depilated, showered and scrubbed, deodorized, anti-perspiranted, cologned, brushed, combed, manicured, cuticled. I had to keep busy. I had to rub away as much of the old Harry as I could. I really wished I could get a nail brush into my brain to rub out the memory . . . the memory . . . of the horror . . . the horror . . .

There was a lovely fluffy towelling dressing-gown under the towels on the cork-stool. I put it on, smelling the reassuring scent of *Fibre Accent*, the post-conditioning re-conditioner that I had pooh-poohed when Les told me about it. You see, he said that it not only renovated every fibre of your clothes but also put back the subtle "just-purchased" scent that washing washed out and conditioning masked. I had to admit that the claim was completely justified. I could smell the Towels Department at *The Floating Bo$co*. And in my experience there's nothing like it.

"Feeling better?" Les asked.

"Much better, Les," I said. He offered me a glass of Export Babycham.

"This dressing-gown is really lovely. Gorgeous scent."

Les smiled knowingly and sat me down in the antique MFI armchair he's so – with justification, it's the only one of its kind – proud of. I sipped my drink and watched the *RealFlame* stove. I thought I saw a picture in the flames. I shivered.

"Don't let yourself get worked up, Harry," Les said. "It was bad, wasn't it?"

"Les – I have never – never – "

"You don't have to talk about it if you don't want to. Now may not be the time. Perhaps you need to let the emotions sit for a while."

I held my hand up. "No, Les," I said. "This thing has to be faced. I've got to pick myself up. I just worry that I may be corrupting you. Do you think you're hubby enough?"

Les just smiled. "Out with it, chuck," he said.

"Well, Hubby Island isn't what I thought. Putting it mildly, that is. Maybe once upon a time it was a place for hubby rejuvenation, but they've diversified. Perhaps you and me, Les, lead sheltered lives. I just had not realised that there were hubbies around who have given themselves over to – and I know I'm being judgmental, Les, but I *feel* judgmental – debauchery."

"They weren't any great shakes in the depilatory department judging from the look of you when you came in here," Les said.

"It wasn't even offered, Les!" I exclaimed. And the thought struck me that Les didn't really know the full enormity of the weekend.

Well, I started from the beginning, told him about Big Yvette and all the other hubbies and Ernest, and me worrying about the smoke-alarms. I stretched it out like mad and I'd finished a 500 ml bottle of Export Babycham by the time I came to the Rock and the Hard Place. But, even through the bubbly alcoholic haze that Export Babycham always gives me, I could see the problem ahead. "Perhaps I should draw a veil, Les," I said. "You know, maybe like they say, 'least said soonest mended' and that."

"I know what's embarrassing you," said Les. "I had a feeling about it. I was introducing Jason to the twin's *Little Hubby Kitchen Planner*. He took to it like a Mrs to Mackeson I can tell you. He did a wonderful little kitchen with the sink in front of the window so he could watch the nippers while he was washing up and the Bosch next to the door so's he can get the washing out on the line without delay. The only quibble I had about the lay-out was that he put the eye-level grill at eye-level. Not a wise move in my experience. Still, your Jason's amazing for his age. He's going to make a great little hubby. Now what was I saying?"

Well, I couldn't help it. That cheered me up no end. For a moment the terrible mental scars inflicted upon me by the weekend on Hubby Island misted over and I saw me – or rather Jason's teachers at his new boarding-establishment – The Little Shepherd School – handing on the torch of hubbydom to Jason in a most efficient manner.

But then the reality of what I had experienced was back. "Les, Hubby Island is a monstrous carbuncle on the sweet face of hubbies past, present and to come."

"They've let their standards slip, have they?"

"Les, they have no standards. None at all. Mind you, the first thing you see when you get on the launch at the Hubby Island jetty is a *Hubby Charter Mark*. Well that should be ripped away from them, and fast – " I knew I was going to have to come out with it or not ever be able to. "Don't interrupt me, Les," I said. "If you want me to stop just raise your hand and I'll stop and we'll talk no more about it. I think I can tell you everything, though I think you'll be running off to the counsellors at *The Floating Bo$co* first thing. I feel guilty at unburdening myself to you. Are you up to it, do you think?"

"Harry," Les said, and he put his hand on my knee. "*You experienced* the trauma. I only have to listen to it. I'd be a pretty poor mate if I couldn't listen."

"Hubby Island," I said, "is a place where hubbies go to play at not being hubbies. There are Mesdames there who are prepared for money to act as if Hubbydom never happened. They have a pub called The Cock and Bull where hubbies drink pints and tell jokes about the endowments or lack of in the Mesdames. They smoke and point at the disgusting waitresses and say "Cop a gander at that pair!" Sorry, Les – and things like that. They whizz beer-mats across the bar. There's a telly in the corner and they play old videos of football matches and the hubbies shout and scream and jeer – they have old copies of *The Sun* – remember that? – sticking out of their trouser-pockets and wear things like t-shirts that are too short so that when they bend down you can see . . . then this waitress started taking off . . . Oh, Les!"

I didn't dare look up in case I caught Les's eye and saw the horror. I also thought his hand might be up to stop me and I didn't want to be stopped. I wanted to get it all out.

"I don't know what else happened in The Cock and Bull because I didn't stay. I just had to leave. I went back to this horrid room, locked the door and wished I could escape from Hubby Island . . . "

"The next day it was all those things that hubbies drew a line under years ago. There were hubbies windsurfing; hubbies comparing pigeons; hubbies fishing; hubbies lifting heavy weights; hubbies doing obstacle courses; hubbies firing guns at seagulls and clay pigeons; hubbies gambling and drinking and pinching the waitresses that brought drinks; hubbies in little groups talking about reinventing their masculinity – whatever that is; hubbies with imitation AK 44s killing one another with paint bullets; hubbies bragging about killings in the City; hubbies calling football managers "big girls' blouses" . . .

"And nobody depilating. Not a word about cellulite or collagen or Mrs-pleasing recipes or child-rearing or why we're here. What has so shocked me, Les, is that there are actually hubbies who would actually *pay* to actually experience all these terrible things. But there are, Les. There are."

I looked up then. Les had his head in his hands. I thought to myself, "That's enough, Harry. Don't try your best mate past his power to endure. Don't mention the malignant Mrs who knocked at my door, offering to take me to the beach with a crate of lager and a set of beach-towels, the strippers, the Miss Hubby Island Competition. Above all, don't mention what Ernest said about role-playing. Spare him. Enough's enough."

FINISHED!

At last Les looked up. I could see he was moved. "Harry," he said, "I had no idea it had been so hard for you. But I want you to know that I can live with it. And I know you well enough to know that you can live with it too. And grow through it."

"Do you think so, Les?" I asked. "I'd like to think so. I really would."

"I'm going to ask you to do something really difficult, Harry," Les said.

I laughed in spite of everything. "Oh, no you're not, Les," I said. "You can't ask me to do anything more difficult than I've already done. Talking about Hubby Island to my best mate. There can't be anything more difficult than that. Not in the whole wide world."

"There is, Harry. Believe me, there is."

"What?" I asked, thinking Les was trying to joke me out of my depression. To tell you the truth he was succeeding. But then he undid all his good work:

"Don't tell Avril what you've told me," Les said.

"Don't tell Avril what I've told you!" I exclaimed. I stood up and the dressing-gown fell open. I don't know why Les has such a resistance to *Monovelc* fasteners; I can't tell you the times I've tried to nudge him towards them. Anyway, for a split second my areas of private access were exposed to view. I quickly covered my embarrassment. "Sorry about that, Les," I said. "Clumsy of me. I hope it doesn't put you off your dinner."

"Think nothing of it," Les said.

"I know you're tired of hearing me telling you this: but I don't understand why you don't go in for *Monovelc* fasteners."

"Did you hear what I told you, Harry?" Les said.

"Yes, I did. I did. But I'll have to tell Avril, even though she's not supposed to know I've been to Hubby Island."

"Well, I remember telling you just after we first met that Mesdames enjoy hearing their hubbies' confessions. It gives them a chance to be magnanimous, chuck. And I know my Barbara doesn't get much of a chance to be magnanimous at the Estuary Nat West. But . . ."

I was completely foxed. "But what?" I asked.

"But I don't think your Avril could take it. Not this. Much too dark."

"She might divorce me for culpable deception. They'd be bound to give her Jason and I'd be sent to the Industrial Nostalgia New Town!" I said.

"So don't tell her," Les said. "You've told me. Let's keep it between ourselves."

I shook my head. "She's bound to find out," I said. "Avril has this uncanny knack."

"And do you remember the swing-bin liners?"

Of course, I did. "Of course I do! How could I ever forget that? I didn't tell Avril about them, did I?"

"And we became best mates after," Les said.

I thought about it for a minute. Then, and I don't know if it was the Export Babycham speaking or not, I said, "You're right, Les. I won't tell Avril."

Well, it wasn't until Tuesday morning that Avril arrived back from Hawaii. Another thought had struck me after I'd left Les that night. If I told Avril about Hubby Island and, if she started litigation proceedings against the Hubby Island people, which I knew for a fact she would, then the whole world of hubbies would know that I, Harry Manley, had spilled the beans.

You see, what had dawned on me was this sudden distrust for the world of hubbies. Having seen what even the most presentable could get up to when out of sight and sound of their Mesdames, I was wondering how many were secretly playing a role in life. Perhaps the whole wide world of hubbies were really just play-acting being good little shoppers, caring spouses, scupulous home-makers. Could it be that it was only me and Les who had really adapted to hubbydom body and soul?

That thought really chilled me as you can imagine. But as usual it was the memory of my mate, Les, that stiffened my resolve not to tell all, no matter what the cost. So what if the whole world of good hubbies, watching me filling my trolley aboard *The Floating Bo$co* hated me for not shopping Hubby Island – if I had Les then I could live through it. Anyway, security aboard *The Floating Bo$co* is top-notch.

I had just left Jason at his new school, than which there is no finer I'm told. I came straight home, rehearsing for the umpteenth time what I would say to Avril. I got to my front gate and blow me, along she came in an Airport limo. We got to the front entrance at exactly the same time.

Avril gave me a peck on the cheek. "Was it a good trip?" I asked her.

"Not for the Hawaiian Sun Oil people, it wasn't!" Avril said. "Still, they were the ones who decided to stay with Factor 15. I told them it was suicide at the time. They're *meat*."

"I see, dear. And that's good, is it?"

"From the perspective of Mosely and Lumumbashi and therefore by extension to myself and so trickling down and down the line to you, it is not only good, Harry, it's fantastic."

"That's good, dear."

"I'd kill for a cup of tea."

"Coming right up, dear," I said.

"I've brought you some Hawaiian pineapple marmalade, by the way. They were doling it out on the plane. No time for presents."

"No, dear. I understand. Having you back is present enough. You must have been rushed off your feet. How was the keynote address?"

Avril scrunched up her face, raised the thumb of her left hand and winked.

"That's nice, dear," I said.

"Where's that tea?" Avril asked. "I've got a meeting at noon, followed by a celebratory lunch at the Astrocaff."

Well, I got Avril her tea, together with a couple of *Powerbite* vitaminised biscuits to see her through to the celebratory lunch.

She was looking through her mail, all stacked up neat beside her place at table, just like she likes it.

"How's Jason, by the way? Did you manage to get him into The Little Shepherd?"

"Yes," I said, "he's fine."

"And how was your stolen weekend on Hubby Island?" Avril asked. Just like that.

I broke down then and told Avril everything. I mean, there was nothing else to do. If you knew my Avril like I know her . . . *I'm sorry, Les!* I screamed inwardly.

Avril was silent for a long time, just drank her tea and nibbled her *Powerbite* biscuit. To tell you the truth I couldn't read Avril at that moment. I knew she was quite capable of sending me back to Dad's for a while. She did that the time I told her I'd got a little job as Care-Assistant at the crèche. Or she might be magnanimous.

"I want you to write an account of everything that happened, Harry. Everything. I also want the complete address of the *Washday Grail* people. What they're doing is not legal, decent or honest. To tell you the truth we've had several Mesdames in complaining about Hubby Island. The problem has been getting the hubbies to give evidence. Hubby Island gets a hold of them. It's a cult, nothing more and nothing less. I can't say I am pleased to hear that you deceived me but it is to your credit that you came out and confessed and were not indoctrinated by Hubby Island. I will expose these people, Harry. It's my duty, pure and simple."

"Yes, dear," I said. "I'm sure you're right."

"I'm sorry, Les," I said. "My Avril *knew*, Les. Don't ask me how."

Les shrugged. "They've got this uncanny knack," he said.

"You never said a truer word, Les," I said.

"What's your Avril going to do about Hubby Island?"

"She says she's going to instigate proceedings as soon as she gets a window of opportunity," I said.

"Its number's up, then," Les said. And he sounded really morose.

"Yes," I said, "and quite right too." Then I remembered. "Les," I said, "here's an irony for you: I still have the sixth plastic bottle of *Washday Grail* Washing-Up Liquid. Funny, Les, when I opened it I knew what I'd find at the bottom. I knew. But, as a sort of penance I suppose, I didn't look until the container was empty. And do you know what I found?"

"No. What?"

I took out the token and showed it to Les. "I'm going to throw it away. I'm going to toss it into the Estuary, Les!"

But Les took it from me and put it in his pocket.

"Don't pollute the Estuary, Harry!" he said.

"But Les!" I said.

And Les started talking about other things. He asked me how I was getting on with my exam prep for "Know Your Way Around Tinned Goods" Module Three. I told him, of course, but I could not take my thoughts away from the token in Les's pocket, warming up and burning a hole in it.

I hope and pray I'm wrong. Of course, I *know* I'm wrong but . . . you know . . .

P.S.

Well, the upshot of it is that Hubby Island is no more. I suspect a good portion of the island, though Avril has never said, belongs to Moseley and Lumumbashi in payment of damages. I don't know what will become of it.

The *Washday Grail* people were forced to make a public apology in all media outlets and withdraw the product advertising the competition from the shelves. I got away scott free, more or less, except that Avril keeps me on a tighter rein these days; and I sometimes turn my head and look behind me with anxiety, wondering if the hubbies who enjoyed the perversity of Hubby Island are after me.

Les, as if you didn't know, has been a great support.

10

Check Out

It's amazing how *Why Not Write, Hubby?* has helped me with my writing. In Chapter Twenty-three the book says that everything is grist to the mill of a writer. I am instructed to go around with my nostrils quivering, alert for the smallest thing that can be turned to literature. And it works. I know it does. I've proved it to myself.

You see, just this morning I was listening to *The Only Music Chip You'll Ever Need of The Floating Bo$co Advert Themes* on my stereo implants and right at the end, there was the theme for the award-winning *Check-Out* series of ads. I was a wet rag when it had finished and I'd be telling you a lie if I said I wasn't.

I can't quite remember when it was that Lady Lavinia Bo$co came up with her idea for the ultimate in Check-Out plastic bags. It caused quite a stir at the time; not all of it favourable.

It must have been roughly the time that she wrote her classic, *The Hubbies Who Floated Away*. If you're a careful reader of Lady Lavinia's work – which I am as if you didn't know – it doesn't take long to tease out the subtext. And not only that, you can, if you've given her words a good soaking in the brain cells, come up with what the next new departure on *The Floating Bo$cos* is going to be.

I'll give you a hint. In *The Hubbies Who Floated Away* Lady Lavinia dared to address a topic which we have always tended to brush under the carpet. I refer, of course, to the vexing problem of hubby wear 'n' tear.

I tried to broach it to Les at the time. "Les," I said, "it has to be faced – " but Les had already put his hands over his ears.

"Don't, Harry. Please . . . " he said. "How's your dad?"

"He's as well as can be expected," I said. "I won't say anything more about it."

Lady Lavinia, however, bit the bullet. She dared to tell the tale of two hubbies who get, pardon me, *older*. They have conscientiously tried everything to delay the onset of the complaint: the whole range of *Silver Hubby* preparations and *Hubby Alert* vitamin, mineral and sea-anemone secretion tablets. Of course, these products undoubtedly delayed the onset of ageing by up to two decades – I mean, look at me and Les! – but at some point even they could not postpone the inevitable evil day. Both hubbies wake up one day to find that they are old.

Of course, they head down to the nearest *Floating Bo$co* straight away to consult the ever-helpful hubby counsellors. The counsellors see a crisis of monstrous proportions heading up. Still, they are well-trained and take time to look up the personality profiles of the Mesdames of the hubbies. Well, you've guessed it, the two Mesdames are not what you'd call tolerant of ageing hubbies – neither of them. The counsellors can see from surfing the *International Mesdames' Wants Organizer* that the Mesdames have been looking for fresh young hubbies worldwide. There is a rather wonderful deviation in the plot here – down a tastefully erotic path – where Lady Lavinia takes time to describe some of the

Mesdames' adventures on the Zambezi estuary. How those Mesdames get themselves into those positions I'll never know.

Anyway we need a bit of light relief because the situation of the two ageing hubbies is looking hopeless. Hopeless!

There's no way out for the ageing hubbies and they know it. There isn't a Mrs in the world who will look twice at a hubby who's lost his looks and his cutting edge in the kitchen. They can always find a fresh young hubby through one of the Find-a-Hubby services.

Anyway, I know what you're thinking: you're thinking, what in thunder can the counsellors tell the poor hubbies? I was wondering that myself, hoping against hope that they'd pull something really startling out of the hat. Well, I was in danger of underestimating Lady Lavinia if I thought she would take the easy way out and not bite the bullet – be it ever so likely to explode in her face.

The counsellors tell tale after tale to the ageing hubbies. They talk of Tosca – whoever she was, apart from an insect repellent – and Achilles and his chum; and allsorts who died for love. Then Lady Lavinia – and she must have made this up, I reckon – started on about hubbies who had decided to slip off to a better place so that their Mesdames could have a chance of something better. It was, apparently, the ultimate sign of affection though, call me daft, me and Les were of the opinion that that was taking affection a bit far.

Anyway, the upshot was that the ageing hubbies throw themselves from the prow of *The Floating Bo$co* while fireworks split the sky and a full moon presides overhead. It was told very movingly and the hubbies go to the Interdenominational Heaven where age cannot whither them further, etc.

Well, Lady Lavinia got a lot of stick for *The Hubbies Who*

Floated Away. All sorts who ought to know better started getting at her. Hubbies for Jehovah, a sect for which I have absolutely no time – leaving as they do a pong of *Know What I Mean?* on my doorstep when they've doorstepped me – tried to organize a boycott of *The Floating Bo$cos*. It collapsed in a week, of course. The Mesdames of every single Hubby for Jehovah put their feet down when confronted with paying over the odds for inferior products at the rump of shops that had swum against the tide and stayed on land.

Well, as I'm sure you've noticed on many occasions, life does have a habit – an irritating habit – of imitating art. Wouldn't you know it but before *The Hubbies Who Floated Away* had sold its first million, *Floating Bo$cos* worldwide were being besieged by ageing hubbies aching to know how to kick off with decorum – and maybe glitter a little while doing it. The problem was that the counselling service of *The Floating Bo$cos* was, perhaps for the first time in its existence, caught on the hop. Nobody had the least notion what to say to the hubbies who wanted to float away. They just said, when the hubbies mentioned Lady Lavinia's novel, "But it's only fiction, hubbies!"

Well, maybe it was only fiction but, as so often before, Lady Lavinia had struck a resonant chord. Who would ever have thought that there would be a demand for, excuse me, *death*? I can't to this day decide whether Lady Lavinia's story so captivated people, so ravished them, that it set the thought off – or whether as is so often the case, Lady Lavinia had her finger exactly on the pulse of hubbies and knew she would be giving breath – and life – to an idea that had not dared before to speak its name.

It's like I said to Les, just as the fuss started getting going, "Les," I said, "we're on the verge of a quiet revolution. You mark my words."

"Definitely," Les replied. "A quieter revolution you'll never come upon. But, and call me daft, I don't see the point of shuffling off before I really have to. I mean, I didn't live through the Great Congleton Mine Disaster – I had to wait about for a week to be rescued in a cavern off number seven shaft with a fellow who was a Daniel O'Donnell fanatic and sang the git's complete repertoire to keep our spirits up – only to surrender myself to oblivion just because the Mrs doesn't fancy me like she used to."

"No, maybe not," I said, doubtfully, wondering if, were Avril to ask me to do the decent thing, I would have the gumption to say "No possibilo, Senora!" To tell you the truth, I wasn't quite sure.

"We'll just have to see what happens," I said.

"Nothing'll happen, chuck," Les said. "Lady Lavinia's smoked a kipper too far this time. I always said that a fertile imagination was a mixed blessing." He turned to me. "You remember me saying that to you, don't you, Harry?"

"I do, Les. I do," I said. I didn't though. It was then I began to fret.

Anyway about a week later, The Little Shepherd school was having a "Mrs Baker Day" – whatever that is – and me and Jason were by ourselves in the rumpus room. Avril was off litigating in Eastern Europe over a consignment of babies that just hadn't been up to scratch. I can't remember the details but it was a case that went on and on. Anyway, I'd plugged Jason into his *Junior VirtuReal*. To tell you the truth I don't really approve of them, but when *The Floating Bo$co* came up with a set of programmes to play on them – all approved by Lady Lavinia for the junior Hubby market – well, I couldn't hold back. As I watched the HomeBo$co channel on the telly, Jason was having his virtual reality experience as a carer in the changing bays on a *Floating*

Bo$co. Anyway, just after the second segment of the new maxi-series, *The Hubbies Demand Free-Range*, instead of the ads for the week's special offers on *The Floating Bo$co*, there was Lady Lavinia herself sitting in her glass office with the whole of the Thames City Hubby Enclave behind her.

She addressed us: "Hubbies of *The Floating Bo$cos*: I am appearing before you this evening in order to announce the introduction of a very special service." I knew exactly what it was, of course, and took the VideoChat off the hook. Well, I didn't want every hubby of my acquaintance ringing me up to tell me Lady Lavinia was on while Lady Lavinia was on, now did I? She went on to say that, since the release of *The Hubbies Who Floated Away*, a huge demand had been discovered for painless, elegant and above all *decorous*, passing-on by hubbies who for one reason or another felt that they had had their time. It was not, she said, her place to look into the reasons why elderly hubbies with nothing to offer their Mesdames and the wider world should have all come to the conclusion that it was time to check out of life's fleeting consumption party. No, she and all the loyal servants of *The Floating Bo$co* were there to supply perceived needs, to *give the customers what they wanted*. Consequently she was delighted to announce that the Undertaking Arm of *The Floating Bo$co* was joining hands with the Travel Arm and the Fantasy Arm to produce a range of *Fun-Floataway* experiences. Over the coming weeks, she went on, the range of these experiences would grow until she was sure there would be one – possibly more – that would appeal, in due course, to every hubby in the land.

Then Lady Lavinia frowned at her audience. I had never seen Lady Lavinia frown before and – I couldn't help it – I gasped a sharp and involuntary intake of breath. "Hubbies," she said, "trust me. I do not propose to allow just any hubby who has something to contribute to avail himself of the *Fun-Floataway Experience*. Call me sentimental, call me a business Mrs with her head screwed on, but I don't want to see hubbies decrease. You are, after all, my toast and caviare. Any hubby who applies will be carefully screened by a team of trained counsellors. His *Floating Bo$co* receipts for the last five years will be perused. Naturally, he will have to have a note of consent from his Mrs."

She smiled and the world of hubbies smiled with her. "In the time remaining in this break between acts of *The Hubbies Demand Free-Range* – and I hope you are enjoying it as much as I am. Isn't Phallo Portillo wonderful as the rogue hubby? He was nothing – NOTHING – when I found him diving for pennies off the Orinoko Estuary Enclave's *Floating Bo$co*! Now look at him! – I wish to show you the prototype *Fun-Floataway Experience*.

Lady Lavinia turned her head slightly, as if to watch a monitor. The screen went blank for a moment and then in black and white this hubby wakes up. He's got inexcusable bags under his eyes, and his hair – what there is of it – is a mess. He gets up. The camera pulls back and the room is an absolute tip. It hasn't seen a *Vac-n-deAlagise* for at least a week. All slouched, he enters the bathroom. He gargles with something pink – shower-gel if I'm not very much mistaken – throws a few drops of undenatured cold water over his ravaged features and, scratching his – excuse me – posterior, slouches downstairs. AS HE IS. Not even a *HubbyCoat* for decency's sake. Anyway, into the kitchen he goes. The assembled family look at one another. The Mrs is trying to care, you can tell. But she's at the end of her tether. All cared out.

Mercifully, we fade out on that scene of domestic desolation. Lights up on a lovely office where the all-cared-out Mrs of the hubby-mess in the last scene is playing miniature executive golf during lunch while talking corporate strategy. They stop. The Mrs looks tired and the other Mrs tries to buck her up by punching her shoulder. Mesdames and their machisma! Anyway, the Mrs's friend tells the Mrs that she knows what's eating her and that did she know that *The Floating Bo$co* has this scheme . . .

Fade out. Then it's all dry ice in rainbow colours. We enter it, go through and there is the hubby seen earlier. He is lying on this lovely swing-seat with tassles and Indian prints – just like the one Plain Waynes's Hubby Supplies had dirt-cheap in that sale, only much better. He looks pale. He is drinking pink champagne. His family – seen earlier – sit around him. Birds tweet and The Joanna Loss Orchestra is playing *Exodus*. As the music comes to a climax the Mrs kisses the hubby. The hubby takes a great draught of the pink champagne, followed by a greengage crystallized fruit and falls back in a dead swoon – though I for one suspected that it was more "dead" than "swoon".

Then, quick as a flash, the swing-seat just swings shut with the happy hubby inside. The family talk among themselves for a moment and then the seat returns only the hubby isn't there any more . . . well he is, but he's all wrapped up in a silver body-bag that has water-wings to give it buoyancy. But the swing-seat isn't finished yet. It yawns open and the body of the hubby disappears. The last we see of it is it floats away into the sunset, viewed by the grieving but plucky family from the first-class deck of *The Floating Bo$co*. End of story.

"Have you seen what they're asking for the *Fun-Floataway Experience?*" Les asked me a few days after the first advert.

"Well, Les, it is quite reasonable for the complete service. A simple funeral costs the earth these days."

"It'll never catch on," said Les.

But it did.

In the weeks that followed Lady Lavinia came up with all sorts of different themes for the *Fun-Floataway Experience*. There was *The Navaho*, which involved the hubby in question ascending to the top of a tree – by lift, of course. He then lies on a pallet under the full moon. Drums sound and the Moon-Spirit – whoever she is – releases the hubby's soul and he climbs up the sky – at least his spirit does – to join the ancestors, while his husk falls back to its constituent parts, aided and abetted by the application of ten thousand volts neatly located in a sub-station at the top of the tree.

Another winner.

And the range on offer just started proliferating. It's the way of the world. I mean, as I never tire of telling Les, there must have been a time when we were all amazed to see one tin of soup for sale. Then we couldn't imagine the range of soups that fill the shelves of *The Floating Bo$co*. That first one seemed like the Ultimate. There could not be any farther to go.

But of course, there was. The range of *Fun-Floataways* mushroomed and snowballed. A few didn't catch on and these you might find yourself winning for nothing by picking up a bottle of something with a special flash. But most were a great success and there were long waiting-lists for many of them, especially the *Fun Floataway On-The-Job*.

However, not every ageing hubby was in the fortunate position to be able to choose his method of demise from *The Floating Bo$co* catalogue. There is many a hubby – and I'd be telling you a lie if I said there wasn't – who finds it hard enough to make ends meet in his lifestyle, let alone his deathstyle.

For a while, among the poorer classes of hubbies – and

they're not all angry undepilated hubbies by a long chalk; there are lots of good, honest souls among them and I hope I haven't ever given you the impression that there aren't – there was a movement to arrange the *Fun-Floataway Experience* on the cheap. This usually involved several six-packs of *Export Babycham*, a beach umbrella in Millennium Park, a Music Centre playing oldies too loud, a packet of Sparklers and a few bottles of *HubbyMorf* if the Babycham didn't do the trick. Well, that's no way to be carrying on in a public park and I'm sure I don't need to tell you that it was a very poor imitation of what *The Floating Bo$co* could lay on for well-heeled hubbies. And they all ended in tears.

Well, I'm happy to be able to say that Lady Lavinia stepped in to assist the hard-pressed hubbies. She knew in her wisdom that the *Fun-Floataway Experience* was not for everyone. She knew that not everyone was in the fortunate position to shell out thousands of estuarios to kick off in style.

Now, at all branches of *The Floating Bo$co* there is the Hubby-Only check-out. Me and Les always looked at it rather askance to tell you the truth. It's like Les said, "Harry, I just don't see the point of a Hubby-Only check-out. I mean, if a hubby hasn't got the guts to pick up a controversial product while he's going round the decks of *The Floating Bo$co*, why do you think he'll be able to do it at some special check-out?"

Well, I just gave Les one of my looks. It was so obvious to me why a shy hubby might be able to purchase intimate items at the Hubby-Only check-out. For a start it had walls around it. "It's not that," I told Les. "What I can't understand is the hubby being able to go in in the first place. I mean, once you're in you're made. You've got a nice hubby-counsellor who will gently find out what you want but daren't ask for, be it *HubbyArouse*, depilatory products or suppositories for various ailments."

Well, Les and me let the matter rest there. I knew he would never come round to my way of thinking. As I keep reminding you, Les is a born conservative and that says it all really.

Anyway, we started noticing while sitting in the HubbyCaff with our hot chocolate that hubbies were emerging from the Hubby-Only check-out with their purchases in a very sturdy black carrier with *The Floating Bo$co* logo on it. I looked at Les in that way I have when I think I'm in danger of missing out on a bargain. And we weren't the only ones. There was this rush from the HubbyCaff when news spread that *The Floating Bo$co* was giving out this basic black carrier at the Hubby-Only check-out and that it would go with everything.

It wasn't until we emerged triumphant with our black carriers that we noticed what was written on the back.

We were shocked for a minute or two. We took a turn around the promenade deck to recover our composure.

"Well," said Les, "I don't *want* to take home step-by-step instructions on how to do myself in – whether matt-black goes-with-everything, or not!"

I knew what Les meant, but . . . "But Les," I said, "it's so delightfully simple. Say you're a hubby who wants to pop off. You haven't got the wherewithal to use one of the experiences for sale at *Floating Bo$cos*. What could be better than a simple plastic bag – with its own drawstring provided – an interdenominational EXIT prayer in luminous Gothic script on the inside of the bag. It's so simple. It's elegant, Les, that's what it is."

"Yes, but what if a kiddie should get hold of it, Harry? What then?" asked Les.

"Just stop it, Les!" I said. "You just can't let go, can you? Lady Lavinia comes up with a simple and virtually free way for a hubby past his prime to float away and you – I'm sorry, Les – carp the whole time. Why can't you be positive, Les!"

Les looked at me. I don't think I've ever spoken to him like that either before or since. When I'd finished I wanted a black check-out bag to open and swallow me up.

We soon made up, of course, and now we take the black check-out bags for granted. They're just a part of the landscape, so to speak. Neither me nor Les plan to avail ourselves of them for some considerable time. They have a specially elongated bio-degradable lifetime, these check-out bags. So they'll stay around until we need them which, being a hubby who is happy with his life with Les, with *The Floating Bo$co*, with my absent, thrusting Mrs – will be a long time hence.

Speaking of which: For some time before this, Avril had been discouraging me from visiting Dad. She reckoned he had a bad effect on me.

"You're a pain in the arse after a visit to your father," she said.

Mind you, she didn't mind me using the VideoChat to keep in touch and Dad could be quite controversial on that – so controversial that we'd been disconnected a few times.

I knew what Avril meant, though. Dad had a knack of making a hubby dissatisfied with his lot. He'd made it the constant study of his declining years to sort out exactly how the world – his world – got turned upside down. Some of his theories were off the wall, of course, but others – well, they made you think and, I suppose, sent you back to the Mrs with questions that shouldn't be asked.

On my last clandestine visit (Avril was somewhere on the Pacific Rim, but she found out; I don't know to this day who betrayed me) Dad said that it was all "the fault" of men pre and post millennium that brought Hubbydom about.

Too many had left all the reproductive decisions to their Mesdames, he said, as I hunted for dust with my finger. "They were so busy with videos, booze, footer and keeping their jobs that they could not take in the fact that all those genetic modifications were splicing away at men's roles. But the women were being given these great long check-lists at the maternity clinics about what sort of qualities they had thoughts on from an offspring and, in the case of boys, they filled them in requesting sweetness and light, lack of aggression, good manners. Anything for a bit of peace. On the other hand, they didn't want the girls to be all put-upon, as in days of yore, so they – "

"Dad," I said.

"What?"

"Bowels OK, are they?"

"What kind of question is that?"

"Well, you did mention that you were a bit worried about – you know . . . "

"They're fine, thanks, Harry. But I was talking about . . . "

"I know you were, Dad. But you're talking complete and utter rubbish. If what you're saying is true, how do you account for Hairy Hubbies, the Angry Hubby Brigade and, God help us, the Underclass in the Unmentionable Regions?"

"Ah," Dad said, "if you recall, by the millennium great swathes of the country had no access to state-of-the-art healthcare. The underclass had to fend for itself. That's why men are men in the underclass."

"Honestly, Dad," I said, "I don't know where you get these ideas from, I really don't!"

"You tell me how it happened, Harry, if you're so clever."

"I don't have time," I said. "I haven't dusted yet."

"You're no son of mine!" Dad said, which may well be

true. Still, I've heard him say that so often that it no longer hurts like it used to.

"All right, Dad," I said. "Hubbydom was just an idea whose time had come. There comes a time in the affairs of men – there does, Dad – when they tire of holding on tight to power. They want to give up all that, to live a quieter life, to say to their Mesdames, 'You do it, dear!' In a way you could say that it was laziness. Men were just getting too lazy to marry and shoulder the responsibilities that come with marriage. There were a couple of generations of nippers with only Mesdames for company. The Mesdames found they could do the whole thing – and hold down a job too. The boys of that time were moulded into the image of their mothers who were, at the same time, throwing off their own dependence . . . being more, if you call it that, manly. I agree that hubbies came along because of Mesdames. It's just that I think it was nurture and accident rather than a considered plot."

Dad had made himself a cup of herbal tea. He threw the tea-bag on the fire. "If that's true, how do you explain YOU?"

"How do you mean?" I asked.

"Well, look at you!"

"Is there something wrong? Is it my hat? Les says it takes ten years off me."

"You never used to be so – so – like you are," Dad said. He really knows how to hurt. "You used to have a responsible job, to be proud of your work and that. What happened, Harry?"

"I don't know what you mean!" I said, though I did really. "I met Avril and then the GREAT RESTRUCTURE came along. Tax breaks and benefits for married couples with only one working partner. It was obvious when Widdecombe Three-Wheelers closed who that working partner would be."

"Yes," Dad said, "but it's a long way from taking over

responsibilities in the home to becoming what you've become!"

"You keep saying that, Dad, but you won't say what it is I've become."

"Do you really want to know?"

"Yes," I said, "tell me."

"You're a sissy, Harry," Dad said.

Well, I had to laugh. Dad was such an old fuddy-duddy. He was forever telling me I was a sissy. To tell you the truth, I took it as a compliment.

"You can laugh all you like – I wish you'd do it an octave or two lower; it really goes through me – I'm not blaming you. All I'm saying is that there's been a conspiracy of social engineering with quite a bit of help from chemical engineering. Of course, I knew there was something up when your mother started going on those Open University weekends, going out with 'the girls', picketing the bypass site. They were up to no good, Harry. They were plotting the RESTRUCTURE. You're not trying to tell me there wasn't careful planning behind everything that's happened. The Mesdames knew in the nineteen-nineties that surfactants were upping the oestrogen level and lowering the sperm count. So what did they do? They set up sperm banks to put it all in the freezer while the going was good. Then, and this was the clever thing, they left the kitchen to get out of the range of surfactants while the men inhaled it by the bucketful. The kitchen, the shops and all the products you love buying – *that's* what's turned you sissy," Dad said.

"Well, if you're right – and I'm not saying you are – how do you account for the fact that I'm so content with my lot? I am, you see, I am!"

"The advertising's got to you, Harry," Dad said. "Once the Mesdames had got themselves into positions of power they just bent everything to their whims and it was 180 degrees away from normal."

"You mean from what we – the former manipulators – considered normal," I said. "Don't forget, Dad, until the Mesdames took over we were pushing our ideas on to them. Maybe we will again. Swings and roundabouts and everything. But you have to admit it was about time they had a go."

"Well, I think it's disgusting," Dad said.

"Well, I wouldn't have it any other way."

"Well, it's not natural. It's not how the world should be," Dad said.

"And how should the world be?' I asked, getting quite aerated, "The world has never turned on 'shoulds' and 'oughts'."

"Well, it should! It ought!"

"It's turned on how things are. You can't say that we worried very much about the world when we had the whip hand, can you? You have to admit that under the rule of Mesdames there've been fewer wars. That's got to be good, hasn't it?"

"But you're a man!" Dad said.

We were two continents, him and me, drifting apart. We'd never jig together again. He would go down the grid, mouthing "disgusting!"; I would sit at a clean work-surface waiting to be loved. But we would never ever come together. It made me go all weepy.

"And a jolly good thing too!' I said, "I'm a hubby! That's what I am!"

"I don't know where it's going to end, I really don't," Dad said.

"It isn't going to end. It's just going to jog along nicely."

"You're too young to remember *Thelma and Louise* and *The Chippendales* and Mary Goldring and Sue McGregor and

Louise Botting and that clever-clogs Ozzy woman and that," Dad said. "The start of the rot."

"You call the enclaves 'rot', do you, Dad? Maybe you'd be happier with those couples trying to make a go of it in the Industrial Nostalgia New Town and the Unmentionable Regions. Everything's just as it was there. Mesdames bringing up the kids – if they've managed any – *and* foraging for food while the men strut about."

Dad shook his head, looking at the floor.

"Fancy a cup of tea? I'll make it," I said.

Dad shook his head, but I decided to make him one anyway. It would give me a chance to inspect the kitchen and do a few running repairs in the hygiene department.

A mess, of course. Luckily I had bought a bumbag full of cloths and cleaners. I aimed the gun-shaped, pump-action pack of *Gotcha Pristine!* and, as I put the kettle on the hob with one hand, liberally fired the cleaner all over the work surfaces and floor. I put all the dirty dishes into the sink and popped in a quick-dissolving *Auto Scrubbo* which – and I didn't believe it until I tried it – completely does away with the need for scrubbing. I laid the tray and still had time to wipe off with *Gotcha Pristine!* and place the dishes in the drainer before the kettle boiled.

"Nice cuppa, Dad!" I said, all bright and breezy.

"I know what you were up to, Harry," Dad said when I handed him the tea. "You've been cleaning up out there, haven't you?"

"Just a touch, Dad. You mustn't let your standards slip, you know!"

"You're a big disappointment to me, son. I'd be telling a lie if I said anything different."

"Don't say that, Dad," I said, trying to hold back the tears.

Dad looked at me, sighed and looked away. "The world's

becoming more and more peculiar. Time for me to shuffle off, I reckon."

"Come on, Dad! You don't mean that!"

By way of reply, Dad reached into the inside pocket of his jacket and pulled out this card. "I've been buying *The Floating Bo$co*'s basic check-out for over a year now. Two more installments and I'm ready."

"A wise investment," I said, before I'd taken in the implications. When I did, I said, "You're not, are you Dad? Not before your time?"

"I've had my time," Dad said. "I want to go before everything gets any more peculiar. I have only one wish, Harry – no, don't interrupt – will you and your mate Les . . . Will you and Les carry my body from the chapel to the Interment Pad above the Estuary? It'll give you a bit of man's work to do for a change."

"Dad," I said, "there are qualified *Floating Bo$co* counsellors who will do that with 'solemnity, dignity and decorum' as they say in the ad."

"I don't want that. I want you and Les. Will you promise me, Harry?"

I thought about it. I'd been to quite a few Check-Out events on *The Floating Bo$co* by that time, but had never heard of such a – well – macabre suggestion before.

"Very well," I said. "Still, I don't think it's time for you to check out, Dad. You've got your health. And don't forget your research. That's important to you, isn't it?"

Dad thought about that. I could tell from the look on his face that I'd struck a nerve. I continued, "After all, Dad, you've hardly dented the vexed topic of the water industry and what that Saudi princess who owned South-East Water going berserk with *Bye-Bye Weeds!* did for the South-East; the nuclear waste farms that went wrong; the genetic harm wrought by Four-Star. You've got so much to do, so much to live for!"

"I've given up," Dad said. "The Mesdames have closed the sources; put a hundred-year ban on everything about those things. It's a shame because I was close to the truth on the water issue."

"So you don't feel you have anything to live for?"

Dad shook his head, sipped his tea. "You do make a good cup of tea, Harry," he said.

And when, six months later, me and Les carried Dad along the promenade deck of *The Floating Bo$co* to the Interment Pad, then watched as he was catapulted into the estuary to the accompaniment of a single rocket and "Comfort Me In The Wee Small Hours" playing over the tannoy, I remembered that Dad liked my tea. But not much else.

Les, of course, was a tower of strength.

"I'm glad we were able to do that for your dad, Harry."

Well, to tell you the truth, I was dying of embarrassment. "How do you mean, Les?" was all I was able to say.

"It seemed right, Harry. Know what I mean?"

"That's it!' I said. "I knew there was something different about you, Les. You're wearing *Know What I Mean?* aren't you?"

Les confessed that he was. And he seemed proud. He did! I really began to worry then.

"We've lost something wonderful with your dad," Les said.

"Why are you wearing *Know What I Mean?*, Les? Don't tell me I've got to take you back to Module 1, Lesson 1 in the Hubby Aroma department." To tell you the truth, I was really quite appalled. Les's giving up on *Know What I Mean?* had been our first really positive and life-enhancing collaboration.

"It just isn't important, Harry. Especially now."

"What do you mean it isn't important, Les?" I said. "Of course it's important. I can't have my best mate taking giant lifestyle-leaps backwards. I can't, Les. If I let it happen who knows where it could lead? It's a slippery slope, Les. Next thing you'll choose price over quality. Discrimination will go out the window. Next thing you'll be going off to the Industrial Nostalgia New Town for day trips!"

And do you know what Les did? To tell you the truth I can hardly bring myself to tell you what Les did. He walked away. There, it's out. My best mate turned his back on me and walked away.

11

Intercourse With The Hubbies-Who-Stay-In

Of course, I followed Les and the aroma of *Know What I Mean?* – I mean, I had to. There was no way that I was going to let the matter of a lifestyle choice get in the way of our relationship. We made up in the HubbyCaff and drank a toast for Dad.

"I've a confession to make to you, Harry," Les said.

"Go on, Les," I said.

"Me and your dad were good mates."

"Were you, Les?"

"We were."

"Now you're sure you're not saying that because of the tragic events, Les?" I said. "You don't have to do it, you know. I was ready for the end. It was what Dad wanted, Les."

"I'm saying it because it's true, Harry. You know your dad used to say that he got the Hubby Home Helps in to keep him spruced up and that and do all the things he wouldn't let you do for him?"

"Yes?"

"Well, it was me who did those things."

I went hot and cold. "Everything?" I asked. "All those intimate jobs?"

"Everything," Les said.

"I don't know what to say," I said.

"It was a pleasure for me to be around your dad and be able to help him out. We had these great chats."

I found that very hard to believe. "I find that very hard to believe, Les," I said. "Dad was such an old rebel. You must know that he was completely against Hubbydom. He actually called me a sissy, Les! On no less than *three* occasions. Work that one out."

"He didn't pull any punches with me either, Harry."

"So all this time you and me've been sharing Dad's care?" I took a sip of my double deCaff. "That really makes me happy, Les," I said.

"He taught me a lot."

"How do you mean?" For the life of me I could not see what Les could have learnt from Dad.

"What I say, Harry."

I nodded. I stirred the froth around in my cup. To tell you the truth I didn't know what to think. I was sorely tempted to call in the counsellors, but I dreaded the upshot. Anyway, the counsellors had enough to be going on with, what with me opening my heart to them about me and Dad's troubled relationship. The aroma – if you can dignify the stink with that term – of *Know What I Mean?* was hitting me really strong. The thought struck me that Les knew exactly what it meant.

Like I've said, no hubby worth the name has been wearing *Know What I Mean?* for yonks. Perhaps Les's going back to it was an anti-fashion statement, perhaps a covert but eloquent anti-hubby statement, too. I thought of Les's denim bumbag. I'd tried to get him to replace it until I was blue in the face. I might as well have been talking to the wall – or Dad for that matter. I shuddered.

"Let's say no more about it, Les," I said.

Les nodded and I thought about for some topic that would help us climb out of the negative morass Dad's *Fun Floataway* and the sorrowful aftermath had let us in for.

"Avril's always telling me what a Luddite I am," I said.

"Is she, chuck?" Les said. He seemed distracted still.

"Yes, she is, Les. Avril thought I was a Luddite over Home Shopping, but I thought then and still think a few hubbies should become Luddites. What's wrong with being a Luddite?"

Les thought about that. Leastways I hope he did. Then he smiled. I smiled back. Like you do. "My Barbara pushed me towards Home Shopping too. Nightmare. Bloody nightmare."

"You're right, Les," I said. "Of course you are. Remember how everywhere you went there were posters showing efficient hubbies at home looking after well-turned-out nippers in a sparkling environment, Home Shopping at amazing speed then relaxing with a cup of *HubbyFruit* in front of the Open University?"

"Between you and me, Harry, I felt cut off," Les said. "If it hadn't been for the Leisure I think I'd have gone daft. And it's like it was at the Congleton Colliery, I just couldn't get my head round all the new technology."

"There was a conspiracy to keep hubbies indoors and stop us fouling the pavements," I said. "It worked, of course. It did for the out-of-town centres in a matter of a few years. The Nirvana Precinct hung on by the skin of its teeth because there were a few hubbies like us who still fancied being social, but the majority – well, they swallowed Home Shopping and all the cut-price intercourse on the Hubby-Net."

"You're right, Harry," Les said, "and, of course, the majority are still at it. When, for example, did you last see Kevin Earnshaw?"

Well, I just nodded sadly, though inside I was singing. I had managed to get Les on to a topic that is dear to both our hearts. And I felt our hearts were beating as one once more. "I haven't seen sight nor sound of Kevin Earnshaw for well over a decade," I said. "I know he's not gone before or anything because his kids are at school with Jason. But Kevin Earnshaw is never seen. The heavy magnolia velvet curtains on his lounge are permanently shut and we think he's inside doing Home Shopping, watching the drippy films on Worldwide Rupert and chatting on the Hubby-Net."

Les shuddered. "And Kevin Earnshaw belongs to the sad silent majority of hubbies."

"You mark my words, Les," I said, "it wouldn't surprise me if one day *The Floating Bo$co* closed up and all hubbies will be stranded at home without a chance of social intercourse. We'll all be like Kevin Earnshaw and those unfortunate hubbies in the tower-blocks of the Industrial Nostalgia New Town."

"You can't stop the march of progress, Harry," Les said. "Look at your poor dad!" And he shuddered.

"I don't call it progress," I said, all militant. "If you ask me there's too much being pushed on us that hasn't been tried and tested. That's why I'll always support *The Floating Bo$co*."

"You're a chip off the old block after all, Harry," Les said.

"Well, I don't know about that, Les," I said. "What I mean is that progress isn't necessarily for the best. I know it sounds odd coming from me, especially remembering how I was when Dad got his really ancient toasting-fork down from the attic and said it'd never been bettered."

"You really gave him an earful, Harry."

"He told you, did he?" I said, remembering. "I could kick myself silly now for buying all those smart toasters. They've gone the way of all flesh and the older I get the more I realise that Dad was probably right. Toasting forks *have* never been bettered."

The hooter signalled our arrival back at the landing stage. Les and me got up to disembark. I felt confident that we had put the trauma of that day behind us. Well, if I'd only known!

Looking back, I know I was neglecting my marriage. I had of course paid close attention to Jason's development and to the beautification of our home, but with Avril absent on the Pacific Rim for so much of the time I suppose I had not taken as much care in that department as I ought.

The trouble was that Avril did not give me much in the way of support. Litigation took up her every waking hour and when I mentioned that I thought it was time she gave her poor deserted hubby a bit of quality time I got this long lecture about how it was her wearing herself to a shadow that was allowing me to live the high-on-the-hog life that I led.

I opened my mouth to protest but Avril waved my account statements from *The Floating Bo$co* in front of me and told me in no uncertain terms that she knew chapter and verse of my spending patterns and that they indicated a great deal of "quality" – she almost spat the word – time with Les at "the floating shop".

She also mentioned the Hubby Island incident, which was a bit unfair.

"Avril," I said, "you said you'd speak no more about Hubby Island. I thought we'd put it all behind us."

"It's the ingratitude that hurts, Harry," Avril said, all cold.

"I'm not ungrateful, Avril. Honestly, I'm not. I know that I owe everything to you. It's just that sometimes I wish we could do things together. You know, like a family."

"I'm going into my office now," Avril said. "You know,

Harry, I sometimes wonder as I go around the globe how I managed to end up married to a hubby who is so – so – *wet*."

"That depends what you mean by 'wet'!" I said, through my tears. "Sometimes I just don't know what you want, Avril! When we tied the knot you said you wanted a hubby who was prepared to give one hundred and ten per cent to his home and family and not count the cost. Haven't I done that, Avril? But something's been missing from our life. Partly, I know, it's due to all the travel you have to do, but when you come home you're really distant."

"Do you want a divorce, Harry?" Avril asked.

I was shocked into silence.

"Silence betokens consent."

"No, it doesn't."

"It betokens anything I choose it to betoken. Bring me a cup of tea, Harry."

"Earl Grey, Mississippi Mountain, Smoky Robinson, Humber Enclave Pride, Darjeeling, ThaiThong Tips or the usual?" I said, on automatic.

"Lapsang Souchong," Avril said.

"Er – we don't have any of that, Av. You said last time that you had it on the Pacific Rim and couldn't be doing with it."

"I'm used to it. I've developed a taste for it."

Avril slammed the door on me. I made my way to the kitchen, wondering what to do. Then I just collapsed into the kitchen chair and wept, my head on the table.

But this could not go on. Avril wanted Lapsang Souchong. I picked myself up and wondered what to do. I didn't dare darken the doors of the Nirvana Precinct – anyway it was too far – and *The Floating Bo$co* would be in the middle of its afternoon QuickieCruise. I thought and I thought, then remembered Kevin Earnshaw. Going to borrow some tea from Kevin Earnshaw would kill two birds with one stone. I could get the tea and see how he was doing.

I put on my outdoor shoes and slipped out the kitchen door. The bin was smelling wonderful. That mango and acacia combo is really gorgeous. I would have no hesitation in bringing that odour into the most intimate pressure points of the home if the product hadn't been specifically designed for bins and only bins.

Kevin Earnshaw's Mrs was a bit like Avril in the travel department. She was the boss of something really hi-tech which, I suppose, was one of the reasons why Kevin had such an automatic lifestyle. I went through the front gate and, before I had got to the front door, it swung open and a disembodied voice told me to enter and go through the second door on the right.

Well, the house was not to my taste, but you had to admire it. Completely magnolia. Chair covers, pots, the lot. I went through the door and there was Kevin Earnshaw behind this bank of monitors.

"I knew you were coming," he said. "I monitor the outside world with a bank of cameras."

"Do you remember me, Kevin?" I asked. "I'm Harry Manley – you know – Avril's hubby."

"And you want to borrow some Lapsang-Souchong, I'll be bound." He gestured to a packet on a sort of magnolia-coloured conveyor belt, covered in a magnolia table-cloth, that led to a hatch. No pictures on the wall. Not a knick-knack anywhere. I shook my head inwardly.

"Gosh," I said, "how did you know?"

"Nothing passes me by, Harry. Charlotte is big in surveillance."

"And you can surveille all your neighbours, can you?" I asked, my heart sinking.

"I can," Kevin said. "I'm sorry you've been having that spot of bother with Avril."

"Talking of Avril – " I said

"Yes, you'd better get that tea to her. I'll be listening in. Best of luck, Harry!"

Well, to tell you the truth I was feeling really bad that I hadn't clapped eyes on Kevin Earnshaw for almost ten years. I was full of questions and was already thinking how I would tell Les everything. I asked Kevin, "How far can you surveille, Kevin?"

"The world's my oyster." He gestured to the bank of computers. "With these babies my reach can penetrate as far as – well there's no limit."

I nodded, and picked up the tea. "I won't forget this, Kevin. May I come and see you again?"

"Of course, Harry," Kevin said. "I wouldn't like you to think I'm lonely or anything. I have friends all over the world, as you can see. But it would be nice to meet the neighbours."

"Must go! Avril will be wondering . . ." I said.

"She already is," Kevin said. "Best of luck, Harry!"

I ran home, kicking myself. How could I have allowed so much time to pass and not popped in on Kevin Earnshaw? He looked so well, hardly changed at all. What was his secret? He was, I thought, as I poured water on the borrowed Lapsang Souchang, the first Hubby-Who-Stays-In I'd met in ages. To tell you the truth, I always tried not to think about them. But was that a mistake?

"Here's your tea, dear!" I told Avril.

"Lapsang, is it?"

"Of course, dear," I said.

Avril hurumphed her thanks. "You borrowed it from Kevin Earnshaw, didn't you?" Avril said, accusingly.

"Yes, I did, Av. How did you know?"

Avril shook her head sadly. "I didn't get where I am today

by not knowing these things. If you weren't such a technophobe, you'd know too."

"I know I'm hopeless, Avril. Sorry."

"Sorry? You are sorry, Harry."

"Yes, dear," I said.

"I'm off in the morning, Harry."

"Are you, dear? I thought you were here until next week."

"It's the Monosodium Glutamate scandal on the concessions along the Great Wall of China Enclave. It's coming to a head, Harry."

"Is it, dear?"

Avril took a gulp of tea. "Has it ever occurred to you, Harry, that I might appreciate it if you took a modicum of interest in my professional life – rather than merely a spending of the proceeds?"

Well, that hurt as I'm sure you can imagine. I could have told Avril that in the old days I had taken an interest but that long ago she had told me to concentrate on what I knew best. From then on I'd made a vow to leave the litigation department of Avril's life to her. Still, I knew that mentioning that to Avril in her present mood would only make things worse.

"I'd better go and do some housework," I said.

"Do that, Harry," Avril replied. "By the way, I don't want to be disturbed again today."

"Yes, dear," I said. And I tiptoed out.

I passed Kevin Earnshaw's on the way to popping in on Les and I thought I saw the curtains move. It disturbed me that Kevin Earnshaw knew everything about my private life. Maybe I was missing out by being a Luddite. I resolved to call in on him again once Avril was safely out of the way.

Les was waiting in the hubby-shelter. We sat down together.

"You're quiet, chuck," Les said after a long silence between us.

"I know, Les," I said. "Me and Avril have had a row..."

I told Les everything that had happened, ending with the observation that I was in despair about the state of my marriage. "Avril doesn't respect me, Les," I said, close to tears.

"It's just jet lag," Les said. "All the travel must get to her. I mean, she's never here."

"It's true, Les. But Avril's been travelling for years. She's never been – brutal before. She said I was *wet*, Les. I'm not, am I?"

Les thought about that. "You are a bit, yes. But we're all wet, we hubbies. In a manner of speaking. Being wet lubricates us, lets us get through it. If we were dry it would be the end of society as we know it. We have to be able to pass through the small space the Mesdames allow us without screaming. It's wise to be wet."

Of course, I knew Les was quoting from the advert for *WetDew* Hubby rejuvenation lotion and all the other *WetDew* products; products which I had introduced Les to, as a matter of fact.

"Well, maybe it is wise to be wet, Les," I said, "but if Avril doesn't like it what should I do?"

"Search me, chuck," Les said. "My Barbara is exactly the same. I can't tell you the number of times she's been at me to be *different*. Well, I say to her, 'How do you mean *different*, Barbara? Can you tell me, please?'"

"And what does Barbara say?"

"She shrugs and goes into her study. To tell you the truth, Harry, I don't take any notice any more."

"I'm going to see Kevin Earnshaw again," I said. "I've got to return the tea to him. Also, in spite of what I said about being a Luddite, I think Kevin Earnshaw knows things that we ought to know."

"How did he look?" Les asked. "All pasty, I expect."

"No, Les, he looked really lovely. Well-groomed and that. He hasn't let himself go to seed in the least. Don't ask me how he does it. I'm pretty sure he never leaves the house."

"It sounds like a contradiction in terms, Harry."

"It does. Still, that's another reason for going to see him, isn't it? Maybe we can prise his secret out of him."

"Well, tell me when you're going. I'd like to come with you," Les said.

We went two days later. I had got Kevin a lovely tin of Lapsang Souchong on *The Floating Bo$co* the following morning. Half-way through the cruise a plane roared overhead and I knew that Avril was probably on board. Was she thinking of me and Jason or were her thoughts all on the Pacific Rim? I don't know why I ask.

Anyway, I happened to mention the Monosodium Glutamate scandal on the hamburger concessions on the Great Wall of China to Justine. She said that she was amazed I hadn't heard about it because it was the talk of the counsellors' staff-room aboard *The Floating Bo$co*.

"Tens of thousands of American Mesdames and their hubbies are up in arms about it," Justine said. "For years they'd come back from China feeling terrible. You see, all the hamburger concessions of the Great Wall stated in black and white that none of their foods contained Monosodium Glutamate while, in fact, they did. It's like Plain Wayne's writ large. The allergic reactions of those Americans will cost China a bomb."

"Americans are great ones for allergies," I said. "You never heard of them until the Yanks started going on about them."

"Anyway," Justine said, "your Avril's going to have her

work cut out for years, shouldn't wonder. You're a very fortunate hubby to have Avril for a Mrs." She looked at my trolley, which contained only Kevin Earnshaw's tea and a crisis-size bottle of *Calm Down Hubby!* "I'd have thought you'd be celebrating your good fortune by filling your trolley to the gunwales, hubby. Have you explored our offers today?"

"I'm not in the mood for shopping, Justine," I said. "Things aren't that wonderful in the Avril department."

Justine looked really upset. "Do you want to talk to me about it, Harry?"

Well, I did and I didn't, but I decided I did a bit more than I didn't. At least I thought I did. "Avril says I'm wet," I said.

"And how does that make you feel?" Justine asked.

"Weepy and insecure," I said.

"Well, that's natural. The problem is, Harry, that your Avril – and many another Mrs – isn't quite certain what she wants. If you want my opinion, I think that 99.999% of Avril wants a wet hubby. But – and blame it on the times – there is still a tiny piece of Avril's personality that wants – and this will probably shock you, Harry – domination."

"It does shock me, Justine, to tell you the truth," I said. "I thought all the fiddling about in genetics and the range of Mesdame Only patches had done away with that."

"Almost, Harry. But not quite. The thing is, you mustn't be completely predictable all the time. The worm can turn, you know."

"I've never understood the meaning of that, Justine. And I'm not sure I like what you're saying. It sounds unnatural."

"That all depends what you mean by natural."

"But I am what I am, Justine. Since the Great Readjustment I've been a hubby through and through. When I think of the old Harry Manley it seems like a character in a book – a character I didn't like that much."

"I understand completely, Harry," Justine said, "but you might try to be a little bit unpredictable occasionally. Just to keep Avril guessing."

"I'll try," I said.

The trouble was, Justine had completely lost me with what she was saying. To please her I went around picking out all the Best Buys on board until my trolley was overflowing. I got home and spent the rest of the day worrying.

It was quite a relief to meet Les the following morning. I'd brought my tin of tea, banded by a magnolia-coloured silk ribbon that I thought would please Kevin Earnshaw, and off we went to make our call.

"Now we must be careful not to mention Kevin from now on, Les," I said. "He's a whizz in the surveillance department."

"It's lovely weather for the time of year," Les said.

"It is," I agreed, "unseasonably balmy."

"Do you think it's the ozone layer?"

"I think it might be the lack of an ozone layer."

"So how do you account for that cold winter last year?"

I stopped. "Les," I said, "not the weather. Please!"

"Any bargains on *The Floating Bo$co*?" Les asked.

"That's better," I said. "Plenty, Les. If you buy a large tin of Algerian-friendly sardines and two small packets of parsley sauce mix, together with a full-price joint of *Tofubaba* reconstructed leg of compassionate lamb, and then fill in a questionnaire about the nippers, you get the chance to enter *The Floating Bo$co's* "Platinum Hubby of the Year" competition."

"I've done that, Harry," Les said, "but Dave says it's all a fix. The Platinum Hubby of the Year is always decided by till receipt."

I nodded. "Oooh!" I exclaimed. "There is an anomaly in pricing that I discovered. It's actually cheaper to buy *Bo$cown* dried soap in single 100g packs than in the multipak."

"It never is!"

"It is, Les. I'm going to point it out to the powers-that-be next time I'm on board."

"You've got to have eyes in the back of your head." Les said.

"You have, Les. You have."

"I've got some news."

"What?"

"Plain Wayne's shut."

"About time."

"And Plain Wayne's Neil has gone off to that Hairy Hubby commune in the Industrial Nostalgia New Town."

"The wages of sin," I said.

"Yeah," Les said.

We arrrived at Kevin Earnshaw's house and went through the front gate. A voice said, "And Plain Wayne's in a shocking state. Come on in."

I gave Les a nudge and in we went.

"This is my friend, Les," I said to Kevin.

"Pleased to meet you at last, Les," Kevin said. "I've heard you a lot, seen you once or twice. Still, it's nice to, you know, see you in the flesh."

"Same here," Les said.

Kevin sat us down in these big magnolia armchairs. I remembered the tea and got it out of my bumbag. "Thanks for the loan. You saved my bacon, Kevin."

"Any time," Kevin said. "Is that tin for me? Well, you shouldn't have, Harry. Really, it's not necessary – and so nicely presented too. Goes with the decor. That really was very thoughtful of you."

"Not at all," I said.

"Now what would you like? A drink? Something to eat?"

Both Les and me said no and patted our tummies.

"Come on, you must have something. I know, a nice coffee. It's about that time."

Then Kevin picked up this little gadget and started pressing buttons. He laid it aside and said, "Won't be more than a couple of ticks."

I only had enough time to say how nice the room was again and out along the conveyor belt from the hatch came a steaming pot of coffee with matching cups, jug and sugar-bowl. All magnolia.

"Ah, here's the coffee," Kevin said. I looked at Les and Les looked at me. To tell you the truth, we'd never seen anything like it.

"You don't go out then, Kevin," Les asked.

"Not if I can help it, Les. All my needs are catered for here. Mind you, I do admire your courage. I couldn't do it." He gestured to the bank of monitors. "Anyway, I hate leaving these. I'm afraid of what I might miss."

"How do you mean?" Les asked.

Kevin smiled a quiet smile I was to get to know rather well. It was always followed by a slick movement of laser pen over a screen and a bank of black boxes that looked like old-fashioned hi-fi tuners.

That first time, and many another time too, you could have knocked me down with a feather. The left-hand screen came to life and I was looking at Avril on the Great Wall of China. She was walking with some Chinese Mesdames, looking at the hamburger concessions.

"How do you *do* that, Kevin? I asked. "I mean, is that really my Avril *live?*"

"It is, Harry," Kevin said. "Course the light's not all it could be what with sunset coming and everything. What I've done is take the signal from the Tiananmen System of surveillance. My Charlotte put it in for the Chinese. It's as easy as anything to pick it up."

"Can you get sound too?" I asked.

Kevin smiled. The laser wand flicked across the black boxes and I heard Avril say, "So per portion of hamburger with Sechuan herbs, you'd estimate that 15 grammes of monosodium gluttamate is added, would you?"

"At least," replied the Chinese Mrs with this big smile on her face. She obviously did not get the full import of what Avril was after.

"It's absolutely disgusting!" Avril exclaimed.

"That's my Avril!" I said. "She's formidable, you've got to admit it."

"Phew," said Les.

We watched a few more minutes of Avril as we drank Kevin's excellent coffee. To tell you the truth it was streets ahead of *Bo$cown* Blend 32, which is the best on *The Floating Bo$co*.

"What else can you do?" Les asked.

Kevin smiled and before a second had passed we were looking at Les's Barbara behind her posh desk at the Estuary Nat West. He put on the volume so that we could hear lots of banking noises, but Barbara didn't do anything except look up from time to time and frown.

"My Barbara's not a patch on your Avril on the telly, is she?" Les said.

"Maybe we've tuned into her at a bad time," I said.

"It's really amazing," Les said, "but Kevin, I hope you don't mind me asking you this, isn't it a bit on the depressing side being stuck in the house all day?"

"Not at all," Kevin said. "Nobody's forcing me, you know. To tell you the truth it's only since Worldwide VideoChat came along that I've really given up on the outside world – and to me the outside world seems *virtual*." He gestured to his equipment. "This is the real world."

Kevin went on to introduce us to his friends on the VideoChat. One by one they came up on the screen . . . Tom from Rotherham, Leroy from Laguna Beach, Abdul-Aziz – complete with veil – from Riyadh. Kevin and his friends chatted away just like me and Les do. They compared prices, nattered about nippers and bargains on Home Shopping. It was all very nice. Still, I thought, they aren't able to get together and just wander about together, have a good old blow on *The Floating Bo$co* and that. There is something definitely missing.

Then I saw it. All the time that Kevin had been introducing us to his friends the monitor showing Avril on the Great Wall of China was going. To tell you the truth I was glad Les and Kevin were distracted. Avril was giving a crowd of Mrs, both Chinese and western, a really shocking time. The volume was down but we didn't need to listen in to know what was happening. The Mesdames stood downcast before my Avril's tirade. Then, a Mrs took Avril aside and gestured towards a car. And Avril smiled and gave the Chinese Mrs a punch on the arm.

Well, I'd never seen Avril's mood brighten so fast. Normally my Avril needs two days' notice in writing before getting out of a bad mood. But not now. The door opened on the car and Avril got inside. Just before the door closed and the car sped away I saw Avril reaching over and embracing what looked, from the crimson of his Mao Jacket, like a Chinese hubby!

"What's wrong, chuck?" Les asked.

"Nothing," I lied. Everything! I thought.

I could hear Leroy from Laguna giving Kevin his recipe for Pineapple Upside-Down Cake. It seemed completely appropriate somehow.

"Something's wrong, I can tell!" Les persisted.

"It's just . . . it's just . . . " I reached into my bumbag and got out my despair-size box of *Calm Down Hubby!* I forced a handful down. "It's just that I've just seen Avril kiss a Chinese hubby!" I stammered.

"Good golly!" said Kevin. "I thought you knew!"

"Thought I knew what?"

"That your Avril is famous up and down the Pacific Rim as a hubby-eater."

I didn't say anything. Instead I reached back into my bumbag and took out my *Floating Bo$co* black check-out bag, in its own slip case. I got it free for spending over 50 estuarios on the Day of the Dead Hubby Cruise. Jason made himself sick on *NoChocChocolate* hubby skulls. I unfolded the bag slowly. Amazing how they've managed to get the crease problem out of plastic bags. I gave it a shake-n-rip to open it up. I looked pleadingly at Les and then popped the bag over my head, drawing the drawstrings tight and breathing deeply to bid farewell to the departing oxygen of my useless hubby life. My eyes couldn't focus on the prayer on the inside of the bag and I thought that that might be something to point out to *The Floating Bo$co* people next time I went aboard. Then I thought, NEXT TIME? ABOARD? THERE WILL BE NO NEXT TIME! I WILL HAVE CHECKED OUT!

Then I heard cries and Les was pulling at the drawstrings of the bag. But I was holding on to them with a determined grip.

Then I heard, "Scratch through it!" from Kevin.

And saw the impression of Les's fingers banded by

stretched-to-screaming-point black plastic close to my eyes. Then one finger whitened. I saw his engagement-ring finger an inch from my mouth. I could have screamed! I could have buried my teeth in Les's importuning finger!

Kevin completed the job of cutting me out of the checkout bag with a pair of nail scissors. They half-carried, half-dragged me to the magnolia sofa, and lay me down. There was Les beside me, so close to my face that I could scent his mouthwash – *Breeze through Pine* unless I'm very much mistaken.

"Why, chuck? Why?" Les asked.

"My Avril . . . " I replied.

"I thought you knew," Kevin said.

"*I* knew," said Leroy from Laguna. "Avril's world-famous. Always gets top ratings from the Hubbies-Who-Stay-In."

Les turned on Leroy. "That Pineapple Upside-Down cake will be burnt, Leroy!" Les said in that voice that always makes me think of the shower-room at Congleton Colliery. Not that I've been there.

That shut Leroy up. To tell you the truth, even through all the pain, I was so happy to have stayed around to hear Les say that. He turned to me. I took his hand in mine. "Sorry, Les," I said. "I know what came over me but I wouldn't have upset you for the world and I know I have."

"Talking about the world," Les said, "it makes you despair."

"I thought you knew!" Kevin Earnshaw said.

"Well, you know now that we didn't," said Les.

"Does that mean you don't know about your Barbara either?" Kevin Earnshaw said.

"What about my Barbara?"

"Hold about," Kevin Earnshaw said. "I'll just call up the recording of her at the Better Banking Conference on Suffolk Island."

"That's a good one," said Abdul-Aziz. "Better call it Better Bonking!"

"I want to go home!" I said to Les. But it was too late; Les was watching a monitor. To tell you the truth I couldn't see what Les was seeing because Kevin Earnshaw was in the way.

"Turn that bloody thing off!" I heard Les shout.

"Language!" said Kevin Earnshaw. Still, he could see how angry Les was. Kevin Earnshaw turned off the monitors. "How about a spot of lunch?" he asked.

"This Pineapple Upside-Down cake is absolutely fabulous!" enthused Leroy from Laguna.

"I'm sorry, Mr Earnshaw," said Les – and at that moment I could imagine the years stripped away and Les being all strict with the British Coal reps, "I'm sorry, but I'm taking my friend Harry away from here. Back to the real world."

"This IS the real world," Kevin Earnshaw said. "If you change your mind and stay for lunch I'll get out the Virtual Reality machine from under the stairs. There's nothing like it to pass a dull Wednesday afternoon between mates. We can have an orgy with any number of exotic Virtual Mesdames!"

Les turned to me. "Do you feel well enough to come with me, chuck?" he asked.

"Or then again," said Leroy from Laguna, "we could watch that footage of Les with that big Mrs down by the ocean."

"Big Yvette in the old Ferry Ticket office. Yeah, that's classic," said Kevin Earnshaw.

Well, I thought Les was going to lash out. "I don't believe this!" was all he said.

"Let's go, Les," I said. "These hubbies have not only allowed their standards to slip in a most deplorable fashion, but have lost sight of what makes the world go round."

"Correction," said Kevin Earnshaw. "We, the Hubbies-

Who-Stay-In, are the ones who see it all. We're the ones who are in touch with reality. You hubbies of *The Floating Bo$co*, who pride yourself on getting out and about – you're the ones who are being taken for a ride. You're only there to provide the Hubbies-Who-Stay-In with their very own soap opera and keep that Lady Lavinia Bo$co in clover. If you could see the footage I've got of that Lady Lavinia Bo$co, you'd – "

"Les, I'm ready – " I said.

"Come on, Harry . . . "

Les helped me out of Kevin Earnshaw's house. As we were walking down the front path, we heard, *"Byeeee!"* through the tannoy, like a raspberry.

"If ever there was an argument for getting out and about, that Kevin Earnshaw is it," I said. "By the way, I'm sorry I got carried away back there."

"Think nothing of it," Les said. "We've got a lot of thinking to do."

"How do you mean, Les?"

"Well, there the Mrss are, playing about in a most appalling fashion behind our backs. What are we going to do about it?"

I thought for a while. "What?" I asked.

Les thought about it. "Search me," Les said.

"If we look sharpish we can catch the afternoon QuickieCruise," I said.

"Let's look sharpish," Les said.

We walked towards the harbour, aware all the time that Kevin Earnshaw could be looking in on us through the surveillance cameras all around. I had this awful feeling that nothing would ever be the same again.

I was right.

12

Hubbies Underground

Well, you can imagine. We just had to find some displacement activity after that shocking day at Kevin Earnshaw's. And for me and Les that meant more time on *The Floating Bo$co*.

Call me slow, but the penny didn't drop at once that if Kevin Earnshaw could tune into our private conversations and the goings-on in the whole wide world as well, then perhaps everyone could. And if everyone could watch everyone else, then everyone could also be watched. Was it possible that only me and Les were blithely going through our lives as honest hubbies saying what we thought when we thought about it?

To tell you the truth, once I'd thought about that and thought that it might well be true, it all began to make perfect sense.

Dave had changed. You just couldn't bond with Dave any more in any meaningful way. Of course, I'd put his sudden distance down to the therapy he'd gone through after falling for the Cult. But there were several others of the hubbies of my circle who were newly distant. I hadn't known what to put it down to at all; Les had said on more than one occasion that all the other hubbies barring Yours Affectionately seemed to be becoming really boring.

But after Kevin Earnshaw and the implications of his stay-at-home activities had had time to sink in, I thought I knew what was what. The penny had dropped with everyone yonks before I went around to borrow some Lapsang Souchong from Kevin Earnshaw. All the hubbies, barring me and Les, *knew* that everything they did and said was being caught by surveillance systems.

Normally, of course, I'd have confided to Les what I was thinking. But if what I was thinking was correct then what I would say to Les would be overheard by goodness knows who and what.

Things had changed. Our chats were no longer the intimate bonding sessions they had once been. But I knew that Les knew and I knew that Les knew that I knew that he knew and knew that I knew how he was feeling and vice versa. And being surveilled is terribly inhibiting, have you noticed?

We didn't give way, though. A brief touch while reaching for a bargain, a rubbing of shoulders, an exchange of glances on detecting a slight dent in a tin of non-cling peaches . . . these became our forms of genuine intimacy beneath the laboured conversations that we knew would be of interest to nobody because they were ever so boring for us.

For weeks we immersed ourselves in a quiet communion on *The Floating Bo$co*. We'd spend ages comparing the labels of identical products, trying to decide why one was differently priced from another. There seemed to be no rhyme or reason to it. It was during that time that Les really mastered the ins and outs of all the complex offers on board and I subdued Tinned Fish. We became so expert about the details and *exact locations* of all the products that we jointly won *The Floating Bo$co* quiz two months running.

Still, I won't say it wasn't a strain, because it was. Something had to give and it gave one afternoon in a bus-shelter near the estuary. Les, without a by-your-leave, reached over and burrowed in my bumbag. He took out my Concordat Personal Organizer – a gift from Avril – and wrote, *This can't go on, can it, chuck?* on the first page of the "Notes" section.

No, it can't; it can't, I wrote back. And that got us started.

I reproduce our written conversation in full because it was important to us at the time.

Les: Have you been thinking what I've been thinking?

Me: What have you been thinking?

Les: I've been thinking that we've been being surveilled for yonks . . . long before we tumbled to it at Kevin Earnshaw's.

Me: You're right, Harry. That's what's been going through my mind. It's terribly inhibiting, isn't it?

Les: I knew you knew. I knew it wasn't only me.

Me: So what now?

Les: No idea, Harry.

Me: Me neither, Les.

Les: The thing is, Harry, that if most hubbies have been able to surveille in the way that Kevin Earnshaw surveilles then the whole wide world of hubbies – not to mention the Mesdames – knows our business backwards.

Me: Not that we've been guilty of anything.

Les: No, of course not. It's just the invasion of privacy. I mean, do you think your Avril has heard everything we've said over the years?

Me: Far too busy, Les. Also, when you come to think about it, if everyone can surveille everyone else then the likelihood of you and me being surveilled at any one time must be infinitesimally small. (Is that how you spell "infinitesimally"?)

Les: Not sure.

Me: Oh, Les, it'll never be the same!

Les: Hold on, Harry. If we could forget that we're being surveilled and just behave naturally then things would be as they were.

Me: But how can that be, Les? The genie is out of the bottle; Pandora is out of her box; the thumb is out of the dyke. Oh, Les!

Les: Hang about, Harry! It may be that you and me are, as you might say, jumping to conclusions. We've only Kevin Earnshaw's word for all this, you know.

Me: Yes, I know. But didn't you think it had the ring of truth, Harry? I mean, it answers the questions that've been on my mind for yonks and yonks.

Les: What question's that, Harry?

Me: I was just about to get to it, Les.

Les: Sorry, Harry.

Me: Don't mention it, Les. The questions are: What do the Stay-At-Home Hubbies do all the time? Why are there so few hubbies – I mean comparatively speaking – who have opted for our lifestyle? And, perhaps most important of all, have you been experimenting with body-odorant blending?

Les: I thought you hadn't noticed.

Me: How could I not, Les? It really is distinctive.

Les: It's a blend of unscented Maine In Fall Plus, Cocoa Petal and . . . you guess.

Me: Lemon Brass.

Les: I knew you'd know. Nobody can beat Harry Manley in the Personal Care department.

Me: Thank you, Les. The Lemon Brass really gives the combo a daring, almost racy, edge.

Les: That's what I thought. I'm coming on, aren't I, Harry?

Me: Les!
Les: What?
Me: LES!
Les: What?
Me: LES!
Les: What?
Me: WHAT ARE WE GOING TO DO, LES?
Les: Well, the question is, Harry, whether we can carry on the way we've been carrying on since we learnt what we wish we hadn't at Kevin Earnshaw's.
Me: We can't, Les. It's awful. I've lost all spontaneity.
Les: I thought you'd say that and I agree with you, Harry. What I think is that we just stuff surveillance cameras and act like we always did. We'll mind our ps and qs a bit, like. I won't catch myself alone with Big Yvette in a hurry I can tell you. But on the whole I think we just carry on. We mustn't let the buggers get us down.
Me: You're right, Harry. Of course you are. But what I . . .

At this point the biro which was supposed to work in zero atmosphere – wherever that is – ran out of ink. It had taken us ages to have our written conversation and when we came to ourselves the sun was setting across the estuary and we knew that Les's kids would be in the holding-bay at school. Still, we left the shelter, talking quite naturally. Of course, I won't pretend that there wasn't the feeling that maybe – just maybe – we were being overheard. But it was no worse after a while than being religious and thinking that The Heavenly Bodies (the supernatural ones, not the shower-gel with loufah that trebles as container, dispenser and disperser) were looking down and taking note. Both Les and me having lived with that for a good many years could learn to accept the idea of a few hubbies surveilling us.

Well, as we were to learn in the fullness of time, the worldwide world of Stay-At-Home hubbies breathed a sigh of relief when me and Les got back to being our old selves. You see, unbeknown to ourselves, Les and me had become cult figures with these hubbies. They tuned into our doings on the surveillance networks whenever they could and were quite prepared to shell out no end in royalties to Kevin Earnshaw's Mrs's company, *The Floating Bo$co's* security network and goodness knows who else for the pleasure of watching me and Les going through our humdrum routine and conversations.

We're absolutely huge in Malaysia apparently and *The Floating Bo$co* on the Straits of Malacca stocks a whole range of *Harry and Les* recommended products.

Now I know what you're thinking, because until I asked Avril I was thinking it myself: what's in it for me and Les? I mean, there we are with our privacy invaded, our little idiosyncrasies spread far and wide, our bits and bobs the talking point of hubbies worldwide, and nothing in it for us!

"It does seem a bit thick, Av," I said,

"It's not a fair world, Harry," Avril said. "Have you finished writing those cards to my Thai Hubbychums yet?"

Avril had continued being huge on the Pacific Rim and had collected all these oriental hubbies as chums who, when they heard who her hubby was, kept writing me letters about odouriser-blending and the merits of *Butch Bags Size 3* versus *Condome* – there's an accent there somewhere, don't ask me where – a French swing-bin liner in primary colours with *Monovelc* fastenings. Needless to say, I recommended *Butch Bags*. As I let slip to Les, confident it would penetrate to my Far East fans and, perhaps, errant Avril, "Product loyalty is something we must hold on to in a world of shifting allegiances".

Nevertheless, I did continue to hint to Avril that, with all her powers of litigation, it might be within her remit to see me and Les, seeing as we are media stars and making money hand over fist for all sorts of corporations, all right in the dosh department. Avril, however, came back quick as a flash with, "Read the back of your *Floating Bo$co* till receipts, Harry," and went off litigating.

Well, I sat down there and then and blow me there at the bottom it said that my custom at *The Floating Bo$co* was conditional on my acceptance, free, gratis and for nothing, that any surveillance, tagging-devices, etc. and the information flowing therefrom should remain the property of *The Floating Bo$co*.

Well, I must say that I was miffed by this and said so to Les the next time we met. "Les," I said, "it seems a bit thick that hubbies are tuning in to listen to us day in day out and we never get anything out of it."

"I couldn't agree with you more, chuck," Les said.

Then we dropped the subject and got back to trying to make sense of the wine labels at *The Floating Bo$co*. They've got this amazing range. The whole world of grapes seems to have been pressed into service to tickle our palates.

To tell you the truth Les and me had been boycotting wines from several countries. Chinese wines – though excellent and very reasonably priced – had been struck off our list because of the shameful treatment meted out to hubbies of a certain age . . . and poor old Taiwan. Anyway, we stick to South Patagonian wines these days. They come in five strengths from 1 to 5. But that's not the end. There are also five flavour combinations and five acidity markers and five tannin strengths. All on the same little label. Well as you can imagine, it took an age to work it all out and come away with a Shiraz, Merlot and Cabernet combo that was 3, 3, 2, 2, 3, respectively and which Les's Barbara manages to keep down.

Still, the time came round when Les and me really felt in need of a good chat away from all surveillance. We wandered over to the bus shelter armed with the personal organizer and a *Bo$cown* discardable seven-colour biro that at the flick of a sensor turns into a roller rugby ball (for italic) and netball (for copper plate). These are wonderful pens, a bit old-fashioned I'll grant you, but fine for our chats. And I knew that if the pen ran out, thereby depriving me and Les of our private chat, a no-quibble redress and a new pen would be available on *The Floating Bo$co*. But wouldn't you know it, when we were nicely settled in the bus shelter there was this discreet little camera looking down at us and robbing us of privacy.

Without a word – natch – me and Les got up and went off in search of a quiet place where we could be on our own. We ended up in Les's outside loo where, I noted, Les had gone all hi-tech by lashing out on the new generation of *Clean As A Whistle* post-evacuation products. They're put out by North West Water, which is owned by a consortium of Saudi Princesses. To tell you the truth, *Clean As A Whistle*, after encountering a good deal of hubby resistance, have taken the toilet hygiene world by storm. Avril and me have had their basic model for years – long before they became accepted and a really long time before a hubby would ever be caught dead talking about such matters as post-evacuation products.

Anyway, I got the pen and organizer out and wrote:

Me: *Lovely loo, Les!*
Les: *Never mind that, Harry! I've got news.*
Me: *What?*
Les: The Floating Bo$co *has been using us!*

Les handed me the pen, a really hard look on his face. It was a look I've only ever seen on Les when he's in the middle of a session of *Get Down to the Vital Hubby Within*, a defoliant, lubricant, emollient and rejuvenating clear-gel that sets on the face like a mask. You have to keep perfectly still, your face set like granite. If you don't – well, I dread to think. It really is a wonderful product. I know for a fact it's lessened Les's smile-lines; not that we've had all that much to smile about recently.

Anyway, that's how Les's face was. I looked at him but he stayed still as a statue, holding the pen out for me to react. At last, my hands shaking, I took the pen from Les and wrote:

Me: Don't, Les. Please!

Les almost snatched the pen from my hand and started scribbling on the Concorde Personal Organizer (it was never the same). I wanted to reach out, take his hand and tell him to calm down. But something stopped me.

At last he finished. Quite calmly he passed the notebook over to me to read:

Les: Harry, chuck, there is no such person as Lady Lavinia Bo$co. She's – how did Barbara put it? – an electronic construct, Harry!

Well, I had to laugh. I seized the pad from Les:

Me: Tee-hee! Pull the other one!

Les, still unsmiling, still with a face like granite – he's really got an impressive face, has Les – he gently relieved me of the pad and wrote at some length. I thought about what he had written, but all I could see was Lady Lavinia's wonderful, caring face, looking sad. I hardened my heart against whatever snares and delusions Les's Barbara had used to snare and delude my mate.

Les: It's like this, Harry. According to Barbara, when Lord Bo$co of Bebington kicked the bucket, the whole of Bo$co International was bought up by Home Shopping. Their futurologists had predicted that some hubbies just wouldn't take to the concept of Home Shopping and staying in. So they came up with the Floating Bo$co idea. Not only would The Floating

208

Bo$co provide an outlet for the minority of hubbies who needed a daily airing, it would also provide the Hubbies-Who-Stayed-In with something worth watching. Still, what they reckoned they lacked was a human face to front the concept of The Floating Bo$co. They put their design projection team and their PR Arm to the task. After months of work they came up with Lady Lavinia Bo$co. But she doesn't exist, Harry!

Me: *But that's complete nonsense, Les! Don't forget, I've met Lady Lavinia.*

Les: *Did you ever touch her, Harry?*

Me: *Of course not! The security was too tight.*

Les: *There you are then. Barbara says . . .*

Me: *Les — and I'm sorry to rip the pad off you like that — but the most unbelievable thing about what you've said is that your Barbara should confide all this to you. That's stretching credibility to incredible lengths, if you want my opinion, Les.*

Les: *She had one-over-the-two-point-seven-five, Harry. But I believe it. After what we've learnt in the past few weeks I don't find it hard to believe at all. We've been duped by The Floating Bo$co. We've become what advertising decided we should become. Lady Lavinia Bo$co is an electronic lie.*

Well, I didn't know what to say. Les handed me the pad and I couldn't put pen to paper. If Lady Lavinia Bo$co wasn't real, what was real? I sat there for ages. Then an idea struck me:

Me: *What about all Lady Lavinia's Hubby Romances, Les?*

Les: *Computer-generated.*

Me: *I see. But why, Les?*

Les: To shift merchandise, Harry. Barbara says hubbies are where advertising has led.

Me: What's that supposed to mean?

Les: No idea, Harry. To tell you the truth, Barbara was pretty drunk by this stage. I'd been testing that new range of South Patagonian wines on her.

Me: I told you they were good value.

Les: You did.

Les passed the pad back to me, but I just looked at it.

Then I looked at Les. *"We can't go on like this, can we?"*

Les looked at me hard, then. He wrote in big letters, covering most of what we'd been saying,

Les: NO, WE CAN'T.

I saw, and nodded. We parted shortly after, without another word.

I walked home, wondering about it all. I'd often wondered before why I was so happy to be hubbied while so many were quietly or noisily dissatisfied. The Hairy Hubbies in the Industrial Nostalgia New Town have never adapted. Nor will they, I expect. There's just no pleasing the underclass. They go around in gangs, drinking more *Export Babycham* than is good for them and making fun of any good hubbies they come across.

But it took the wind out of my sails, to put it mildly, hearing Les telling me all that. I kept swallowing handfuls of *Calm Down Hubby!* but they didn't work their magic. The magic seemed to have gone from life completely with the doubt sown in my mind about Lady Lavinia Bo$co.

It was quite possible, of course it was, that every word Les had said was true. But I repeat, if Lady Lavinia Bo$co wasn't real, what was real?

Well, I thought, I won't think about it today; I'll think about it tomorrow. I passed a surveillance camera and tried to look my best. Well, you've got to, don't you?

13

Les's Second Crisis

Around about that time – well, the following day at 10.33 a.m. it was actually, on board *The Floating Bosco* – I was pretending to look confused in front of Chilled Deli, always a prime site for confusion. You see, I sort of wanted a Hubby-counsellor to approach me and ask what was wrong so that after an initial bout of bashfulness out it would all come. Naming no names, of course.

I'd had very little sleep during the night, this not helped by a long distance call from Avril in China on the VideoChat. Was I behaving myself? she asked; what was I doing awake at that time of night? Did I have anything I thought she ought to know? Not being able to see Avril's face – she always puts her Gucci Executive Module in front of the VideoChat camera – I felt really vulnerable. I said that no I hadn't anything to say, except the usual and that I did wish she'd let me see my beloved Mrs on the VideoChat once in a while.

Well, I don't know what was happening on the Chinese end of things but Avril didn't reply at once. Then I heard her voice: "Don't you dare, Lin Po!"

But obviously Lin Po did dare because all of a sudden the Gucci logo disappeared from the VideoChat screen to be replaced by a full frontal of Avril with two Chinese hubbies lying next to her. In bed. Then, in a trice Avril had placed a sheet (silk if I'm not very much mistaken) back in front of the camera.

"Av!" I cried.

"What, Harry?"

"What I just saw!"

"You saw nothing Harry," Avril said.

"But I did – Oh, Avril!" I cried through the uncaring ether.

"So what if you did, Harry? It'll never stand up in a court of law. You're too wet to know how to record VideoChat."

There was a sound of high-pitched giggling. Then Avril: "Lin Po, cut that OUT!"

"Avril!" I called.

"Should be back in three weeks."

"Avril!"

"Kiss Jason for me!"

"Av – "

"Over and out," Avril said.

And that was that.

From then on, all through the night, the state of my marriage to Avril and the state of my private-but-public relationship with my best mate, Les, warred for my attentions. I tried to empty my mind by breathing deeply. I don't know why I even tried. I was so busy thinking about breathing deeply while worrying about Avril and Les that I didn't know what to think.

Still, all was not lost. Thanks to my diligent work over the years in the Personal Care department, I had discovered this fabulous range of inhalers in pretty pastel-coloured titanium containers – suitable for bumbag or purse – which you take a sniff from for any and all of life's little crises. They offer an amazing range. There are sixty-eight all together and, of course, Yours Aromatically has the lot. To tell you the truth, by buying them all, even though some of them are not exactly up my street in the psychological department, I saved 20 estuarios and they all came in this gorgeous mock-croc carrier.

The name of the product is *GrandMrs Hetherington's VegOdour Mood Swings* and, though a lot of people say their effect is all in the mind, I always come back and say that, seeing as I've heard tell as how moods tend to originate in the mind, that's where their effect ought to be, which shuts the cynics in the HubbyCaff right up.

The trouble with *GrandMrs Hetherington's VegOdour Mood Swings* is that it can be the devil's own job deciding which mood you want changed and which inhaler you need. I mean, I've seen hubbies sticking one after another of the inhalers up their noses in the hope that one will do the job.

And you've got to have some sympathy for these confused hubbies in a way. I mean, it isn't always easy to decide what's eating you. Is it *fear of the unknown* (sprout tops) – *fear of crowds* (parsnip) – *fear of change* (celery) – *fear of fear itself* (cabbage) – *irrational fear* (spring onions) – *fear based on a real threat* (chicory) . . . ? Well, you can see the problem. And that's only FEAR! The other moods that *GrandMrs Hetherington's VegOdour Mood Swings* has taken it upon itself to cope with also include *Uncertainty* (ten types); *Lack of Interest* (eight varieties); *Loneliness* (four); *Despair* (nine. Nine!); *Over-sensitivity to influences and ideas* (five) and – and this is the section that I seldom if ever use – *Caring Too Much for the Welfare of Others*. Now, if you want this hubby's opinion I think that *Caring Too Much For The Welfare Of Others* is not a set of moods that a hubby worth the name should be inhaling out of his system. I'd throw away those bottles if I didn't hate breaking the set.

Still, that night worrying about both Avril and Les I inhaled quite a selection of the whole range I don't mind admitting. And I have to say that I felt much better for it, though the bedroom smelled like school dinners and I had to get going on the remedial re-odorizers. STRENGTH FOUR! So you can see how bad it was.

In the morning I awoke like a new hubby. I knew the problems in my life which had to be faced but somehow I was looking at them in an objective way. Harry Manley, Hubby, was standing on top of a high hill looking down at all the bickering world of hubbies, Mesdames and the unacceptable pace of change below me, and I was thinking. "I am a part of all that, but I am still me, Harry Manley; in it but not of it; of it but not in it. In it up to my neck yet detached in a deeply caring sort of way."

Thus recharged, I went off to meet Les for the Morning Cruise on *The Floating Bo$co*.

I saw him there on the landing-stage, chatting away to Big Yvette as if Big Yvette was a hubby. As I approached I could hear Les saying as how, given a level playing pitch, a Mrs didn't stand a chance against a hubby in the netball department. To tell you the truth, I could see Big Yvette was looking at Les a bit oddly. I was looking at Les a bit oddly myself. Big Yvette has seen some things in her life, but a hubby talking about netball and fancying a hubby's chances must have been a first.

"Here's your mate!" said Big Yvette.

"Morning, Mrs Yvette," I said.

"Morning, Harry!" boomed Big Yvette.

Then Les boomed, "Morning, Harry!"

And I do mean "boomed".

Big Yvette looked at Les, then at me. She seemed stuck for words. Then, chewing her bottom lip, she told us to get on board sharpish.

As we were going up the gangplank, Les held back to let me go first. I thanked him – we always defer in turns; I saw nothing odd about it. Then, when I was halfway up the gangplank, Les pinched my bum.

Well, of course, I was shocked. I turned, appalled. But Les was looking back towards Big Yvette, shouting, "Nice arse! Always liked Harry's arse!"

Well, I didn't stay to see what Big Yvette would have to say to that. I didn't have to. I knew how she'd look. Big Yvette may be a big tough Mrs on the outside; but she's not past shock. I tripped straight up the gangplank with Les in hot pursuit. When I looked back at the landing-stage, Big Yvette was talking into her lapel tannoy.

I cornered Les by the entrance to Chilled Deli.

"Les," I said, "why did you do that just then?"

"What?"

"You *know* what."

"It was just a bit of a joke, Harry."

I looked at Les severely, "To you, Les, it may have been a joke," I said, "but to me it was humiliating. You know full well that hubbies don't ever, ever, do that to other hubbies. It's just not decent, Les."

"Where's your sense of humour?" Les asked. And I swear a leer flashed across his face. "Christ, Harry, there's nothing naffer than a hubby with no sense of humour."

"I have a sense of humour!" I said, though to tell you the truth I don't think I do. "But there are jokes and jokes, Les. And that was no joke in my book."

"You've got *On The Crimson Side Of Natural* lip salve on, haven't you, Harry?"

I pouted, wondering what that had got to do with anything. "What's that got to do with anything, Les?" I asked.

"It suits you, Harry. It really suits you."

"Do you think so?"

"I do," Les said.

Well, Les just isn't capable of staying in my bad books for long. "That's nice to know," I said. "But Les, you oughtn't to have done what you did to me on the gangplank. Big Yvette could report you to *The Floating Bo$co's* HubbyPsychology Department and if they think there's a problem that can't be solved by a careful diet of specific and rigidly-enforced products from *The Floating Bo$co's* Hubby Rejuvenation Department – and the stuff in there costs an arm and a leg – you know what they'll do?" I paused. "They'll send you to the Harmon Hubby Reorientation Hospital, that's what they'll do, Les. It's not a fate I'd wish on my best friend and it's a bugger – excuse me – to get to. Three EcoBuses if you're lucky! And getting away from it is just as bad."

"I don't care, Harry," Les said. Just like that.

"How do you mean you 'don't care'!"

"I've given up on all this hubby stuff. It's just not me."

"Is it what Barbara told you about Lady Lavinia Bo$co? Is that it? I was hoping to find Justine so that we could sort that out. I'm sure it'll turn out to be one of those Enclave myths."

"Lady Lavinia's part of it, it's true," said Les, "but I've been yearning for something different for yonks." He gestured around: to the ship, the quay, the Enclave. "None of this seems right and proper, somehow."

"Les, you can't change society. You can't fight progress."

"Remember what that Ernest said to you on Hubby Island?"

"How could I forget, Les?" I said.

"Well, while you were telling it I was playing at being shocked. I wasn't really shocked; I was just wishing that I'd had a chance for a weekend at Hubby Island. I'd have really had a great time."

"Come on, Les!" I said. "You and I are are going to have a good long chat with Justine! Right now!"

Les shook his head. "You go, Harry," he said. "I'm staying here."

Well, I couldn't let my best mate ruin his life without a struggle. "Come on, Les!" I said. "You'll see, everything will feel better after a few minutes with Justine." I took hold of his arm and he pulled away really roughly.

I looked at Les and Les looked at me. Then I noticed a surveillance camera to our left.

Well, there was nothing else for me to say. I turned on my heel and walked through the automatic door into Chilled Deli. I tried to calm myself by looking at the gorgeous display of cooked meats. But I was not thinking of Chilled Deli. I was not thinking of anything except the terrible change in Les.

I was devastated. I reached into my bumbag and inhaled the complete range of *GrandMrs Hetherington's VegOdour Mood Swings* that covers despair, but I was still in despair and if it hadn't been for Justine coming upon me just at that moment, Well, I don't know.

"Having a bit of a break-down are we, Harry?" Justine said in that voice that really inspires confidence.

"Oh, it's you Justine!" I babbled. "Me? A breakdown? Whatever could have given you that idea, Justine? No, I was just having a good think about dry-cured bacon smoked in hickory/oak/recyclable softwoods or unsmoked versus spring-water cured bacon smoked in the above plus juniper leaves, camomile flowers, or birch leaves. I'd narrowed it down to the spring-water cured smoked in hickory with juniper leaves, but I hadn't been able to make up my mind which kind of spring-water to choose. It's the usual hubby quandary, Justine. Some things never change. *"Show me a hubby that can make up his mind and I'll show you a Mrs wearing pink!"* As true as it ever was. No, Justine, what I should probably do is call on the help of the Chilled Deli counsellor and then everything in the garden will be lovely – "

"Something's eating you, Harry!" Justine said. "I can tell."

Well, I broke down completely, then. "I'm in despair!" I said. "My whole life is falling apart!"

"Don't say another word, Harry!" Justine said. "To the Interdenominational Chapel with you right this minute!"

I don't recall my journey from Chilled Deli to the Interdenominational Chapel, to tell you the truth. But I do remember arriving there and seeing a steaming mug of HubbySoothe waiting for me at the same table where, back in the mists of antiquity, Justine had redirected my feet away from the Nirvana Precinct and towards *The Floating Bosco*.

Anyway, Justine sat me down and said straight out, "It's about Les, isn't it?"

"Yes, it is, Justine. He's been really odd today."

"That's because he's started kicking against the system, Harry!" Justine said.

I acted surprised. "What makes you say that, Justine?"

"Come on, Harry," said Justine. "You can't expect me to accept that Les hasn't told you all about it."

"He did not!" I contradicted, quite truthfully. "He didn't tell me he was kicking against the system."

"Well, he wrote to you about it. With a Bo$co pen." said Justine.

I didn't say anything, but I realised all at once that in all probability – and don't ask me how – *The Floating Bo$co* have developed the wherewithall to monitor anything written with one of their pens. I mean, I didn't know that for a fact, being, as Avril so rightly says, hopeless in the technology department, but – and I know this sounds terribly ungrateful after all I've said in the past – I wouldn't put it past them.

"But," I said, "if Les is having problems, what can we do about it?"

"There is nothing to be done about it," Justine said. "It's a free country – as long as you mind yourself. Les is a hubby of mature years. If he wants to ruin himself by spectacular dissatisfaction with his lot, then, regretfully, there's nothing anybody can do about it."

"It just goes to show . . ." I said.

"It does," said Justine.

"But I'm not ready to give up on my best mate, Les," I said. "Without him, I've got nothing."

"What about Avril and what's-his-name?"

"Jason."

"What about them? A family's always a great aid when hubby-pals let you down. Which, in my experience, they invariably do."

I just nodded. I didn't think I could bear to get into the problem with Avril as well as the rest. I sat there, picking at a loose thread on my jacket.

"Penny for your thoughts?" Justine said.

"I wasn't thinking of anything in particular."

"What I would advise, Harry, is that you keep well away from Les from now on. A rogue hubby is better off – excuse me – cast out into the area of gnashing teeth and that. You know, I trust, the place to which I refer."

"I think so," I said. "You mean the Industrial Nostalgia New Town, don't you?"

"I do," said Justine. "And you wouldn't like that, would you?"

"No, I wouldn't," I said. "Very much I wouldn't."

"So think about it, Harry. Find yourself a good upstanding hubby for a friend and not one who takes to the old laddish ways at the first crisis."

"But, you have to admit, we've been given a hard time, Justine!" I countered. "That surveillance is a bit much."

"It's for your own good," Justine said. "Honestly, Harry, if you could see the amount of bacon that's been saved in the HubbyCare department through surveillance."

"I expect you're right," I said. "But tell me, Justine. Is Lady Lavinia Bo$co a real person, or just an electronic construct?"

Justine laughed, but it was hollow and went on too long. I knew she was playing for time, trying to think up an answer. She glanced ever-so-quickly into the eye of the surveillance camera. "The very idea!" she said.

"Is she or isn't she? Is *The Floating Bo$co* just an arm of Home Shopping, just another way to extract money from us, to keep us consuming? Or is the caring desiderata of Lady Lavinia, as outlined in the *Hubby Romance* novels, true?"

Justine looked at her watch. "You've just time for a good shop before we dock, Hubby!" she said.

I looked at Justine icily. Then I was missing Les. I wanted to find him wherever he was. At that moment – and don't ask me what happened – I was just completely tired of myself, of Justine, of the sweet orderliness of it all . . . above all – and you're going to be shocked – tired of *The Floating Bo$co*. "You must excuse me, Justine – and I don't wish to be rude – but I really must continue my shopping."

"You're going to look for Les, aren't you?"

"I don't think Les is past saving."

"I warn you, Harry, don't. You know, of course, that Les's Barbara has severed all connection."

"Already?" I said,

"Les's Barbara finally broke. Les has been discussing his family's private conversations for years! And she told me she can't tell me the times Les has been unfaithful. Your Les has been a rogue hubby for ages! He takes testosterone. By patch.

He gets it from a Hairy Hubby pusher and sticks them on in the Hubby Comfort Station aboard *The Floating Bo$co*. Spends a great deal of the housekeeping on it. Did you know that?"

Well, that did it. "I don't believe that for a moment, Justine!" I said. "And I'll tell you for why, shall I? Me and Les have been best mates for years. There's nothing Les doesn't tell me."

"Did Les tell you how he seduced Big Yvette?"

Of course, I had to laugh, in spite of everything. "Les! Seduce! Big Yvette!" I exclaimed, through my chuckles, "You must be having me on, Justine! I mean, *HONESTLY!*"

"I have Big Yvette's deposition in front of me as I speak."

"I don't care if you've got a video of the whole thing," I said, thinking that Kevin Earnshaw had said he had one.

"I dare say that a video could be obtained, though it would, as I'm sure you'll agree, not be in the best of taste to show it. But don't forget, Harry, that I am a counsellor to *everyone* who has to do with *The Floating Bo$co*. Big Yvette came to me and informed me what had happened. She's said she just couldn't resist Les's animal magnetism – especially when Les got her in an armlock. Of course, I smelled a rat straight away. It was then that I called in Les's Barbara for a three-way comforting and reconciliation session. And Barbara told me everything. She'd been having anxiety attacks about you and Les's relationship, to tell you not a word of a lie. It's been worrying her sick."

"So, Justine," I said, trying to get it straight in my head, "all the time I've known Les he's not really been a hubby in the strict sense at all?"

"That's about it, Harry. Les reverted to the Old Lad Adam some time ago. He was just very good at concealing it."

"So what happens now?"

"There's only one thing that can happen," Justine said. "He'll go off to the Industrial Nostalgia New Town – Barbara is seeing to the details as we speak."

"Then what?"

Justine shrugged, "He'll do what they all do in the Industrial Nostalgia New Town, I expect."

"Yes, but what DO they do, Justine? Can you tell me please? I haven't the faintest idea."

Justine looked down at her hands. She keeps them well, I have to say. Those nails have seen some *Hard As Nails* in their time. "They go downhill, Harry. They fight one another, they drink home-brewed poisons, they go to the Unmentionable Region, looking for willing SubMesdames and come to bad ends. Some, I suppose, look back across the Estuary and think of what they've lost."

I didn't say anything. To tell you the truth, I was too stunned. The thoughts went round and round in my head. I kept thinking that, if Les had never really been a proper hubby, what did that say about us being best mates? I mean, I just couldn't see how we'd shared all we'd shared while all the time rogue male hormones and a terrible unhappiness with being a hubby were going through him. What did our friendship say about me?

"What does that say about me, Justine?" I asked quietly.

"Speak up, Harry!" Justine said. "You've got a lovely little voice, let's hear it!"

"What does that say about me?"

"I was just about to address that, Harry. Clearly you are the innocent party in all this. But the question remains as to what it is in your personal make-up that caused you to bond with a rogue – albeit a covertly rogue – hubby like Les. It is difficult, Harry. None of the other hubbies would go near him; they sensed that something was not normal about him.

Just observing Les's demeanour aboard *The Floating Bo$co* made me think he was not really a hubby. But I couldn't quite put my finger on it."

"But I *really really like* Les!"

"I dread to think what your Avril would have said had she been here."

"It's the truth," I said. "My Avril is not only *my* Avril, Justine! She's lots of hubbies' Avril."

"You must have driven her to it."

Well, I couldn't think of anything to say to that. To tell you the truth, I couldn't think. "Can I go now please?"

"Of course," said Justine, all cold still. "You might still be able to fill a trolley before we dock."

"Fill a trolley?" I said, really shocked. "You don't think I could possibly shop feeling the way I do, do you!"

And do you know what Justine did? She shrugged. Then she opened her folder and started making notes. No more time for Yours Despairingly.

I left the Interdenominational Chapel and stood, looking at all the hubbies shopping like mad. I wondered where Les was, and set off looking for him.

There was a crowd of hubbies around the "Fresh For A Day" bargain produce counter. On a normal day I'd have been there in the middle of the scrum to rescue the produce-on-the-edge from oblivion and save a bundle in the process. But not today. Those hubbies not intent on their shopping looked at me oddly – they could probably see that I was as vulnerable as the produce they were pushing into their trolleys. Those leaving the area swerved out of my way as if I'd give them something nasty if they got too close. They know, I thought. Word is out. I'll be the talk of the HubbyCaff by now.

No sign of Les. The ship juddered, always a sign it's about

to dock. Lines were forming at the check-outs. I passed along the line with my empty trolley. There was nowhere for me to get out without a trolley – there never had been, though I'd not noticed before. All the hubbies with their brimming trolleys seemed suddenly really – you're going to be shocked, but I don't care – really stupid. Without Les, nothing *The Floating Bo$co* had on offer could offer me anything.

At last, not being able to find an exit through the checkouts, I left the empty trolley – something I've never done before – and pushed past the line of hubbies at the Express Super Checkout. A buzzer sounded.

"Hubby Harry Manley, return to line immediately!"

I didn't, of course. I just walked straight to the exit and down to the reception deck, where Big Yvette was standing, waiting to lower the gangway.

"Mrs Yvette," I said, "have you seen Les?"

"Don't mention that Les to me, Harry," Big Yvette replied. "He's left me traumatized. I'm a psychological wreck."

Well, I didn't believe Big Yvette for a minute. "Just tell me where he is, Mrs Yvette. Please!"

"Can't you guess?"

"If I could guess, I wouldn't be here, asking you, would I?"

"He got off at the Industrial Nostalgia New Town landing-stage," Big Yvette said. And she spat. "Best place for him if you want my opinion. That Les is a pervert!"

Then, without another word, Big Yvette turned away, jerked her big shoulders and lowered the gangway to the usual accompaniment of admiring *oohs* and *ahhhs* from the crowd of disembarking hubbies.

I waited for the crowd of strangers to get off and then followed them ashore. I've never felt as hopeless as I did at that moment. I didn't know what to think nor who to go to for help. I started walking.

But that was no good. Every step reminded me of my loss. I'd look to my right, hoping that by some miracle there Les would be, saying, "I bet that fooled you, didn't it, chuck! Any day's April Fool's Day for some!"

But I knew that it was impossible. Les was on the other side of the Estuary in the place I'd always told Jason that bad hubbies went who wouldn't eat their *CocoCornBran*. I stopped and looked across. *The Floating Bo$co* was heading back out for the afternoon QuickieCruise. I resolved that the following day I would go on the Morning Cruise and get off at the Industrial Nostalgia New Town to look for my mate Les.

I felt a bit better after making that decision. After all, what did I have to keep me here? Faithless, faraway Avril? Boarding Jason who wasn't mine anyway and certainly never gave any sign that he thought much of me?

I turned into our road. As I was passing Kevin Earnshaw's house his voice came over the door-tannoy: "All alone are we, hubby? I've been watching you on your walk. You looked like the last scene of *Hubby On The Corner* or maybe even the opening credits of *My Hubby's Long Road Back*!"

Well, I wasn't feeling much like company, especially Kevin Earnshaw's company. Before I'd met up with that Hubby-Who-Stays-In everything in my life had been bouncing along like the steady beat of a well-filled bumbag. But not any more. I walked past, then stopped when Kevin Earnshaw said, "Maybe I can help!"

I needed all the help I could get, I thought, and turned back. I went through the front gate and the door opened for me.

"Hello, Harry!" Kevin Earnshaw said. He was sitting exactly where I'd last seen him. "Take the weight off your feet. I don't know how you hubbies who like to get out manage it! I've been watching you trudging the streets looking all depressed."

"Thanks, Kevin," I said.

I sat down and straight away the magnolia conveyor belt started moving and in no time at all there was this steaming cup of *HubbyBroth*. I picked it up and started drinking. I hadn't realised how hungry and thirsty I was. And, of course, *HubbyBroth* is balanced liquid nutrition, complete to the very last milligram of vitamins, minerals and amino acids, as well as all important roughage. It comes in a range of flavours, both fruit and savoury and taste-neutral which, I hear, is the most popular among discerning hubbies.

"Now, that's better, isn't it?" Kevin Earnshaw said.

"Yes. Thank you very much, Kevin. To tell you the truth I was in a bit of a state."

"And not only you, Harry! All the Hubbies-Who-Stay-In are in a bit of a state on your behalf – except Leroy from Laguna, that is. He's still nursing a grudge about Les. You are in a state about Les, aren't you?"

"Right first time," I said. Then I broke down and had a good cry. Well, that's not quite right. A good cry always makes me feel better; this cry just made me realise how bad I felt. It didn't help at all, actually.

"That's it," Kevin said. "Better out than in."

"I'm beginning to think it's the other way around," I said. "Better in than out. I mean, if I'd stayed in like you and the other hubbies none of this would ever have happened."

"Perhaps you're right there, Harry. I've never regretted my decision to be a Stay-At-Home Hubby. You know where you are when you're in. Mind you, we do need outside hubbies too, I suppose."

"Why do you say that?"

"It's obvious, Harry: if all hubbies were Stay-At-Home

Hubbies, what would we have to look at? You can take only so much of the doings of Mesdames and Hairy Hubbies. And you can get a bit cheesed off with Hubby dramas. Also, there's that frisson when Hubbies-Who-Go-Out turn to the bad. It all comes down to the harmful chemicals, Harry."

I finished off my *HubbyBroth* and in a trice a second cup was making its way along the conveyor-belt towards me. I sipped it – strawberry and juniper – making it last.

"You can watch Hairy Hubbies?"

Kevin Earnshaw nodded.

"In the Industrial Nostalgia New Town?"

"If I've the stomach for it. A little goes a long way, Harry. Mind you, between you and I there's many a Stay-At-Home Hubby who's addicted to watching Hairy Hubbies. There but for fortune, I suppose, and a bit of voyeurism. Mind you, Harry, any Stay-At-Home Hubby who says he isn't a voyeur is – excuse me – a big fibber."

I didn't understand much of what Kevin was saying. I finished off my *HubbyBroth*. Then I said, "Can you watch the Hairy Hubbies in the Industrial Nostalgia New Town?"

I wanted to get Kevin to click his clicker straight off. But I knew, after what me and Les had seen of Kevin, that I'd have to tread carefully. You see, I wasn't sure – in spite of the two *HubbyBoths* and the interest – whether Kevin was really my friend. After all, being a Stay-At Home Hubby meant in my book that he had completely sold out to the Mesdames, and was dependent on them for his housekeeping and that. Same as Les and me, I suppose, but at least they're as dependent on us as we are on them for the going out and doing the necessary. Also, I had the distinct impression that Kevin Earnshaw would do anything for a thrill. That's what most of me thought I was doing in his lounge. I was just a passing character who had come off his hi-definition monitor. What thrilled him about me was that for once in his life he could manipulate the way this character acted. Pull strings and that. Not just be a helpless spectator but play at real life.

For years, you see, we were able to change the plots of soap operas as the mood took us. The technology was nothing like what there is now, but it seemed pretty impressive at the time. You came to a certain point in each episode's story-line and we were interactively able to press a button for the plot-shift you wanted. It didn't last. If the programme was unpopular thousands chose to kill off all the participants just to give the writers a real challenge. The Thespian Union put a stop to all that.

Anyway, that's a long way of saying that that's what I thought Kevin might be up to. Only for Kevin it would be real life. But I also knew that if he could help me for the sake of Les I was prepared to let him pull my strings and observe the results.

"Show me!" I said.

The monitors lit up before I'd got the breathless exclamation mark out.

I saw shot after shot of mean streets. Not a tree. Not a blade of grass. A dog. A mongrel! It squatted – no sign of *Good Doggy-Doggy Diapers* about his person. Then a couple of Hairy Hubbies passed and didn't take a blind bit of notice of the mess on the pavement.

Kevin Earnshaw was flicking from shot to shot of depressing sights of the Industrial Nostalgia New Town. I had to tell him to slow down. I just couldn't take it all in.

"Sorry, Harry," Kevin said, "I keep forgetting how hard it is for Hubbies-Who-Go-Out to speed-read visual imagery." He handed the clicker to me – it was really complicated – showed me the buttons to press and said I was free to have a go.

Well, I soon got the hang of it. I flicked from the

Millennium Arch to the Portillo Dual-Carriageway Cul de Sac to the Gorman Depilatory Centre – a burnt-out ruin, natch – Blatch Passage, Patten Vocational School . . . on and on. I was beginning to get as good as Kevin Earnshaw on the clicker. Then, in Lilley Street, I saw this great big tourist bus with darkened windows moving slowly along. Flashes, dulled by the dark glass, showed where Pacific Rim hubbies were taking snaps of the desolation all around them as they passed.

"They've come to see the Hairy Hubbies' Wheel-Barrow Sale," said Kevin. "If it's Friday, that is. Is it Friday, Harry?"

"Yes," I said.

"That's it, then. The Pacific Rim hubbies can't get enough of Hairy Hubby Wheel-Barrow Sales."

"But there isn't a wheel-barrow anywhere in sight, Kevin!" I said. "Just those miserable-looking hubbies selling *Goblin TeasMades* and Record Turntables. What's interesting about that?"

"It's all part of the Industrial Nostalgia New Town Experience, I expect," said Kevin Earnshaw. "I don't know why they come, but I expect it's the old thing. Poverty is interesting to look at through the windows of a tour bus. They haven't had much of it on the Pacific Rim, you have to admit."

I was going to ask why the Hairy Hubbies didn't get angry at being looked at like that. Then I thought of how me and Les were looked at each and every day of our lives without even knowing it. Still, one hubby on the monitor seemed to be angry – or maybe he was drunk. Anyway, he made a lunge at the tour bus and beat the coachwork with his fists. There was a series of really bright flashes and the hubby fell back senseless into the gutter.

"They never learn," said Kevin Earnshaw. "The tour buses have an electric charge passing through them to save them from incidents like that. Every hubby knows that."

"I didn't, Kevin," I said.

"And I suppose you didn't know that since last year Hairy Hubbies get an electric shock if they stray from their own designated parts of *The Floating Bo$co*?

"No, I didn't know that, either."

"When did you last come across a Hairy Hubby in the Deli, or the Luxury Foods department?"

"Now let me think . . ."

"Not since the Angry Hubby Brigade had that campaign of filling trolleys and then abandoning them."

"It's true, I suppose. Once you've left Tinned Goods, The Econo Boscown Range deck and Washday Requisites you almost never see a Hairy Hubby."

"Not seldom, Harry. Never."

I thought about that. The Hairy Hubby who had punched the Pacific Rim tour bus was still dead to the world in the gutter. I clicked on, looking for Les. "Is there any way to get into places?" I asked. "The pubs, churches and that?"

Kevin Earnshaw took the clicker from me with one of his looks. "Honestly . . . !" he said with a sigh. "Look, Harry, when you see a building you want to go into, press these two buttons together. I tell you, the more I stay in the more I realise what you miss by going out." He gestured to the room. "The whole world comes to me, Harry!"

Seeing what I was seeing on the screens, knowing that I was going to have to venture into the hell of the Industrial Nostalgia New Town on my quest for errant Les, I could see Kevin Earnshaw's point-of-view. To be spared all the aggravation, decision-making and consumer choice in the full glare of the public felt at that moment like a wonderful thing. As long as Les stayed at home with me some of the time.

Of course, I'd have decorated my lounge differently. Magnolia would have to go to be replaced by something a bit more sunny. What? I wondered. Well, maybe I'd go for *The Gay Sixties* range that I'd seen once at Plain Wayne's Hubby Supplies. I mean, it's time for African Orange to have its turn in the sun after all those years – not to mention swirls of black and white that made you dizzy. They deserved an airing too . . .

Then I realised that I was wandering from my path. I was not a Stay-At-Home Hubby. No, on the contrary, I was a hubby who would soon be venturing out on the most important quest of his life. I saw what looked like a pub on the screen, pressed the two buttons on the clicker. The screen went blank, though, as I looked harder, I thought I could see shadows of people through the blackness.

"That's not much use!" I said to Kevin.

"They've covered the camera lens, shouldn't wonder. The surveillance inspectorate just can't keep up. There's been a lot of that recently. An edict goes out threatening withdrawal of the benefits if the lenses aren't cleared at once. Things are back to normal for a while, but then the lawless element take over. It's hard to credit the Industrial Nostalgia New Town is only half an hour away. It might be a million miles."

"You're right, Kevin," I said. "It's amazing how little I knew about the Industrial Nostalgia New Town. It doesn't turn up much in the news, does it? You never hear of hubby charities or the *Bo$coBag Appeal* appealing much for it, do you?"

"It's past charity, Harry. It's the end of everything. If I were you I'd forget about Les. I know you're looking for Les, Harry. I stay in, remember. If Les is there, he'll not come back. Go and ask your Avril – nicely – if you can become a Stay-At-Home Hubby like me. My Mavis will point her towards a system that fits your needs just right. You'll see, when you get used to staying at home you won't want it any other way."

"I know what you mean, Kevin, but – "

"Home is where the heart is."

"But – "

"A place for everything, everything in its place and lots of lovely things to watch. Above all, Harry, home is comfort. Comfort is what it's all about, Harry."

"I've got to find Les!" I said.

Kevin Earnshaw shrugged, like he'd given up on me. "Try inside that building. On monitor Number 7."

I clicked like Kevin had shown me. This time the camera worked. I was looking at a sort of waiting-room. Rows of benches with no backs. Hairy Hubbies smoking cigarettes and rubbing their stubble. A big display with numbers on it, like in the Deli queue. When the hubby's number came up he would stand up, scratch his area of private access and slouch off to this really hard-faced Mrs behind a grille. Truly, it was a really pre-millennial scene.

"That's the Benefits Office," Kevin said. "Can you see your Les there? He's bound to end up there to register. There'll be nothing from Barbara. She's absolutely incandescent with rage, I can tell you. Already put an ad for a new hubby on the HubbyNet. Hubbies are queuing up to take Les's place. She's a real catch, Les's Barbara. Have you seen the Nat West's *Armchair Banking*? Every time you use it you get a free pizza. Delivered."

I was all ready to click on to another section of the Industrial Nostalgia New Town when the door opened and in walked Les!

"There's Les!" I cried.

"Knew he'd show up. Barbara cancelled all his cards," said Kevin Earnshaw. "That woman revives one's faith in banking."

The sight of Les startled me. Though it was only a few hours since I'd seen him, he was greatly changed. All the advice I'd given him in the Personal Care department had gone straight out of the window, unable to survive just a few hours of the Industrial Nostalgia New Town. "I hardly recognize him," was all I could say.

"He's made his bed . . ." said Kevin Earnshaw, just like Avril says. Then he took back the clicker. "Let's see something different. Wouldn't you like to see how Barbara is doing?"

"No," I said, "I need to know where Les will be staying so that I can find him tomorrow."

"No problem there. He'll be back in the Benefits Office. But look, Harry, you mustn't try to stop me from following the story. That's what we Hubbies-Who-Stay-In like doing best." He switched one of the monitors to a view of Barbara's office at the Estuary Nat West, but it was deserted except for a Mrs pushing an Ioniser Vacuum Cleaner – a really old-fashioned one – about the floor. Then he switched to Barbara's house and we saw Barbara standing in her kitchen looking all puzzled, a microwave instructions book in her hand. She had a face of thunder on her. It took me straight back to the swing-bins incident.

"Nothing much there," Kevin Earnshaw said.

He clicked to scenes of hubby-life around the world. Tokyo and Singapore hubbies carrying swank designer bags and looking pleased with themselves, as well they might; Hubbies on the Plate Estuary *Floating Bo$co*, Leroy from Laguna Beach making *Ultimately Devilish Texan Chilli Beans* and looking as crazy as ever . . . but it all seemed a world away to me. I could only think of Les. Les, I screamed inwardly, *Why? WHY?*

Well, I would find out. I would dose myself with enough *Calm Down Hubby!* to calm a dozen Hubby Cheerleaders and I would do what no other hubby of the Estuary Enclave had ever done before: I would go to the Industrial Nostalgia New Town. And I would return!

Kevin Earnshaw seemed to know what I was thinking. "Don't go," he said. "I'm being a good friend to you, giving you this advice. A part of me wants you to go, the stay-at-home side who likes a good story – and you getting off at the Industrial Nostalgia New Town would make great viewing – but I like you, Harry. I want you to be happy. As soon as the Hairy Hubbies clap eyes on you, you'll be meat. They hate well-behaved, depilated hubbies. Also, not to put too fine a point on it, they've been deprived of contact with Mesdames . . . they'll gobble you up."

"How do you mean?" I asked.

"Think about it, Harry. More liquid refreshment? A meal, perhaps?"

"Thank you, Kevin. But, no. I must go home and think."

"Leave it, Harry."

"I stood up. "Thank you for everything," I said.

"Well, I've done everything I can," said Kevin Earnshaw. "Now all I can do is stay in and enjoy the show."

As I walked home I thought that if I could get Les back he and me would be happy as anything to be Stay-At-Home Hubbies. We wouldn't watch all those monitors, though. No, we'd stay at home, bonding nicely in a simple way.

But could I bring Les back to the Estuary Enclave and, if I could, would Barbara take him back? Would Les go back? The questions just went around and around.

I didn't sleep a wink that night, not helped at all by a late call from Avril, all triumphant, from China, about her win in the Monosodium Glutamate case. I *"Very Niced"* and congratulated her, like I do. I don't think she noticed that my heart wasn't in it.

"When are you coming home, dear?" I asked.

Avril said that she and a couple of other Mesdames from the

Moseley and Lumumbashi legal team were popping over to Formosa for a bit of R and R and to follow up on some litigation leads involving faulty Taiwanese battery-chargers. I wished her luck, and waited to be asked about my news. I wasn't, though. She had to go, she said, back to the celebration.

I put down the receiver of the VideoChat on to its cradle and my smile back in its box. Lying in my soft bed looking about me, I knew I was the envy of 99.9% of hubbies. I had everything a hubby could want, didn't I? No!

The following morning, instead of getting off at the Industrial Nostalgia New Town, I could take the Morning Cruise across the Estuary, fill as many trolleys as I liked and justify my extravagance safe in the knowledge that I was making wise purchases to welcome my Mrs home and relieve her of the necessity of giving any thought to domestic matters. I was a hubby in clover, wasn't I?

But that was not how it was going to be. Instead of behaving sensibly, I was about to risk everything for a mate who had gone off the rails. What I would do once I'd found him I didn't know, but I did know that all the comfort around me, all the things, filled me with a really queasy feeling when I thought of the Industrial Nostalgia New Town in general and my mate Les in particular. I couldn't wait for the morning to come so that I could be off. In fact, I didn't wait. I made myself useful by reading the instructions book of the laser-book diary. I wanted a hard copy of my work. I wanted to read it – call me daft – on paper.

I must have been first in line to board *The Floating Bo$co* for its Morning Cruise. When Big Yvette let me on board I made straight for the Bare Necessities deck and bought the sort of things I thought I'd need. Lots of *HubbyWipes*, vitamins, *HubbyBoost*, a conference-size pack of *Calm Down Hubby!* and a range of the strongest depilatory products for use on Les if I managed to convince him to mend his ways. I also bought a humble holiday diary to replace the tasteful laser-voice diary which I'd emptied out the night before. I had two hundred pages secreted about my person! It soon adds up. All I needed was the ending.

I paid for everything, saying to the counsellor that I was feeling a bit off-colour and wanted to spend the rest of the cruise relaxing in the HubbyCaff.

Well, to tell you the truth, I did go into the HubbyCaff, drank a cup of coffee and loaded my purchases into a Trueblue-Hubby bumbag, the top of the range – and largest – bumbag put out by the *"Lighterload"* people of Rotherham. I then looked around at all the gossiping hubbies comparing purchases, swapping coupons and gobbling up cakes. I knew that I had been one of them for ever such a long time but – and I know this sounds impossible to believe – I found it impossible to believe – Harry Manley was a completely new hubby – a lone hubby. I was frightened about what I was about to do. But I was elated, too.

The hooter sounded, announcing the docking of *The Floating Bo$co* at the Industrial Nostalgia New Town landing-stage. I drank up my coffee and quietly bade farewell to the HubbyCaff, *The Floating Bo$co*, my whole former life. The gangplank clattered down and a noisy rabble of Hairy Hubbies started boarding before I'd had a chance to disembark.

"Excuse me! Sorry! Pardon me!" I called as I fought against the tide, smelling the smells, seeing the undepilated chins inches from mine.

Then the tide had passed and I stood alone on the landing-stage. A toot from *The Floating Bo$co* and off it went, back across the Estuary. I watched, across the clear blue water, Home glittering in the sun. Beautiful. Safe.

I turned my back on it and walked away quickly into the Industrial Nostalgia New Town. Looking for Les.

14

Into the Heart of the Industrial Nostalgia New Town

I wandered the Industrial Nostalgia New Town in a terrible state for most of the afternoon. Swallowing a *Calm Down Hubby!* every few minutes, I managed to keep one foot stepping in front of the other, but it wasn't easy and I'd be telling you a lie if I said that it was.

You see, from the moment my feet touched the alien landing-stage I had felt under siege. The Hairy Hubbies gave me looks and said things to me, but really to their mates, if you get me. They seemed to hate me for just being there. It was as if I was the freak. Gangs of men and women working on scaffolding shouted down remarks, and whistled. I suppose it's ages since they got a good whiff of *Maine In Fall* which, with thoughts of Les on top of my mind, I was wearing as a – call me daft if you like – talisman. In short, the sight of a well-turned-out hubby with manners was something new for them.

Groups of Hairy Hubbies followed me – they've nothing better to do, I suppose – as far as the Millennium Arch, which I was shocked to see had been allowed to deteriorate alarmingly. Bricks had fallen off – the whole thing was done in brick to get the brick industry off its back – and Hairy Hubbies had built themselves makeshift shacks from them.

The whole area was a real tip. I don't know what the Queen would think, I really don't – cementing the last brick in place was just about her last public act before she made a bolt for it.

I tried to keep my thoughts anchored on my quest for Les. I watched the way the Hairy Hubbies carried themselves and tried to imitate their walk, but it didn't seem to do any good at all. I was still attracting all this unwelcome, unkind, attention.

At one point I plucked up all my courage and went up to a Hairy Hubby to ask him the way to the Benefits Office, where Les would still be waiting, He was sitting at the sack-covered door of his millennium brick hut and had, I thought, a smile on his face.

"Excuse me," I said, "can you tell me where the Benefits Office is, please?"

He didn't say anything by way of reply, just lifted the sack over the door of the hut. "I don't have time to stop to chat, I'm afraid," I said. "I'm looking for my friend, Les."

Then the Hairy Hubby reached into his pants and produced his area of private access. Undepilated. I backed away, while he shook himself about like a monkey in a zoo.

I walked for mile after mile through wrecked, wretched landscapes. I could have kicked myself for not having learnt the location of the Benefits Office. Kevin Earnshaw would have been sure to know. Still, there was nothing else for it, I had to keep going.

Night was falling. Across the Estuary, the Enclave twinkled. I watched it, completely at a loss. My comfy life over there was just a memory. The Benefits Office would have closed for the night. I turned away from the mirage of the Estuary Enclave and found myself back at the Millennium Arch, but did not know how I'd got there. I have no sense of direction. Never had.

I'll draw a veil over that night. Suffice it to say that I spent it sheltering between two shacks by the Millennium Arch. I didn't dare talk to any more Hairy Hubbies. Not after what had happened. The place seemed to come alive after night fell. Raucous noise, singing, moans and screams filled the air. It was like that advert for *Peace of Mind* mattresses.

I tried to sleep, but it was no good, so I planned my strategy for the next day. I decided that my *Lighten Your Load!* bumbag and my tasteful clothes were making me stand out – like the manufacturers promised – but at the Industrial Nostalgia New Town it wasn't the thing to do to stand out. No, I should try to blend in. I resolved at first light to hide some of my things under bricks and leave my nice jacket there too. Though I had my depilatory kit to hand I would not use it, in the hope that I'd blend in better.

That only left my voice. I spent quite a bit of the night trying to sound like a Hairy Hubby. It wasn't an easy job, I can tell you. A deep rough voice is everything Harry Manley isn't. It felt like a betrayal of all that was best in me. Still, if I was going to avoid being laughed at, stared at, and violated in ways I could hardly imagine, desperate measures were called for.

I set off again at dawn. Snores and sighs and nightmare-mewing came from the shacks all about. My ablutions consisted of spreading brick-dust on my clothes and some more on my face for good measure. I fancied that if Kevin Earnshaw was surfing the surveillance network at the Industrial Nostalgia New Town he'd have trouble recognizing me. Why, even me – and I've known myself for years – had trouble recognizing me. I looked at myself inwardly and saw a stranger: I was a Hairy Hubby.

It was half an hour before I saw anybody. A man was opening this really dingy corner-shop, Still, I was hungry and, thinking that if I bought something from the chap he might feel grateful enough to answer a question, the only question I had to ask, I went in.

I asked the shopkeeper for some *HubbyBulk, Low Cal.*

"Don't do 'em, mate," said the shopkeeper. "No call for them round here. I've got crisps in thirty-six flavours, if you like."

"Crisps!" I said, in what I knew was my normal voice. I couldn't help it; I was really shocked. I tried to retrieve the situation. "OK," I said, all deep and rough. "Give me three packets."

The shopkeeper looked at me. He had this really awful salt and pepper beard. We recognized one another at exactly the same time.

"Harry Manley!"

"Neil!"

"What are you doing here, Harry? You're the very last hubby I'd ever have expected to turn up in the Industrial Nostalgia New Town!"

"What about you? Where's Plain Wayne, by the way?"

"Wayne left me after the shop shut. That business was the glue that held our relationship together. I realise that now. When I think of the years I gave to Plain Wayne! The best years of my life . . . " Neil stopped, thought. "Still, maybe not."

To tell you the truth, I felt guilty at that moment. Don't ask me why. "Look, Neil, I'm sorry I stopped coming into Plain Wayne's Hubby Supplies, but after I'd read Plain Wayne's *Black Diaries*, I just couldn't in all conscience continue as a customer."

"Plain Wayne's Black what?" Neil asked.

"That notebook he kept. I'm surprised you never saw it, Neil. It went on for page after page and it was very nasty about us hubbies."

"Hold it right there," Neil said, frowning. "Where did you see these notebooks?"

"In the Interdenominational Chapel on *The Floating Bo$co*."

"That's funny, in a peculiar sort of way. Were they in Wayne's handwriting?"

"They were."

"Harry," Neil said, "Plain Wayne never kept a diary, black, white or any other colour. He'd always had trouble with his letters. I was the brains of that outfit."

"But Justine – "

"So that's why we never saw you. I used to say to Plain Wayne, 'We haven't seen that Harry Manley since he bought that three-for-the-price-of-two on *Butch Bags Size 3*.' We thought the *Bo$co* dirty tricks brigade had got at you."

"How do you mean, Neil?" I asked, going hot and cold and red and pale.

"I'm not sure exactly. Just that Bo$co was always poisoning our customers' minds against us. We tried to sue once over a letter *The Floating Bo$co* sent to one of the Stay-At-Home Hubbies who took an order from us every week, but Lady Lavinia engaged Moseley and Lumumbashi and once your Mrs had been to see us, throwing writs about, we just decided it wasn't worth the candle. The family business doesn't stand a chance. To tell you the truth, we thought it was your Avril who'd slapped an injunction on you coming to Plain Wayne's."

You mean," I said, "that the *Black Diaries* weren't true!"

"Well, if they were anything like the graffiti campaign or the rumours on the InterHubbyNet or the disgusting fax shots – no, they weren't true. Plain Wayne and me were in business to make money, I suppose, but we enjoyed the work, too. You don't stand a chance against Bo$co's. They were determined to destroy the Nirvana Precinct."

"You mean, you never put new date stamps on old food?"

"Never."

"Never overcharged?"

"Never."

"Never – expressed contempt for hubbies?"

"Never ever. Definitely. We really liked the hubbies. Both

me and Plain Wayne thought hubbies were an idea whose time had come."

"I can't believe it!"

Neil laughed. "Why would I lie, Harry?"

"But Lady Lavinia would never have approved of such low tactics."

"Where have you been, Harry?" Neil said, severely. "Every waking moment of Lavinia Bo$co's life is devoted to serving the self-interest of Bo$co's. You know she owns Hubby Island and has the concession on the Benefits Offices here at the Industrial Nostalgia New Town, don't you?"

"No, I didn't, Neil."

"Well, you know now. She's trying to close me down here, too. Luckily, I do have a few loyal customers."

"They do say," I said, "that Lady Lavinia Bo$co is a computer construct. That's what Les says. In a way I'm glad it wasn't actually Lady Lavinia who was doing all those terrible things, but the Home Shopping people."

"I think I'm well out of it," Neil said.

"But how can you stand it, Neil?" I asked. "I mean, it's all so common."

"It takes all sorts," Neil said. "There are worse things to be than common."

"I feel really terrible that I'd believed the *Black Diaries*."

"Don't worry about it. It's the times," Neil said. "The big conglomerates can make the world dance to their tune."

"Neil," I said, "could you help me? I'm looking for my mate, Les. You remember Les, do you?"

"How could I ever forget him? He used to be a miner, didn't he? To tell you the truth, Harry, I always wondered about him."

"How do you mean?"

"Don't know really. I just never thought Hubbydom suited him."

"That was very perceptive of you – you're right. He's here, Neil. He got fed up with everything at the Estuary Enclave."

"Send him around!" Neil said. "I always fancied Les. And a good man is hard to find, even here on the Industrial Nostalgia New Town. So many have let themselves go, you know. They just give up."

"I've got to find Les. That's why I'm here."

"You won't get him to go back to the Estuary Enclave, Harry. The Industrial Nostalgia New Town may not look like much but it gets a hold of you. There's a real sense of community here – when they're not beating hell out of one another, that is."

"I find that hard to believe, Neil."

"If you'll excuse me for saying so, Harry: you find quite a lot hard to believe."

"I've encountered nothing but rudeness since I arrived," I said.

"You've got to get used to their little ways. After all, Harry, you've been living the pampered life of a hubby for years. But give it a few days and you might just decide you want to stay over here with Les. I know I'd give my right arm to have a friend like Les."

"Can you help me find him?"

And do you know what Neil said? He said that the Benefits Office was in the next street. He gave me directions and I left him, saying I'd pop in on him before me and Les went back across the Estuary.

But when I got back into the messy street the full enormity of all Neil had told me stopped me in my tracks. To take on board what he had said to me meant that all my time on *The Floating Bo$co* – all the products, the books, the counselling – had been there only so as to bring me under the control of Lady Lavinia Bo$co. And my Avril was involved in it all, too!

I won't think about it today, I'll think about it tomorrow, I thought. Today I had Les to find, Well, I thought, maybe Lady Lavinia doesn't exist, doesn't give a damn – but if I find Les, I can live with that and grow through it.

I popped back a handful of *Calm Down Hubby!* and went off to the Benefits Office.

It was Les who saw me. I had been going frantic searching for him, while Hairy Hubbies nudged one another, pursed their lips and imitated what I thought they thought were my mannerisms.

"Harry, chuck!" Les called out across the room.

"Les! Is it you?" And the crowd of Hairy Hubbies, hearing my tones, went all hushed. The whole Benefits Office watched in silence as we excused our way towards one another.

"Put it there, Harry!" Les said, offering me his hand.

I took it and his hand held on to me as he went around the Benefits Office introducing me to all the Hairy Hubbies.

"If you're with Les, you're all right!" said an elderly Hairy Hubby with no teeth to speak of.

I smiled at him. "Les," I said, "I've come to take you home."

"I am home, Harry," Les said.

"But what about Barbara and the kiddies?"

"They'll make other arrangements."

"You can't mean that, Les!" I said. "What about all that work in the house?"

"I've forgotten it all, Harry. My benefits are being processed – I feel really good about everything."

"Have you missed me?"

"Yes," Les said. "I've missed you. Have you missed me?"

"Every moment, Les. I mean, where would I be without my best mate?"

Les smiled. Like he does. "I knew you'd miss me, Harry,

but I wasn't sure you'd be able to pluck up the courage to come over here. It's not everyone's cup of tea. You're your dad's son after all."

I looked around me. "Well, it's all right. For a visit. To see how, you know, the other half live and that. But it isn't very – and I don't mean to be rude – very comfy, is it Les?"

"No," Les replied, "it isn't a bit comfy. It's life in the raw over here in the Industrial Nostalgia New Town. There's an allotment, though."

"An allotment, Les!" I said. "You sound just like Dad."

"I always had a lot of time for your dad," Les said.

"Yes," I said, "you said."

"Harry," Les said, "you know, Harry, ever since the GREAT RESTRUCTURE I've been feeling really bad about things. It wasn't just the surveillance and that Kevin Earnshaw; it was the whole thing. Something was missing all the time, Harry."

"What, Les?"

Les gestured around the Benefits Office. To be perfectly honest, I couldn't see among all the Hairy Hubbies and their Mesdames how this might provide what Les had been missing. On *The Floating Bo$co* you could watch just such types from a safe distance.

"Harry," Les said, "if what I'm going to say doesn't ring any bells with you then it's probably better if you go back to the Estuary Enclave today . . . "

"Les," I said, "I've come to take you back!"

Les shook his head. "I'm never going back, chuck."

"But Les – "

"Hear me out, Harry. We've all been freaks on the Enclaves. Freaks, Harry. Not just us hubbies but the Mesdames as well. We've all been enslaved by *The Floating Bo$co*, by Home Shopping, and the rest. We were consumers. First and last. We consumed the chemicals, the global economic shifts, the advertising. We swallowed the notion that the Industrial Nostalgia New Town and similar places were deprived, almost barbaric. We just accepted everything as the way the world was going. Upsides and downsides. Restructuring. Well, I've decided not to accept that any more. An allotment is a great thing, Harry."

"Les," I said, "you can't be serious!"

"Never been more serious, chuck. And I'm not the only one, you know. There are as many Mesdames as Hubbies coming over here."

Les must have seen me looking really incredulous. "Of course, you haven't heard that. We didn't hear anything over there, Harry. Only what they want us to hear. But a lot of those houses we passed that had their curtains drawn, where we thought the hubbies were spending their days enslaved to their gadgets – they were empty all the time, Harry. Come and see my allotment!"

"All right, Les," I said, though to tell you the truth I didn't really want to.

Les led me out of the Benefits Office. We walked along the depressing streets towards the Estuary. We didn't speak. I had nothing to say. Les was too busy whistling – whistling! – to be able to say much. I caught sight of a surveillance camera perched high on a pole. It stared down at us like a surprised crow, swivelled its neck to watch us walking down Mawhinney Passage.

Finally, at the end of a street of really depressing terraced houses, we came upon this great expanse of green. A patchwork which, if you kept your eyes half-closed, could have been that duvet-cover I bought at Beloved Bygones just after me and Avril tied the knot. Every green you can imagine. And in the midst of it all, like stitches holding it all together, Hairy Hubbies and their Mesdames, working away like their lives depended on it.

Les opened this little wooden gate and in we went. Birds

were singing. Call me daft if you like, I'd quite forgotten that they did that. There was this funny smell which, I'd have sprayed with a good blast of Personal Space Organizer, if I'd had one on my person. Still, it wasn't unpleasant when you got used to it.

Les was still whistling. We walked on and on until we were completely surrounded by green. Roses were blooming up trellises between the allotment patches. Little sheds with flowering creepers and names in fretworked letters . . . "HOME SWEET HOME . . . DUNROMIN . . . IAIN-N-TONE . . . CHRISTOPHER AND FELICITY . . . JONNY AND BARBARA . . . DOM-N-EMILY . . . VELVEL AND JOHN . . . " And, in each hedged and wattled section, a variety of crops was growing, all in these different greens.

"Close your eyes!" Les said.

"How do you mean, Les?"

"Just close your eyes. I've a surprise for you."

Well, I did as Les told me. He took my arm and led me along the path between the allotments in the dark. We turned right if I'm not very much mistaken, then left. Then we walked on what seemed like some very uneven ground. Les put his hands on my shoulders.

"You can open your eyes now, Harry," Les said.

"Before I do, Les," I said, "is that *Maine In Fall* you're wearing?"

"I'm not wearing anything, chuck," Les said.

"So what's that lovely perfume?"

"Open your eyes, Harry."

I opened my eyes. There was Les in front of me. He stepped aside, smiling. I found myself looking at one of the little sheds I'd seen already. Only this one was standing at the edge of a bare plot of weed-covered land. On the door was written, in white paint:

"LES and HARRY."

In spite of everything, I was touched.

"What do you think of it, Harry?" Les said.

Well, to tell you the truth I didn't know what to think.

"Course, there's a lot of work to be done. You've seen what the others have managed, though, Harry. Are you game?"

I wasn't sure. But I was sure that I was happy to be here in this really rather lovely place with my best mate. Also, I could see exactly what I'd do with the shed. With a bit of thought . . .

"You know, Les, if you let me do one round trip on *The Floating Bo$co* – just one, Les – I could really make something of this."

"No, Harry," Les said. "We can find everything we need from the dump. Everyone else has."

"The dump, Les?"

"Yeah," said Les. "The dump. We all have to put in a few hours each week excavating it. Look what I've got already!"

Les swung open the door of the shed and there was this really old-fashioned bed of the sort that even Dad wouldn't have been seen dead in. Next to it stood – or more accurately leaned – a wardrobe of great antiquity but little charm.

I stood looking around. I didn't know what to think, to tell you the truth. At that moment I heard the hooter of *The Floating Bo$co* sound across the green expanse of allotments. It might have been another world.

"Give it a try, Harry!" Les said.

"How do you mean, Les?" I asked.

"The bed, Harry."

I walked into the shed. The floorboards creaked. I sat down on the bed and smelled *Maine In Fall* – a really strong blast of it.

"What do you think?"

"It's really lovely, Les. And don't try telling me that isn't *Maine In Fall* because I know it definitely is *Maine in Fall*."

"I used the last of it to sprinkle on the bed," Les said. "It masks the smell of damp."

I thought of the amazing range of deodorizing products for the home aboard *The Floating Bo$co*. Then, just at that moment, I heard the ship's hooter sound again and knew it would be nosing out into the estuary for the afternoon QuickieCruise. I imagined I could hear Lady Lavinia Bo$co's voice on the tannoy, welcoming everyone aboard. She would be running through the facilities on offer, itemizing the offers of the week, congratulating the hubbies on their good taste in choosing to make *The Floating Bo$co* the centre of their lives.

I excused myself and popped outside Les's hut. I noticed that he had already cleared the ground around it. In a year or two the desolation that stretched from here to the ruin of the Millennium Arch and on down to the Industrial Nostalgia New Town landing-stage would be a chequer-board of green. The question was: would rhubarb leaves, climbing roses, walls of beans and sweet-peas mask the sound of *The Floating Bo$co*'s hooter? Or would I, every day of my life with Les, be tempted by its siren call to pull up stakes and run back to the old certainties?

I knew that I was a hubby on the crossroads. I thought of Plain Wayne's Neil. Then I thought about Avril coming back from the Pacific Rim and finding her hubby gone. I could not for the life of me imagine her reaction. Would she miss me? I wasn't sure she would. After all, what was there in me to miss?

I turned and walked back into the shed. I saw Les sitting on the bed looking anxious.

"You wouldn't have something as mundane as a broom, would you, Les?"

Les brightened. He fished about under the bed and came out with a dustpan and brush. I parked my bumbag on the rickety table next to the wardrobe – stripped pine! – and set to work.

"You're staying, are you, Harry?"

"Yes, I am, Les," I said. "I couldn't leave my best mate all on his ownsome, now could I? You know how hopeless you are in the Household Needs department."

"I'll go and get on with the garden," Les said.

Half an hour later when the place was spick and span, I went outside. Les saw me and paused from his work. He'd been mixing a load of cement in a wheelbarrow. He was sweating. I made my way towards him across the corrugated soil. We stood side by side. We didn't say anything but I reckon that moment was our greatest bonding experience ever.

"I'd better get on," Les said at last. "We need a good firm path to get to the privy in all weathers."

I nodded. Then I had a thought. "Les," I said, "I want to bury something under the path. Is that all right?"

Les nodded and I went inside the hut, where the laser-voice diary – that gift of Lady Lavinia which started me off – sat in the bottom of my bumbag.

I have now written the last lines of the *Story of Harry Manley, Hubby* – apart from the ones I'm writing now, if you get me. Soon I will wrap the manuscript in a *Bo$co Check-Out* plastic bag, have Les shovel a bit of cement around it and leave the rest to posterity . . . though it's awfully hard writing for posterity, have you noticed?

I bite my pencil as I moon, wondering about Kevin Earnshaw watching the end of our story on one of his screens, the magnolia conveyor at his elbow. Will he be shaking his head, tapping up Leroy from Laguna to tell him about the scandalous happenings at the Industrial Nostalgia New Town? Or will he be glued to me and Les, poor as corner-shop mice, about to set sail towards the future in the fragile barque of our new home . . . and be secretly wishing he was us?

Who knows? Who can tell?

The End